T0248045

BECOMING A COMPOSER

ERROLLYN WALLEN

———

BECOMING A COMPOSER

faber

First published in the UK and the USA in 2023
by Faber & Faber Limited
The Bindery, 51 Hatton Garden
London EC1N 8HN

Typeset by Faber & Faber
Printed and bound in the UK by CPI Group (UK) Ltd, Croydon, CR0 4YY

A CIP record for this book
is available from the British Library

ISBN 978–0–571–37013–9

Printed and bound in the UK on FSC® certified paper in line with our continuing
commitment to ethical business practices, sustainability and the environment.
For further information see faber.co.uk/environmental-policy

2 4 6 8 10 9 7 5 3 1

Dedicated to the memory of Rory Allam

CONTENTS

FOREWORD

It was late at night as, arm in arm, my friend Michèle Mendelssohn and I laughed and skipped down the path beside King's College Chapel, past Gibbs Building and along the Backs. We were both postgraduates at Cambridge. I burst into one of my spontaneous nonsense songs and Michelini joined in:

We were singing for the pure joy of being alive, for the gift of friendship – and for all the adventures we knew, that night, were ahead of us.

Twenty years later Michèle suggested that I write the book that I kept saying I wanted to write. Although I have kept a diary since I was twelve, jotted down this and that, written poetry, lyrics, shopping lists, set lists and libretti, contributed chapters to books, and even *thought* about writing a book, the reality of an entire book written by me alone seemed daunting. Books are for proper writers, people for whom the word is sacred.

Then, just a few months later, the auspicious publishing house Faber and Faber asked me if I might consider writing a book. I was taken aback. My first shattering introduction to modern literature, poetry and plays occurred in my school-days and was almost entirely because of Faber – Harold Pinter, Sylvia Plath, Ted Hughes, Philip Larkin, T. S. Eliot. These writers' words remain to me not only sacred, but as sacred as an eremite's prayer.

Since becoming a professional composer I have often longed to demystify the act of composing. I hope that by sharing stories of my working life alongside those of my personal life and upbringing I can encourage anyone from anywhere to make music. Any apprehensions I might have felt about my limits as a writer have been conquered by this consideration.

There are many different types of writing in this book. A few chapters are drawn from essays, diaries and contributions to other publications or broadcasts. The reader should feel free to dip in and out of the book in the same way as I dip backwards and forwards chronologically. I have tried to avoid musical jargon wherever possible but when it appears, I have given explanations that I hope will lead to further exploration of the world's infinite treasure trove of sound and music. What I write about my childhood is purely from my own direct experience and no one else's. It is important to remember that each child in the same fam-ily can have strikingly different relationships and memories of those relationships.

My parents are now dead and are no longer able to speak for themselves. In relating my experiences I have tried to remain true to my thoughts and feelings as a child because at the time I felt unable to do so. It has not been an easy task to articulate these memories. I am aware that there are many children who find themselves separated from their parents for a variety of reasons – through custom, neglect, culture, death or necessity. May some of my words help other children and their parents.

Writing this book has made me realise just how many questions I have to ask my mother, father, aunt and uncle, and just how much I have to thank them for my life in music.

Errollyn Wallen
Strathy Point
January 2023

Egg
to Mora Beauchamp-Byrd

When you get there, you breathe out.
And, I suppose, going by Darwin's calculation,
We did pretty well to travel this far,
Through the seas of so many names –
German, Abyssinian, Jewish, Scots,
Spanish, Mayan.

Family tree.

Your name sounds French to me . . .
And you sing the blues, Mademoiselle Longhair
You sing the blues!

So, friend, we are connected by ships,
And rice, and sing-song stories of vanished mammas
Who couldn't be mammas to themselves

And our new gleaming world,
So nearly impossible. Blinding. Bejewelled. Impossible.
Encircled. We are
History circling. Forever. Impossible.

For she is dancing fearful
Jaguar whispers
At our strong, smooth backs, and
She is coming for us.
She is
History

In an ermine coat.
'Take what you need, girls.'

And so, at last, we did.

Before planes, telephones,
Answer machines, paper.

Or the knowledge of water

Brought us again
To this.

*

I am beginning this book carrying only what I can hold
in my hands: manuscript paper, pencil, eraser, words to a
friend that will open the latest work in progress – a solo
show that opens soon.

I am starting from now. Now I am folded into myself and
my dreams are mixed with all the music I have ever written
or will ever write. For I am writing time for myself. I am
lost in time, making space. I am in the strange solitude of a
composer. A midnight plane.

'Why wait? Write something down.' This is how it always starts. And then the sound of a dripping tap, a door slam, a motorboat, breathing, a distant laugh; all of this becomes *material*. You enter the subway of your unconscious and start writing from memory. You stay home all hours and share secrets with yourself. You get yourself to a point where you can't turn back; you trick yourself; you sit still. I can't turn back.

*

When I was nine I was walking along the road with my Uncle Arthur – we were on our way to Ridley Road Market to buy fruit and vegetables for the week. I told Uncle Arthur that I could hear 'all these sounds in my head' but I didn't know what to do with them. Uncle Arthur suggested that perhaps I was a composer.

I am a composer. A composer of classical music. As I read that sentence again, I am not completely sure how this happened to a girl born in Belize and brought up in Tottenham. My life has often felt as if I've been walking backwards and forwards through a maze of a thousand reflecting glass doors with no handles. Nevertheless, here I am. Composing found me. It crept up on me, tapped me on the shoulder, tackled me to the ground and wouldn't let me out of its grasp. As a baby lying daydreaming and singing in my cot, or as a little girl, trailing off mid-sentence while talking to someone, as a fledgling dancer, moving to whatever music

I heard, as a recalcitrant schoolgirl walking along the road singing intervals, making up imaginary television jingles for washing-up liquid as I stood at the sink doing chores for my parents, I always lived in a parallel world – gripped in the vice of the immortal, invisible world of music. As I dreamed about playing the piano, dreamed of myself as an opera singer on an imaginary stage, as the fire raged inside, I was composing. There has always been music and sound in my head and I have always tried to shape those sounds, whether consciously or unconsciously. I was making up music way before I recognised that that was my essential activity and purpose in life. I am glad that I didn't ask permission for any of this as I would have faced even more derision and ridicule than I did. I am glad that I eventually *gave myself the permission* to do this thing, which, to me, is as natural as breathing.

But it has made 'normal' life tricky.

*

There is not one way of being a composer, just as there is not one way of living on this earth, or of walking on it, but being a composer is a distinctive way of inhabiting and looking at the world:

Tree. I am looking out of a window. I am looking at a tree. I am looking at a line of trees.

To the edge of my vision is the Thames, a faint gash of

4

blue-grey. People walk up and down the long path, passing the line of trees. Some limp, a few sway from side to side as they walk. A woman stops to check her phone. Three people stand chatting. Children skip and hop their way along the path. A dog leaps.

What can you see? This is a question I ask my students when I instruct them to notate the rhythms of the movement of the wind in the trees.

Everywhere is motion at thousands of different speeds. And that doesn't include the layers upon layers upon multilayers of motion and micro-motion which is the River Thames.

I tell my students that they can focus on a single leaf or the movement of a clump of leaves, a branch, the whole tree or the entire line of trees. I say, 'Write down the rhythm of the movement that you see. You can collect these over several sessions. Come back next week with bars containing only rhythmic patterns; forget about pitches. This is a looking exercise.'

*

Because my acceptance as a composer has not been a straightforward journey (perhaps because of the colour of my skin and the ingrained perceptions of what a composer is and can be), in my work and teaching I feel impelled to fling wide open the doors on my world for others to walk through with me, sharing the pathways and practicalities of creating music, as well as illuminating the personal experiences that shape it. It gives me pleasure to share the joy.

It is rare for me to keep a detailed record of the process of composing a piece right up to the performance but in a demonstrated talk I gave for ResCen (a research centre founded with fellow artists Ghislaine Boddington, Shobana Jeyasingh, Richard Layzell, Rosemary Lee and Graeme Miller) at Middlesex University and later at our conference *NightWalking: navigating the unknown* at the Southbank Centre, I decided to document, as honestly as I could, all the stages of composing and rehearsing a new work in order to shine a light on this activity for a non-specialist audience.

Dervish is a piece that was inspired as much by the sound of the word as by its meaning. I worked my way into the music from the word 'dervish' and what it meant to me. Early in the year 2001 I had received a call from Matthew Sharp inviting me to compose a cello and piano piece for him to perform with Dominic Harlan at the Wigmore Hall. This piece would form part of a series of miniatures. Matthew is a dear friend and as he was speaking on the phone – asking me if I would compose something for him – I came up with a title immediately: *Dervish*. I had no idea where it came from but it was as if I immediately *knew* what sort of piece would capture his and Dominic's personalities. I could somehow sense the piece without having a note of it written. From Matthew's commission to the point of me actually sitting down and composing it was six months. To be precise, I started putting notes on the page only three weeks before the concert. Here is the programme note I wrote for it. It describes what I wanted to achieve:

> Dervish dances are different from many Westerners' perception of them. There is absolutely no hedonistic wildness; the swirling skirts move from rapt and still devotion. An intense, trance-like state is where the music begins. I wanted to capture this atmosphere and also set it beside the passion that is in speed. The Sufi dance is solely for worship; my *Dervish* is in celebration of the rapturous sound of Matthew and Dominic playing together.

In the months before composing the piece I'd listened to a recording of Turkish Sufi music and had been struck by how spellbindingly concentrated it was. You could *hear* that prayer was at the heart of it. At the time, I was finishing off an opera and was highly frazzled, yet there were just weeks to go before the Wigmore Hall concert. Would there be enough time for Matthew and Dominic to learn it?

Once I move my attention to the actual notes, I am immersed in a world of almost overwhelming practicalities. Which instrument, which range, how long? Where in the programme? Where to put the page turns? How many beats to the bar? How loud, how soft? How fast, how slow? Errollyn, you are no longer alone in your head with your sound-dreaming; you are now in the world of humans, of fingers, breath and muscle. Knowing exactly *who* I am writing for greatly influences the music regarding what technical and expressive challenges I decide to set the performer. The personalities of the musicians will seep into the music in any case, so when composing for specific people I try to be sensitive to their qualities as human beings and to let those qualities inform what I compose.

I rarely trace my process as closely as I did in these notebook jottings made while composing *Dervish*:

— Matthew was leaving nice messages on my answer machine. By the ninth message I could detect the slightest quiver in his voice.

— I sat down on 5 June and started simply in my notebook from Mexico. As I sat at the piano I could hear Matthew and Dominic's sound in my head and I could see them performing in my mind's eye. I love how Matthew plays high on the cello. He is also a singer and brings this experience to his playing. The piano's first chord is a semitone and in this piece I seek ways to make the piano bend its notes the way a cello or any stringed instrument can. This bending, this getting between the cracks of notes, is what is so striking about Eastern music. Later in the piece I clash notes (a B against B flat, for instance, which gives the effect of microtones. The opening statement sets up the patterning of these tritones (a tritone – an interval of three whole tones – is considered the most enigmatic combination of two notes), which gives the piece a dreamlike quality, and I was also remembering the sound of the drum in the Sufi music I'd heard. Later, I made direct reference to this drum in my music by getting Matthew and Dominic to tap on the wood of their instruments.

- In the early sketch I thought that I'd come back and fill in more gaps but I decided to see what the gaps sounded like. I had to keep reminding myself that instruments in the live, acoustic environment fill the space with their harmonics and breath. There seemed to be a lot of octave doubling and unison playing, something I don't usually do.

- Wrote bits that got chopped out as they proved extraneous. Everything needed to be condensed as Matt had asked for a 5-minute piece. I had to cut to the chase and find a way of instantly establishing and maintaining the atmosphere.

- Started sending piece off in bite-sized chunks to Matthew and Dominic.

- Read an account of Dervish dances by Will Self then forgot it. My *Dervish* is fantastical and not factual or musicological. Half-known or half-remembered things more easily liberate my imagination. Much thinking, listening and research can occur before I compose a work such as *Dervish* but when it comes to the actual committing of notes on a page I have to push the facts aside, accepting the filter of my whole self, with all its predilections and foibles, and embark on a spree of invention – fuelled though it is by knowledge.

- Whirling section. Half of me wanted to avoid a mad, fast bit as being too obvious. But . . . I went there. Wondered if it might sound a bit bald. In the sketches I see that this section was much shorter and later I introduced its repeat with a key change. I had also thought of doing something different in the piano part. Matthew and Dominic played it down the phone to me and when we got together we experimented with various types of bowing and piano articulation.

— Time was fast running out, so I switched to writing straight onto my computer from the piano then editing it. Rather than from hadwritten sketch book to computer. A few mistakes in cutting and pasting actually improved the piece. Time was running out.

— Wanted to end the piece drifting into the air, as if it could still be going on somewhere . . .

— Rehearsal with Matthew and Dominic a couple of days before Wigmore Hall. Worked a lot on getting the right sort of glisses.*

— Concert. June. Not sure it was good enough. Bit depressed.

— October. Purcell Room concert and rehearsals. In rehearsals talked more about the atmosphere we were trying to create. Asked Dominic to try knocking piano at different places. Asked Matthew to look at the rising harmonic glisses as in bar 43. Added one little bar towards end to make the phrase more asymmetric, less expected – bar 158 (I think). This section had been bugging me since the Wigmore Hall concert. In the Southbank Centre concert we ran my opening piano piece (*Louis' Loops*) into *Dervish* and worked out the different states of lighting to change mood from me to Matt and Dom.

---

* Gliss = glissando, a note that slides – think swanee whistle!

– Recording at Potton Hall. Dominic and Matthew asked for a night-time slot to help with the vibe. They had wanted to spend part of the day walking by the sea to prepare. Piece continued to grow at each take, not least with the startling revelation that *pp* made the opening truly work at last. A world of difference between *p* and *pp*.* Turned pages for Dominic in the live room and witnessed the intense concentration and electricity between Matthew and Dominic. Worried that my presence might inhibit them, but they're true performers and relish connecting to the ether.

Dervish was recorded on my album *The Girl in My Alphabet* and has been performed all over the world by different musicians. As I sit reading my account of composing *Dervish* years later, there are performances scheduled by Yo-Yo Ma and Kathryn Stott in South Korea and Japan. I will never compose a piece quite like this again. I had wanted to put a secret message in the work to someone I was enamoured of as well as wanting to encapsulate my response to Sufi music. I believe these things give the work a special energy.

*

One of the lesser discussed aspects of musical composition is the way in which the performers influence the journey of a piece *after* the work has been composed. That is not to say

* p = piano (quiet) and pp = pianissimo (very quiet).

that the score isn't precisely notated and the conception fully worked out and made clear by the composer in terms of the notes on the page but rather that the performers bring their individual personalities, their lifetime of thought, interpretative experience and technical prowess to breathe further life to the work. Without fully acknowledging and embracing this stage the composer's development is hampered. For a composer the rehearsal period often feels like starting again from the beginning. It can be a nerve-racking time; all the dreams and hopes and doubts that are the foundation on which music is built are laid bare – in sound. The composer has to wait patiently (and with empathy) for the musician or musicians to learn the music. But by listening to a musician learn a work, aspects of the now disappeared world of its stumbling creation – those hesitant, hidden corners – come back into view. All the questions a performer asks me as they are learning a work force me to think about how clearly I have notated the music in the first place.

Several years ago I accompanied a friend, the viola player Rita Porfiris, to Miami where she was rehearsing with the New World Symphony, conducted by Michael Tilson Thomas. As usual, I had music to write for some urgent deadline so I would grab a practice room when it became free and compose there. All around me was the sound of practising of individual instrumental parts of the orchestral music due to be performed in a few days' time. Passages repeated over and over, at different speeds, slow notes turning into fast, repeated again and again with varied phrasings

12

and dynamics. And there and then it fully came home to me that I was eavesdropping on the secret life of devotion of a musician, the lifetime of thought and private, solitary preparation. All this before a new work is presented for the first time to an audience. All this before even a tried-and-tested, centuries-old work is presented to an audience.

On hearing a new work for the first time a composer can be full of doubt as well as optimistic anticipation and, as happened with the first performance of *Dervish*, I was not entirely sure of the work's construction as it contained things I hadn't tried before. Now, years later, after hearing it performed by countless cellists and pianists, I would not change a note. To hear *Dervish* live and breathe in so many ways, to hear the kaleidoscope of timbres and colours brought to bear by performers, has been an education. The rehearsal period with Matthew and Dominic was a life class for me and I will always be grateful for their frankness and honesty. The piece exists because of their unique energy, love and commitment.

*

One does not always work with friends. As a recovering shy and lumpy introvert, I've had to find ways of walking into rehearsal rooms and concert halls without immediately turning round and bolting for the door, although I still find it surprising the way my enthusiasm for music actually overrides any awkwardness as everyone in the room settles into the shared endeavour of music-making. I remember walking into a rehearsal for a work for two orchestras. I was full of trepidation since one of these orchestras was quite poorly behaved – rude and disrespectful to the conductor and clearly not inclined to play my new work – but I had counselled myself beforehand to smile whenever possible and to say thank you . . . a lot. I was astonished at the difference it made to the atmosphere in the room to put my own nervousness to one side in order to convey my genuine thanks to everyone.

It isn't enough to spend months or years composing a piece of music; the composer must sometimes bring hundreds of people with them through how they carry themselves. A composer must often persuade, cajole. Yet we have no training for this. I did my theory exams, studied orchestration, practised ten hours a day, read books, wrote essays, analysed scores, attended lectures, concerts, masterclasses, auditions, rehearsals; but it would also have been invaluable to have had, as part of the course, the opportunity to study psychology, anthropology, geology, philosophy – and to have gone into therapy – in order to understand oneself and others better, and to make sure of being fully equipped with the requisite amount of emotional intelligence. But we tend to stay inside, in small rooms, while we reside in the lonely palaces of our minds.

BEGINNINGS

You walk towards light when you listen, when you pray, when you look out, when you love, when you put your hands on the keys – like this.

*

She had a stern, cold uncle as another absent father. Her aunt sent out for jellied eels every Sunday and her parents were set free in New York. Things couldn't carry on in that Tottenham-tense atmosphere without something breaking. Eventually they all splintered off into harsh, fragmented lives. She tried suicide first.

Her aunt is making her stand up against the wall. She is three years old. Her aunt is trying to cure her of what she doesn't realise is her African heritage – a sticky-out bum. 'Don't stick out your bottom, Linny. That's it – try to press all of your back against the wall.'

Her uncle is saying, as she is about to leave to go to school, 'Look at you. You're slovenly – call that cleaning the kitchen floor?' He beat her for throwing away a piece of soap that had fallen into the dustbin. She must have been about ten years old.

Now her father is dead and her uncle is grief-stricken into Alzheimer's.

She loved her family.

She survived her family.

CHRISTMAS EVE 2020

An early-evening drive from Thurso to Strathy listening to the Choir of King's College, Cambridge, tells me that another year is coming to an end. There is a particular point, just after crossing the border from Caithness to Sutherland, where the landscape suddenly opens up wide and becomes wilder. The sky is enormous. The clouds roll across the mountains in the gloaming and the dark calls out to the deer and small creatures huddled in holes. I drive through Reay, Melvich, then straight on to Strathy Point.

A solitary eagle wheels and I drop off my presents to my friends Patsy and Don. The drive from them to the lighthouse on the narrow pot-holed single-track road takes me even further out to sea. Maybe I will put up some decorations for my own eyes. After a week of tense contractual negotiations for my latest opera, I am ready to sink into the peace of this place. No one else is here except for me. I hoover and then admire my new chair made by a local craftsman out of a single birch tree.

Later, after watching *Carols from King's* on BBC Two, I learn that all the choral scholars were quarantined because of Covid-19 and that the King's Singers were brought in with just one day to learn the music before filming. I am particularly moved by the service this year with its absence of congregation and I remember the completely empty Albert Hall I sat in for the premiere of my piece *Jerusalem: our clouded hills*, at the Last Night of the Proms just a few months ago. I silently toast Christmases past and those to come. My mother's birthday was yesterday.

It is peaceful here, yet I am aware of the increasing danger all around the world. The United Kingdom has finally made a post-Brexit deal with Europe the same day that my old passport is returned in the post, now useless. My new one is blue.

The Festival of Nine Lessons and Carols offers comfort. Each mouthful of music is remembered as carols we sang as children. I reflect on the many boxes of Haribos I sent the boys of the Choir of King's College, Cambridge, after they had recorded my EP (*Peace on Earth, See that I am God* and *PACE*) last June for release this November. It was one of the last recordings made by their musical director, Stephen Cleobury.

Like so many people, I get tense coming up to landmark days: Christmas, New Year, birthdays, anniversaries. We can do nothing about the relentless ticking countdown. Earlier in the Co-op I watched a grandmother fretting over which chocolate to buy for herself as a treat for Christmas. She seemed fractious; her grandson was patient and loving, as if he understood that she felt so keenly the piercing grimace of time. My questions to myself include, 'Have I been alive enough?'; 'Have I paid sufficient attention?' I decide to commit to five hundred words of this book every single day. I commit to writing it as I write music. Two different parts of the brain will have to accommodate each other somehow.

DO IT

Do it. Do it. Do it. Stop. Stop thinking. Don't stop to think.
Bad luck.

Trick yourself or be forced into writing something very
fast and you will see just how quickly you become an animal. All nerve endings and responses, ears on wire stalks.

You know it all already.

*

Once upon a time there was a little girl who was forced to
make her own way in life from an early age. Her mother
gave her up to an aunt and uncle living in England and went
to live with her husband (the little girl's father) in New York.
The little girl learned to field the emotional demands of four
adults who behaved like noisy toddlers one minute and then
would suddenly become very strict and beat the little girl the
next. The grown-ups told the little girl that she was stupid,
lazy, slovenly and ugly, and that she would never amount to
anything – she would certainly never get married or have
children. Her job was to look after them – make breakfast,
clean the stove before school, fetch tea and coffee, clean the
floor, wash the dishes, do the laundry, pick up all the bits
from the carpet, look after her younger siblings and never
ever answer back. 'Children should be seen and not heard'

is what her uncle would say. The little girl was scared of her uncle. Uncle Arthur. The little girl's job, as the eldest, was to wear sensible colours (brown and navy blue), help her sisters cross the road and to assuage her mother's guilt at leaving her children by doing everything she could for her aunt, Renee, who she called Kenee or Kene. The little girl loved her aunt so much, even when her aunt told her that she was nothing special and that other girls she knew did much more at home to help their mothers, like making Sunday dinner. The little girl never ever answered back.

Often the little girl would come home from school to see her aunt sitting on the couch, looking very sad, staring and smoking into space. When her uncle came home the air would hold its breath because if there was too much salt in the rice or if the dinner was late the uncle's quiet, simmering anger and resentment would shudder throughout the whole house. It was best to keep out of his way.

One Saturday the uncle was making the girls their Sunday lunch of soup and coffee. There was laughter. The coffee was made in a percolator on the gas stove. The uncle took the percolator off the stove and poured it into the little girl's cup but most of it was pouring, accidentally, onto her leg. The little girl was too frightened to call out 'Stop!' and sat there in agony. Eventually she had to get up and ran into the garden so that she could cry.

*

I know what I've done.

INTUITION

Nelson's Victory

I am looking for something. Like a private detective or unwisely curious explorer, I have the faintest scent, a curling wisp on the air, a trill caught in the breeze as I bend to tie up a shoelace. I am looking for something I have neither seen nor smelled before. But how, in the myriad of possibilities of sound and combinations of sound, will I know when I have found it? And why am I looking for it in the first place? In these early stages of a work, when all I know is the timescale and date of the first performance, it is as if I am inching my way down a long, misty road. Trees hang their frowsy heads in the wind, reaching out rheumy, breaking fingers to each other in order to keep safe. Tired and alone I am caught up in the limits of my body. Half blind I navigate the unknown. Eventually, after I have become accustomed to the overwhelming solitude and have surrendered hope of find-ing anything at all, I begin to see sparkling patterns dancing right ahead of me on the path. My heart leaps. I squint and they are gone. I rub my eyes. What can I do to bring them back? Did they go away or is it just that I can't see them any more? Maybe I never saw them in the first place.

Intuition, as I once copied down from a long-forgotten dictionary, is 'the power of the mind by which it immediately perceives the truth of things without reasoning or analysis; a truth so perceived, immediate, instinctive knowledge or belief'. Intuition is a 'knowingness'. Knowing when something is right or wrong, knowing when a piece of work is finished or needs revising. Knowing when the joins don't join. Intuition is an awareness of patterns, above and below the surface, seen and unseen, heard and unheard. For me, the act of intuiting can involve doing nothing – listening, waiting (like Lara and her alethiometer in Philip Pullman's *His Dark Materials* trilogy) and just being alive to the moment. It is the mental leap that takes us out of ourselves, allowing us to connect to atavistic principles and to a collective unconscious. When a work is completed, however, amnesia sets in and I forget the details of the intuitive process.

I often dive into composing a piece of music without consciously knowing the structure. I believe and trust in my intuition and the fact that I do *know* at a deep and non-linguistic level exactly what it is that I want to achieve. I have learned that starting is what is important and that it is how one manipulates the material that defines the process. It doesn't lessen the fear that is concomitant with voyaging out into new terrain, but the knowledge that intuition will be my compass and companion in the wild maze of creation is a source of reassurance.

When I was a young girl, I remember reading a biography of a composer whom I greatly admired. I came across a passage in which the biographer described one of the composer's abilities as being able to 'see the wood for the trees'.

This made a significant impact on my own thinking and approach to music-making and I have realised that I am best able to 'see the wood', that is, to have an overview, a bird's-eye view, of a work by using intuitive perception. I tried to activate this perception when composing my large-scale work *Our English Heart*. This work demonstrates intuition in operation at various levels. Looking back at this work I can see the influence of intuition on historical research, social perception and interpretation, in the writing of words, music and in musical structuring. This reveals to me the interplay between intuition and learned craft – tuition.

Our English Heart is scored for soprano, men's chorus and orchestra and lasts approximately thirty-five minutes. It was co-commissioned by George and Janette Wilkins and the BBC to commemorate the two hundredth anniversary of the Battle of Trafalgar and the death of Admiral Lord Nelson on 21 October 1805.

It was a work that required a level of historical research before I wrote a note. I knew very little about Nelson and his naval or amorous adventures, but my fascination with the sea has been a continuing source of inspiration for me. This was a different sort of commission from most of my others in that it was a 'public' piece, marking a major historical event, as opposed to a work based around a set of preoccupations of my own choosing. My work was to be broadcast live from Portsmouth Cathedral on BBC Radio 3 in a concert commemorating Trafalgar Day. Because of the historical focus and the narrative aspect of the work, I initially considered working with a writer who would provide me with a text, but in the end I wrote and compiled the text myself as well as composing the music. I wanted to let the music drive the text and to be free to react quickly and instinctively to the material as it grew and changed. I have increasingly realised that the raw material of my compositions very often gives rise to the structure of a work, enabling it to grow organically. This organic growth ensures that the macro is related to the micro and this supports my desire to create a finished entity that is authentic. *Our English Heart* presented new challenges for me, and in these relatively straitened circumstances when I was not completely free to follow my own predilections regarding subject matter, how would intuition play a part in my process?

Every new work involves decisions about how one is going to use that particular opportunity and how long that piece will take to write. Before I began *Our English Heart* I knew that I wanted to try something new – to give myself a sea of time, time I could luxuriate in, time to do the very best I could, time to refine. I decided to stop many other activities, including performing, so that I could place all my focus on creating this new work. For a freelance musician this was a hard decision, but I knew, both rationally and intuitively, that unless I seized, with both hands, this rare opportunity to write for huge forces, I would miss out on a new journey of discovery. I wanted to give myself time to really 'finish' this work, to allow time for the fine-tuning of details.

I feel things before I understand them. I walk towards a sound before I can hear it. I can *know* what a work is before I find the notes. So it was with *Our English Heart*. Before starting I had a strong sense of the atmosphere of the work without knowing anything of the structure or the details of its harmonic and melodic language. I imagined the sea swirling through the orchestra; I heard in my head the texture of voices pitted against that sound. There was a notion about a variety of new techniques to learn and employ carried over from previous works – it is as if each work I compose seems to open up new questions and technical possibilities for the work to follow. All this as well as the usual, fervent wish to make this my best work so far. But how would I construct the sea in musical notes? What words would I put into the mouths of the men at sea and the woman left at home?

The act of composing, while being an act of faith, determination and imagination, also involves active learning. One learns by doing and many of the problems to be solved are set by oneself and are thus unique to that particular musical situation. So, while intuition enables the possibility of 'knowing', one has to discover the 'making' skills required to bring forth the known. One example of this, in *Our English Heart*, was in the battle scene (bars 382–500). I had to find a way of conveying the tension before battle commenced and the bloody chaos and noise of the battle itself, culminating in the fatal gunshot that was to kill Nelson. It took a while to build patterns that would be perceived as random, reinforced by the percussion, signifying cannon and gunshots.

The use of ostinato, counterpoint and vivid ever-changing orchestral colours were all techniques used but the details were built up instinctively, note by note.

When I work, it is as if I am operating in at least two dimensions. My head is spinning among the billions of stars while my feet are wedged firmly in mud. I navigate between these two worlds by listening to the voice of magic, spurring me on to think and bring forth the impossible, and then there is the 'sensible' voice of distrust, constantly urging me to think of practicalities. Most major leaps in the learning curve happen through hearing what you have composed. For me, it is important to try new things in every piece and then to listen carefully in rehearsal, so that I can fully gauge whether or not my calculations have worked. Throughout my life I am conscious of building an ever-growing cata- logue and mental archive of sounds. This happens through taking risks, which for me come from 'composing with a hunch' and lead to the formulation of new ideas and new sound worlds.

In creating a new work one is often working backwards, from an imaginary sound world where everything is per- fect, sparkling and bright, a world of pure energy, through to its actualisation. In the case of *Our English Heart*, this meant months of drudgery, uncertainty and painfully slow progress even in the act of refining and detailing. But in those months, there was also the opportunity to explore other composers' music to see how they had solved partic- ular problems.

There were two works close to hand while I was composing *Our English Heart* – Wagner's 'Ride of the Valkyries' and Britten's opera *Billy Budd*. I knew that strong melodies and evocative textures in the foreground and background would play an important part in my new work. In studying Wagner, I admired the way that the texture of the accompaniment, the woodwind trills and string figuration, gives this piece its thrilling excitement – even though it is the famous tune in the brass that we remember. In *Billy Budd* I wanted to look at Britten's handling of male voices with an orchestra, as those were my forces too. I was also very much interested in his particular use of percussion in evoking both the sea and naval life on a ship in 1805 – the same year as the Battle of Trafalgar.

What makes a composer turn one way and not another? What led me to alight on certain scenes to set and not others? I believe in using curiosity, chance and everyday synchronicities as my guide in learning. Most things we need to learn are at our fingertips, particularly with the resource of the Internet. A lot of research for *Our English Heart* was carried out on the Internet, right down to investigating what music was played on Nelson's ship, HMS *Victory*, before the Battle of Trafalgar commenced. But it was the actual and physical – not the virtual – that gave me the strongest drive to write my work: the visit to the *Victory* with my commissioners, George and Janette Wilkins, who also lent me rare books containing Nelson's letters to Emma Hamilton; and the trip to meet Clive Richards who owned the largest private collection of Nelson memorabilia. There I held the last letter from Emma Hamilton to Lord Nelson and looked at everything from signal books written and drawn in by the sailors themselves, to Nelson's silverware. These were the significant, formative experiences that led me to include and highlight specific historical moments. I wanted to find a way of connecting these events and figures from history to those people living today who remember and revere them.

What makes writing and speaking about intuition difficult is that it is essentially non-linguistic. We use words such as 'hunch', 'gut feeling' and even 'gift' to describe a sensation of knowledge from deep within ourselves. I believe that we are all born with it in abundant supply but we are encouraged to shut it off as we get older and we gradually lose touch with our younger, more instinctive and truthful selves. As an adult I find that the best work I do is first thing in the morning, when the last remaining blankets of sleep are still on me. That is when I make the sharpest decisions and feel most fully 'in the zone' of creativity. Finding my way as an artist has meant that I work to my own dictates, and I have chosen a life where I can have the maximum freedom to explore and to learn. And each work requires different working methods. When I was composing *Our English Heart*, it felt right that I should work for a short period first thing in the morning, immediately after breakfast, before I got dressed or embarked on daily rituals, interfacing with the world. I found that in this alert yet relaxed state many compositional problems were solved and many new pathways opened up. And I could carry on thinking about them throughout the day.

I used this method in refining the end section of *Our English Heart*, which took a long time to get right. It is only twelve bars long, but I played around endlessly with the words and notes of the soprano's last entrance and with the heterophonic burbling figurations in the orchestra, which were designed to evoke a different sea, a twenty-first-century sea. The work had to feel as if it were coming to a close, but a closure of hope and tranquillity. The harmony was relatively static, but it was the details that would make it work. I used the percussion very differently here and introduced gentle, ringing sounds. As in the battle scene, I contrived to make everything sound spontaneous – guided by instinct for the atmosphere required and advised by the technique of my training. I grew grateful for these mornings.

I believe that it is my responsibility as an artist constantly to evaluate and adapt my working methods. One has to be aware of one's temperament and I find that I sometimes have to trick myself in order to get the best from myself. This is where intuition plays an important part. There are times when my concentration span is short and there are other times when I can work steadily and undistracted for long hours. Taking the advice of a friend, I used a stop-watch when composing *Our English Heart* and decided on a minimum number of hours I would work each day in order to complete the work by the deadline. I could thus accom-modate my short bursts of compositional activity, knowing that I would get the required amount of time in and not be caught out by a last-minute scramble to the deadline. For all the wonderful ideas I might have, for all the thinking and dreaming I might do, my thoughts would be realised only through sitting down and putting the notes onto the page. What is written gets heard. What is not notated doesn't get played. It is simply not heard.

The hard fact of notes on a page is what remains of the storm of ideas. That's not to deny that thinking and pondering occur all the time but to reaffirm that using Western notation to write music to be performed by others takes time and foresight. Deciding how one is going to actualise the formless inspiration involves the day-to-day 'housework' – the placing of one note after another. I roughly estimate that in *Our English Heart* there are over a hundred thousand notes, all of which need to be placed in the right order. At the end of a work I sometimes calculate how long it would take me simply to copy out that work in an automatic fashion, without the sweat of making it up. In the case of *Our English Heart* it could take up to a couple of months. For labour on that scale I believe one has to keep checking in with oneself to ensure that the ideas and fundamental conception are worth the time and effort.

I have chosen a life of searching: searching for questions, answers and an artistic habitat where I can be myself and create freely, happily, looking for opportunities where I can continue to grow. It has been my own intuitive choices as to what I need that have made that life possible. We are all, to varying degrees, caged beings, whether we make those cages ourselves or whether we are locked into them involuntarily or without noticing. We can all find ourselves without control. Writing music is thinking in time and, often, thinking in public. When I was composing *Our English Heart* I confronted the reality of this and was able to grow comfortable with its awesomeness because, in this instance, the story of Lord Nelson, Lady Hamilton and the Battle of Trafalgar is so well known. Before I wrote a note, the story was familiar to many, which meant I didn't have the burden of explaining my characters and situation but could concentrate on casting my own light on history. The work is shaped in a single movement that falls into several sections. This form grew through instinct and I responded to the pictures in my head rather like a film-maker. Music is experienced by the listener in linear time – the same domain as for a film, and I soon decided to approach the structure of my new work as if I were making a film: the work moves from scene to scene, and from one emotional state to another. I wanted to depict the drama in its actual, imagined moment and to convey the atmosphere and sensation of life at sea and the feeling of passion and personal sacrifice.

I started composing first at the piano. The piano is my instrument and it is the best instrument for working out harmonies. I start by improvising, playing around with the notes and possibilities I find beneath my fingertips. The work begins with a short orchestral introduction, evoking the majesty and nobility of the sea and of victory. As in

Wagner's 'Ride of the Valkyries', I use the brass for the main theme and employ the woodwind and strings for flourishes and swooping figuration. The next section (from bar 28) sees the entrance of the male voices accompanied by the cellos and basses. I heard these voices as those of Nelson's sailors. They sing of the terror and uncertainty of being at sea, knowing that they must do their duty:

The sea craves us,
The waves taunt us,
The wind calls for us.
Do your duty, sailors, hoist the pennant. Heave, heave-ho,
Hold to the sea.

The work is about an episode in British history when to be a hero was to be a man who carried word through to deed in epic fashion and in the unquestioning service of his country. But I needed to show both the public and private moments – the tough and the tender. Horatio Nelson, Emma Hamilton and Nelson's sailors on the *Victory* are at the centre of the piece and the research I did enabled me to connect with these historical (and near-mythical) characters as real, living human beings.

As there are innumerable composers, so there are myriad ways of working. I believe each composer starts on the physical work of a piece (by that, I mean physically putting the dots on the page) at varying points along the way to completion. For some, the conscious working-out of possible pathways is important before they start the work proper and these people make sketches. For others all the gestation is done, sometimes unconsciously, in their heads, so that when they sit down, as in the case of Mozart, it is simply a matter of getting the notes on the page quickly enough.

Personally, I regard each new work as an adventure and try to come to each piece as if I am an alien from outer space and am discovering music for the first time. I take nothing for granted, whether it is a scale or a chord, an interval or a phrase, an instrument or a hemi-demi-semiquaver, a style or a genre. I see my job as making sure that each note within my piece has earned its place and is there for an irrefutable reason. The experience of writing that work should bring me greater knowledge, illumination and understanding. I am aware of a sense of having worked a great deal out beforehand, but in a wholly non-verbal manner – in fact, in a manner that eludes any language. It is as if I have mentally worked through and rejected various sets of materials and possible pathways, all of which will impact on the overall essence of a piece, before I sit down at my piano. Therefore, when I start the physical realisation of a work, or when I *think* I start, I have actually already started. The strength of my conviction in making crucial decisions leads me to believe that this is so.

Right now, I find myself thinking about an opera that will be performed next year. Running through my mind, unbidden, are glimpses of the sound world. The metallic cry of electric guitars seemed incongruous at first but my mind is connecting the strands of ideas in the story so that the orchestration itself connects with every detail of the emotional logic of the opera. It is as if I start with the sound and work backwards for its reasoning during the actual sitting-down at my desk. Intuition is the snapshot – the flash of insight – and the craft is in the slow unpacking of that flash.

When I was a fledgling composer I placed greater value on inspiration and ideas. It was working on *Our English Heart* that confirmed a change of approach. I dived head-long into the piece and let my intuitive sense guide me. I was able to witness the role of intuition even in the drudg-ery of the work. I would be working on a passage and would get a nagging feeling. I learned to trust that this physical discomfort was almost always due to the fact that there was a small detail in an earlier part of the piece that just wasn't right. It could be one note within a flourish of a myriad of notes that might barely be perceived amid the whole orchestra, but until it was fixed I couldn't concentrate on the current passage.

As I continue to work as a composer, I grow ever more to trust my physical reaction to sound and to my working process. Physical motion is a crucial part of a day's work. It solves problems. It is no accident that walking is so import-ant to composers, mathematicians, philosophers, writers. I also find that washing up is very good for switching down the gears of conscious thinking and allowing intuitive thought free rein. Just recently, while stopped at a red light in my car, I was caught by the rhythms of the vibrations of the engine. I listened, captivated, and I am sure that one day those ever-changing patterns will find their way into a piece. The wonder of sound is all around us.

As I put the last note into the score (an ecstatic coda that grows out of a solemn section depicting Nelson's funeral), I happened to look out of my window in Greenwich, overlooking the River Thames, at the very moment a black-canopied barge passed by on the water. I knew it was Nelson's funeral barge. Historical accounts tell us that it arrived at Greenwich on 23 December 1805 and that Nelson's body lay in state in the Painted Hall at Greenwich from 5 to 7 January 1806. More than fifteen thousand people came to pay their respects and many more were turned away. Nelson's body was then taken from Greenwich up the Thames to Whitehall on 8 January. The next day it was taken through the streets, filled with twenty to thirty thousand people, to St Paul's Cathedral. Was what I had just glimpsed, by chance, a rehearsal for the re-enactment for 21 October? But it was not yet October . . . Whatever it was that I had seen, I took it to be a magical sign that my work, commemorating one of the greatest naval heroes, was done.

In short, intuition, perception and craft are the essential ingredients for inspiration and spontaneity. For me, intuition is about seeing patterns that are already there and about creating new ones; perception is about understanding how to apply them and craft is the development of technique in order to communicate. All three provide the space and satisfactory environment for inspiration to flourish. The greatest enemy of intuition is fear. We don't always want to see or hear what is in front of us. We don't always trust the light of our calling. But there is endless treasure if we can but dare to walk the path that opens up for each of us individually, alone.

CAKE

I like to eat cake for breakfast. My Second String Quartet aspired to the condition of fruitcake and *Fondant* is a recent work for Royal Northern Sinfonia to celebrate its sixtieth birthday. Cake has been my inspiration and guide since schooldays when, aged around thirteen, I came up with the brilliant idea that if you wanted to lose weight it would be much easier to starve in anticipation of eating your very favourite food – in my case, cake. So began what I now realise was an eating anomaly, if not an honest-to-goodness disorder. At this point I was at Hollington Park School for Girls, St Leonards-on-Sea, East Sussex. ('Holly Park' is what we called it.)

After my first term there, devouring the diet consisting mainly of English stodge served to us, I put on ten pounds. I needed to do something about it. I came up with a slimming diet. I came up with a ruse. As the young girls marvelled at my weight loss, I put the girls on low-calorie, *healthy* diets, instructing them to part with their cakes in return for extra portions of my vegetables, fruit and meat – the non-stodge elements of our diet, that is. So it was that I spent whole terms eating nothing but three or four cakes a day (iced buns, Eccles cakes, doughnuts, Bakewell tarts). Anyone who has known me since my youth will refer to my 'cake diet'. It was highly effective and kept me thin for a long time. It was just common sense to me that if a person wanted to lose weight they must focus their eating around the food they were passionate about and omit everything else. I would, no doubt, have made millions if I had written a book about it. The cake diet saw me through the Urdang Academy, the Dance Theatre of Harlem training, my dance degree at Goldsmiths, University of London, all the way through my career with PULSE (the alternative-comedy band I was with), my career as a keyboard player (how else could I have squeezed into my PVC dress?) and the period when I was running my recording studio in Camden. The thing about the cake diet: it was very, *very* strict – if eccentric – with regard to portion size. I was permitted half a cake a day – half a Swiss roll, half a Battenberg cake, half a box of French fancies, half a birthday cake. Cake with icing was the optimum and I became a leading authority on every type of shop-bought cake.

Today I eat more conventionally though there are still reminders of my former lifestyle.

London Fields Primary School has a class named after me – the Wallen Class. Recently, on my first visit to meet the nine-year-old children, among the many questions I was asked was what I liked eating. I replied that I loved cake for breakfast. The next day a parent tweeted that her nine-year-old daughter now expected to have cake for breakfast, just like me. Not quite the role model, EW! My eleven-year-old goddaughter, Ariana, is still psychologically scarred because I ate her cake eight years ago. Her grandparents told me it is still often spoken about at home in hushed tones of shocked incomprehension. Ariana advised me to title this book *Why Did Errollyn Eat My Cake?*

I have always had a sweet tooth, which in many ways was encouraged by the dull food on offer in the British Isles for main meals when I was growing up. Today there is a vast array of ingredients, herbs, spices, recipes and restaurants from every culture. Back in the day, the most excitement came from our Sunday dinner of Belize spiced chicken with rice and beans, plantain and potato salad. A world away from sandwich spread, lumpy gravy and slithery cabbage. My sweet tooth was something of a rebellion against blandness.

When I was making my very first album, *Meet Me at Harold Moores*, it was lemon drizzle cake that kept Gerry O'Riordan and me in tip-top recording buoyancy. When my aunt, Kene, was dying, my friend Cathy Lewis made an orange and almond cake and brought it across London to the hospice. I will never forget that act of kindness, nor how much comfort it brought us. My students at the Royal College of Music knew to bring me either a double chocolate muffin or a KitKat. At Trinity Laban Conservatoire of Music and Dance it was a Danish pastry or a KitKat. Only a couple of days ago, I made sure before returning home from an evening concert in St John's Smith Square including the premiere of a work of mine that I had bought a pastry for my breakfast the next morning. Cake still remains on my mind at all times. In lockdown I have learned to make Dundee cake and a knockout cherry and almond cake. Happily, I have just found a caramel iced apple turnover in my fridge. That will be tomorrow's breakfast.

When I was on my cake diet I would carry my daily allowance around in my bag – which is how Peter Gabriel got to be offered a Kipling's French fancy. We were mixing a track he'd sung in a multi-star line-up for the concert at Wembley Stadium in honour of Nelson Mandela's seventieth birthday. My studio was responsible for overseeing the mixing of all the tracks. What should have been most memorable about that session at Peter Gabriel's recording studio in Bath was meeting Donny Osmond and Georges Acogny (who had recently produced a Youssou N'Dour album). But this voluntary parting with cake – this star-struck altruism on my part – was a *very big* deal. It wasn't just everyone who got a French fancy. Donny didn't.

An ambition held since childhood has been to have my own sweetshop or tea room.

When I was at primary school, I was always more interested in chocolate than those annoying sweets you have to suck. I also have very strong opinions on the cakes I would serve in my tea room. There would need to be a *lot* of fondant icing on a variety of cakes filled with jam and buttercream, and not too many mille-feuilles or chocolate eclairs.

*

As a black person I seem to have to do more thinking – personally, culturally and historically – than my white counterparts, often having to think for them or to imagine their viewpoint without reciprocity. When I stop to consider, I find the subject of sugar both complex and painful. The sugar in my iced cherry Bakewell tartlets is the reason I am not a size 8, but it *is* the reason I am a British citizen. Sugar's presence in the United Kingdom is directly rooted in slavery. The craving I developed as a schoolgirl was as nothing compared to the inexhaustible demand for this culinary sensation centuries before I was born. This was an indisputable factor in the exploitation of the twelve million Africans who were transported via the so-called triangular trade right up to the late nineteenth century.*

As Daniel Defoe, the author of *Robinson Crusoe*, wrote, 'No African trade, no negroes; no negroes, no sugars, gingers, indicoes [*sic*] etc.; no sugar, etc., no islands, no continent; no continent, no trade.'

It was when I was working with the record producer and drum 'n' bass artist A Guy Called Gerald† that I started to play the game he played. His game is actually a simple question: 'How did I get here?'

---

* The triangular trade was a cycle that drew together different parts of the world. Between 1505 and 1888, approximately twelve million Africans were enslaved and transported to the New World for financial profit. Plantation agriculture – and sugar in particular – drove the African diaspora. Slaves of Caribbean sugar plantations produced molasses that was transported to New England for distillation into rum that was then shipped to Africa in exchange for the slaves who would endure the final leg of the triangle, the Middle Passage to the sugar islands.
† Along with Buggy G. Riphead, we were commissioned to create a new work for Nottingham Now festival.

When I composed *When the Wet Wind Sings* for forty una-commpanied voices, I sat at my piano in Greenwich, looking out on the Thames, and whispered to myself, 'How did I get here?' *When the Wet Wind Sings* goes some way towards answering that question. The work is about memory and forgiveness. The longer we and the world live, the greater the imperative to confront our past with full emotional engagement, so that in acknowledging its pain and complexities, our present may be seen through a more vivid and compassionate lens – and our future be shaped with wisdom and maturity. This was my own personal and artistic imperative when composing *When the Wet Wind Sings*, a work that, through its use of text and music, gesture and aural imagery, weaves together strands and fragments of the history of the Thames in a musical celebration of Greenwich and its sea-faring heart across five centuries.

Over several months, while looking out on my own stretch of the Thames, I assembled a selection of texts in Latin, English, Twi, Spanish and Portuguese by Cicero, Ovid, Elizabeth I, Francis Drake, John Hawkins, Shakespeare and myself. The texts of Cicero and Ovid frame the work and provide a philosophical commentary throughout:

Animi labes nec diuturnitate vanescere nec amnibus ullis elui potest.

Stains that affect the soul are not removed by time, nor can any rivers of water wash them away.

– **Cicero**

Nihil est toto quod perstet in orbe.

Cuncta fluunt, omnisque vegans, formatur imago,

Ipsa quoque assiduo labuntur tempora motu,

Non secus ac flumen.

> *There is nothing in the whole world that does not change.*
> *All things are in a state of flux, and every shadow passes away.*
> *Even time itself, like a river, is constantly gliding away.*
> *Time rolls on and on.*

– Ovid

Through the opposing meanings of these verses, the paradoxes of memory and the complexities and wonders of living history are explored. What stories are whispered on the breath of sea winds?

In 1562 Captain John Hawkins (later Sir John) initiated the English slave trade by sailing from England to Sierra Leone, capturing three hundred Africans and exchanging them for hides, ginger, sugar and pearls, which were then sold. On his third trip he was joined by Francis Drake, and on the return journey they were driven off course by storms and trapped by a Spanish fleet, losing several ships and many sailors' lives.

When the Wet Wind Sings alludes to the violence and majesty of the sea and to the new lives brought about by misadventure and migration across water. My music uses polyphony, chant, speaking, antiphonal techniques, sea shanties and spirituals to commemorate those lives and events that shaped Greenwich and the world of today, by way of its river, by way of its sea.

When the Wet Wind Sings

Nihil est toto quod perstet in orbe.
Cuncta fluunt, omnisque vegans, formatur imago,
Ipsa quoque assiduo labuntur tempora motu,
Non secus ac flumen.

> *There is nothing in the whole world which remains.*
> *All things are in a state of flux, and every shadow passes away.*
> *Even time itself, like a river, is constantly gliding away.*
> *Time rolls on and on.*

– Ovid

Animi labes nec diurturnitate vanescere nec amnibus ullis elui potest.

> *Stains that affect the soul are not obliterated by time, nor can rivers of water wash them away.*

– Cicero

Owuo fa me Bah

> *Death has come and taken my baby from me.*

Umma wo na Nsuom

> *The sea will never let you sleep on its bed.*

Oh haul away, Oh haul away
Steal away
Haul away

When the wet wind sings,
When it sings,
When the wet wind sings,
The salt wind.

C ni ABD Nom

There is no letter C in the Alphabet.

Do not take them without consent 'which would be detest-
able and call down the vengeance of Heaven upon the
undertakers'.

— **Elizabeth I**

A ship she was rigg'd and ready for sea,
and all of her sailors were fishes to be.
Windy weather! Stormy weather!
When the wind blows we're all together!

— **Trad. Sea Shanty**
('The Fishes')

A ship was set to sea

   Eko   *War*

   Sum Sum   *Ghost*

Blow, blow the wind

   Apo, Apo   *The sea, the sea*

When the wet wind sings

Blow the man down, bullies, blow the man down!
Wayay, blow the man down,
O blow the man down in Liverpool town!
Give me some time to blow the man down.

                     – **Trad. Sea Shanty**
                     (**'Blow the Man Down'**)

Steal away, steal away,
Steal away to Jesus.

                     – **Trad. Spiritual**

A Agua o dá, a agua o leva

    The water gives it, the water takes it.

                     – **Portuguese Proverb**

Blow the wind

    Sum Sum   *Ghost*

    Eko   *War*

    Apo, Apo   *The sea, the sea*

Haul away from the land of the Thames and steal, steal away

Blow the man down

Ave Maria, gratia plena: Dominus tecum

    Hail, Virgin Mary, most highly favoured, the Lord is with
    thee

                     – (**Music attrib. T. L. de Victoria**)

CAKE

Animi labes nec diurturnitate nec diurturnitate amnibus ullis
elui potest.

> *Stains that affect the soul are not obliterated by time, nor*
> *can rivers of water wash them away.*

– Cicero

Steal away home

> (I captured them) 'by the sword and partly by other means
> . . . (For spices), ginger, hides and gold . . . (bringing home)
> silver and jewels and pearls . . . sugars (and profit in) gold
> . . . (So we prospered in our adventuring), capturing,
> burning and spoiling their townes.'

– John Hawkins

    Ansio   *Water*

'Does the Queen still live?'

– Francis Drake

    Weroanza Elizabeth
    Lady of the sea!

The sea, all water yet receives rain still
And in abundance addeth to his store

– William Shakespeare (Sonnet 135)

. . . mi corazón se desató en el viento

> *. . . my heart broke loose on the wind*

– Pablo Neruda

Tossed to the sea,
My heart was flung to the wind

    Apo   *Water*

And the first three hundred men are here

Steal away

    Awura de Nyame   *God Almighty*

Owuo fa me Bah

   Death has come and taken my baby from me.

Death has come.
It is come,
And taken my baby from me.
And never more to see my brothers,
   my home, my name.
Never more to see land

    Sum Sum   *Ghost*

Lost forever

Me ma wo Yaako

   I give you all my sympathy for your loss

My child is dead.
She is dead.
He is dead.

They came and took them.

Wo ma me yen Ahyam

    You have just given me the shock of my life

They took them.

This is the beginning of war

Umma wo na Nsuom

    The sea will never let you sleep on its bed.

Steal away to Jesus

C ni ABD Nom

    There is no C in the Alphabet.

    Awura de Nyame   *God Almighty*

Nihil est toto quod perstet in orbe.
Cuncta fluunt, omnisque vegans, formatur imago,
Ipsa quoque assiduo labuntur tempora motu,
Non secus ac flumen.

    There is nothing in the whole world which remains.
    All things are in a state of flux, and every shadow passes away.
    Even time itself, like a river, is constantly gliding away.
    Time rolls on and on.

                             – **Ovid**

Animi labes nec diurturnitate vanescere nec amnibus ullis elui potest.

> *Stains that affect the soul are not obliterated by time, nor can rivers of water wash them away.*
>
> — **Cicero**

Nothing remains,
But nothing remains.

Apo no oyi afuno to koko su

> *The sea will always reveal its dead to the shore.*

Love's fire heats water, water cools not love
> — **Shakespeare (Sonnet 154)**

When the wet wind sings.

*

So, how did I get here? How did I get to England? How do I reconcile the underlying brutality which governed my arrival here – with my love of cake?

FREEDOM AND TRADITION

Going to New Mexico

'I want to fly!
I want to fly!' said the Princess to the King
One day.

'I suppose you know that it is a
Craft and not a science.
Your temperament
May not be suited. Anyhow, you belong to the sea.'

'I tire of the fish
And long to stretch up
Beyond the mirror of the sky
And beyond my own longing.
If you would teach me to fly
I would be Queen of the World.'

The King said, 'If you were to go
Up above the world,
Beyond yourself
And looked down,
Like a little lily bird,
You would only know disappointment,
You would only know fear;
You would know only the limits

Of the world, its greed and rancour.
These things would only dull your
Longing for knowledge.'

The Princess, in anger and frustration,
Locked her teeth together and stamped her glassy feet.
'I do not want to be with the fish,
I belong in the air above
Deserts and canyons.
I need to see the world.
To know the whole realm of its disappointments.
Then I can begin.'

The King shook his weary head.
'I have given birth,
Not to a sweet, docile girl
Who would comfort her father in his
Old age, with grandchildren,
Sweet treats and gentle gossip,
But to a raving adventurer.
A betrayal indeed.
You belong to the sea – with me.'

For two long, leaden months the Princess
Starved herself.
She reckoned that by going into the heart
Of her longing she could
Set herself free to fly,
Bear less weight and that sort of thing.

But instead she grew weaker
And found herself one day lying in the sand,
Nose pressed to a rock sheltering a starfish.

He said, 'You are reduced.
It is time for you to leave this place.
Don't be like me. Get bigger.'

The Princess went to the King.
She kissed him goodbye,
The tears chasing streaky lines down her face.
'I am thin. There is very
Little left of me. Some miscalculation.
But what strength I have I will
Use to make my own life.'

Then, from nowhere, came a tremendous pain
Tearing across her back
And the King called, gasping and weeping, after her.

The Princess, now a new lily bird
Looked down at the King of the Sea.
'I am going to a place of
Red deserts and orange Mountains
And Beans and Maize
And a Mathematics
Recognizing Zero.'

Up into the white foam
Folding into the blue,

A brilliant Lily Princess Blackbird
Clutches a new beginning and
A skeleton fish
Under her wing.
The brilliant, recently brilliant, recent Lily Bird.

So many of us yearn to test our limits. In my somewhat elusive poem, 'Going to New Mexico', I am trying to convey the spirit of countless young girls who have an innate instinct for freedom, for adventuring – and who naturally assume equality of travel. In the era in which I grew up, it seemed as if my wings were constantly being clipped if I ventured to speak of aspirations that no one around me had experienced. Later, when I started on the serious path of my music future, I was constantly being told that I needed to know the rules before I could break them. But what if some things have been left out of the rule book to begin with? What, then, is a reliable set of 'rules' to pass on to my students?

My job as a teacher is twofold: to accept these (mostly young) people for who and where they are and then to prepare them for a world the like of which I can't imagine. This means that while I have to think about the principles I believe remain constant in music I must also allow those in my charge to fly high, away from me and away from many of the things I know.

Here are some of my trusted rules, hard-won and ingrained after my own early stumblings:

- Being a composer is a long game. Don't be distracted by vicissitudes of fortune, especially in the middle years.
- Develop your ear and believe your ear.
- Be pleased that you are dissatisfied with standing still and want to push at your edges.
- The quest to capture the spirit and details of sound in notation is a holy one.
- You can be self-critical and still be your own friend.
- I repeat, develop your ear. It is your trusted friend, guide and provocateur.
- There is room for everyone.

However hard I try, I can never capture or convey all of music's endless variety or emotional force. There are no words in any language that begin to describe what it really is and what it really means. Therefore, to be a musician means one is living in a world impossible to describe accurately. I have spent and will continue to spend most of my life being absorbed by both the practical details of its performance and by the depths of its utter unfathomability. In musicology, many lifetimes are spent poring over a single composer's sketches, or in documenting a song form of a single African tribe. The study of music is rather like the study of a shell by the ocean, washed up on the sand. You can memorise every curve, indentation and pattern but you will still know only that shell and not the soul of the animal that was protected by it. You may never know the soul of the sea but you will keep searching for it.

Composing is as much a way of thinking as it is an activity and there are no two composers, even if they are working in the very same tradition, who think, or even hear, alike.

Every composer walks their own destiny, regardless of their parents, teachers or ancestors. And then a lucky accident occurs – we pick up a single shell among the thousands gleaming on the beach – and we listen anew to the ancients.

AMERICA

Subway

What is the sound *behind* the sound? What's the pulse *beneath* the clanking of the train? What key is the sidewalk? These trees, those skyscrapers, this bridge – what notes do they hum?

Motion is sound and the world is always moving. By composing, I am trying to understand the patterns of movement in sound. It can beat the hell out of your ears, but the New York subway *is* the perfect place to start for ear-training exercises. First, there is the *breathing* of the entire underworld, its vast metal tributaries, its ghost towns of forgotten, disused tracks and stations, its seething inhabitants, anxious to get to water or air but caught in a trance induced by the sheer volume of sound pressing down on and around them. Hard surfaces reflect the noise and harpy shrieks battle with grid-iron hiccups for the attention of the underworld gods of war. Agonised cries of grimy metal and steel locked in a furious embrace for our transport. It sounds like a fight to the death, not a simple journey to Atlantic Avenue. This could be Hades but it could also be hell. After a time, after getting lost in the subway, and walking miles along tiled corridors in search of the right portal or exit, after becoming accustomed to shuffling hopelessly in the dank air, after pushing against turnstiles and their fanning, splayed, rusted teeth trying to bite and steal your belongings, trap and possess your entirety, after the whistling dark has left your train behind but taken the rats and your re-routed, pounding anxiety with you, it suddenly becomes clear. This is a civilisation, a lost, subterranean nation of the urban soul. This is a whole world, singing and dancing beneath the skin of the earth. Where the rulers are ferric, feral ghosts of wind and power calling to the mortals who walk above their heads. This is music. *This is America*. There are many Americas, so many of them hidden below ground, and in un-united states. So much of the living history of this country is to be found in secret, unexpected places.

And there, in a ready-made performance space by one of the exits to Broadway subway, were six tumbling boys, of varying degrees of black, aged between three and twenty-five years old. They somersaulted, isolated limbs, ate fire, walked on the moon and the air, accompanied by a sound system and the ecstatic waves of applause erupting from the gathered throng after each jaw-dropping stunt. We paid our money and couldn't find a show above ground that equalled the one we'd just witnessed.

So it was then, down in the bowels of 42nd Street a few years ago, that I decided to write a piece for solo percussion based on the idea of the New York subway's sound, which is buried beneath the immediate din. I tried to discover other layers of rhythm without setting out merely to mimic the sound of trains in tunnels, though I am fascinated by

tunnels themselves and by the sensation of being underground, moving through darkness. As a key, or mental
torch, I tried to carry the atmosphere, the peculiar burdened
environment, in my mind's senses as I worked back home in
England. The transformation and transference of memory
to sound, of reality to fantasy, of atmosphere to psychological states was what interested me.

And so I spent as much time as possible in the New York
subway, not only as a means of understanding the sound
and atmosphere but also as a way of understanding people
and culture. The world we live in is made up of fleeting,
yet often powerful impressions. There is nothing we see or
hear that doesn't get stored somewhere in us. This is what
makes composing such a rich experience for me: uncovering
forgotten memories and atmospheres and creating new ones.

I have had a lifelong, umbilical relationship with New
York ever since my parents went to live there when I was six.
I tend to wear the United States of America like a second
winter coat. My father went there first and there's a photograph of my sisters and me at Heathrow airport, dressed
in identical outfits and our Sunday-best shoes to see our
mother off. While we remained in London, those first few
years were lived in a not unpleasant sort of limbo, waiting to
be 'sent for'. In the meantime, we conjured thrilling images
of America, a land of blazing lights, giant buildings and
Cracker Jack. Cracker Jack was a slim box of caramelised
popcorn with peanuts sent in parcels from my mother. These
parcels also occasionally contained glittering party frocks

unlike anything you could find in Tottenham (or the rest of England, for that matter). My favourite was a pale green chiffon and lace dress with a full skirt that I wore proudly for my eighth birthday.

As a child, whenever I saw footage of the New York skyline on television and film, I hugged these images to myself, enthralled by the glamour of a place so different, so enormous and so inviting. This unvisited place was my second, imaginary home. I craved information and when we spoke with my parents on the telephone or when I read letters from them, I noticed the new words creeping in – 'garbage', 'movies', 'elevator' – all spoken in their lilting Belize creole. To this day, after decades of living in New York, and even after becoming US citizens, there is not a trace of an American accent in their voices.

And then there was the music. My parents adore and cannot live without the American standards, the songs from the Broadway shows, and whenever I'm with them they are always either playing records or singing Bing Crosby, Ella Fitzgerald, Sarah Vaughan, Nat King Cole. It's been this way since I was a baby – the first song I ever sang, aged two, was 'When I Fall in Love'. This music is part of me. Years after my parents moved there, we finally visited New York and were taken to Broadway to see the shows and to Radio City Music Hall. As an undergraduate music student in London, steeped in the music of the Second Viennese School – Schoenberg, Berg and Webern – it was to the Americans I turned for a breath of fresh air and for a dance – Copland, Charles Ives,

John Cage. Despite their individual differences of expression, I sensed the underlying 'showtime' energy that imbues their music and the sense of space and unselfconscious delight with the world around them. Before I knew I was to be a composer, I felt the need for a new music that could combine the 'twang' of the vernacular together with a classical sensibility. From America I heard the first possibilities of interweaving these stark sonic contrasts. In Copland's 'Hoe-Down' from *Rodeo* the dancing fiddling folk music is brilliantly evoked in the open strings and piano while the orchestra hurls us into the air with its brass and cymbal flurries. As a young composer looking to my own future, I glimpsed colliding worlds rolled into one huge map of sound.

*

As children, we didn't grow up in the United States but from the age of about twelve, together with my siblings and aunt, I would spend every summer in New York. My parents lived in Brooklyn – the black part of Brooklyn. I remember my first subway trip travelling from Manhattan to Park Place, watching how the passengers changed from mainly white to only black. This was my first experience of segregation and these yearly trips dispelled my glamorous myths but signalled the beginning of a new intellectual journey and fascination with my 'other' home.

I have watched the gradual Americanisation of England and I remember the first Kentucky Fried Chicken and

McDonald's arriving here. Today, many black people in the United Kingdom aspire to the American way of life and model their lives and music-making on what's happening in Black American culture on the East and West Coasts. It seems that a very great number of young white and Asian people aspire to be the Black British who are themselves aspiring to the customs of the US. Indeed, the underground culture – the subway life now emerging – appears to be Middle America, as American youth culture from the coast visibly pervades the entire world. It is cool to be black.

Scratch a little harder, though, and any number of recent events will testify to something different. Find yourself in the South, for example, a boy aged twelve, a member of my own family, falsely accused of fondling your white fellow classmate, and suddenly you are the wrong black. You are not cool, and you'll be shackled in chains. And when a clerical error occurs, depriving you of a lawyer, though only twelve years old, you will be forced to defend yourself in court. Cool trainers or not, you are the wrong black in the wrong place.

*

I am three-quarters of the way through a cycle of operas, *ANOTHER AMERICA*, which are all set in the States at different periods of history. I was originally inspired by the work of my American painter friend, Peter Edlund, who I met at MacDowell, the artists' colony in New Hampshire.

At the time, Peter was working on a series of paintings also called *Another America*, which sought to reveal the hidden, unacknowledged history of its people. Revisiting and reworking the pictures of nineteenth-century American landscape painters, the Hudson River School, Peter uses vivid colour on large canvases and, in tiny detail, inserts actual events that would have been taking place at that time in history. Using this idea as a springboard I set out to invent imaginary situations in order to explore my own thinking about America's history and also its future.

The second opera in the cycle, *ANOTHER AMERICA: Fire*, is about a black woman astronaut preparing to go on the first voyage to Mars. I began composing it in Houston in 2004 and it was there that I was introduced to the astronaut Steve MacLean who has been into space twice and who greatly helped me in my research, showing me personal footage of his orbital adventures.

On the day I met Steve in Houston I went to a performance by a mariachi band. Later that evening I went to the rodeo where George H. W. Bush gave a speech and where we were entertained by country and western music after the bouncing cowboys. Only in America (well, Houston, actually) could I have stepped into this many earthly worlds – and outer worlds – in a single day.

It is this thrilling, constantly changing hybrid that attracts me to America – its rich confusion of peoples and then the sudden way in which you can stumble across the very essence of a completely different culture, wholly intact. I remember walking with a friend in Greenpoint, New York, where for two entire blocks we might as well have been in Poland; every sign on every shop was in Polish. We ate Polish food in a Polish cafe while all around us everyone spoke in Polish.

Back down in the subway, on the platform, at nearly midnight, a virtuoso musician from South East Asia is playing music from home on a stringed instrument the name of which I don't know. The music is highly intricate and ornate. I am mesmerised. Then, at the end of the piece, without a moment's pause, he launches immediately into a version of Tchaikovsky's *Nutcracker*.

*

The United States of America is made up of a continuing stream of people from other lands who hold passionately to their culture but the minute they step onto American soil are also passionately American. They can hold these two concepts without becoming confused. Yet, find yourself on the wrong street at the wrong time, the wrong black, and suddenly you own nothing; you are nothing. You are a threat. Amadou Diallo from Guinea was standing on his doorstep in the Bronx taking in the night air when he was gunned down by police. They thought the wallet in his hand was a gun. Which of the forty-one bullets ended his life isn't certain but that night the hopeful twenty-two-year-old immigrant had his romance with the New World abruptly terminated. And if the world is progressively adopting American sensibilities as its own, then higher standards should be set.

Most of my closest Belize relatives moved to New York in the sixties and seventies seeing America as the land of endless opportunity and prospect. The contrast between the two countries couldn't be greater. Belize is still a tiny, slow paradise where no building is over two storeys. There are no elevators, no motorways and no McDonald's and it is only in the last few years that there has been more than one television channel. I often ask my mother, who grew up by the sea, who came from a family of fishermen, how she could bear to leave the source of her being. How can holding your hands in a Brooklyn sink compare to bathing in the iridescent beauty of Belize? But Americanisation is gradually coming there too. On my last visit to Belize City I saw a new sandwich cafe, one of an American chain. It's called Subway.

WORDS, MUSIC, STAGE

In 2002 I was commissioned by the Royal Opera House and Nitro to compose a fifteen-minute opera as part of a triple bill with two other black composers, Dominique Le Gendre and Clement Ishmael. These new commissions were part of a weekend at ROH called 'Nitro at the Opera', celebrating black composers and singers. The project was the brainchild of Felix Cross, composer and theatre-maker and then artistic director of Nitro, a music theatre company. The weekend was co-produced by Nitro and the Royal Opera House and was intended to encourage a black audience to the Linbury Theatre (ROH's smaller theatre for new music and dance) and to the world of opera.

This wasn't my first opera, as years before I had been commissioned by Royal Opera House's 'Garden Venture' to compose *Four Figures with Harlequin*, for which I wrote the story and libretto. In 2001, a year before I started work on *ANOTHER AMERICA: Earth*, Broomhill Opera had commissioned me to compose an ambitious community opera, *Homeward Bound*, for the unsuspecting people of Gravesend. Librettist Atima Srivastava, director Netia Jones, musical director Stephen Higgins and I told a story of immigration and the SS *Empire Windrush* arriving at Tilbury Docks from Jamaica in 1948. In fact we took over Tilbury Docks, and the opera began with audience and cast sailing by ferry from Gravesend to the vast elongated stage at Tilbury Docks that Netia had installed.

I decided that for this new opera for the Linbury Theatre I wanted to invent my own story and write my own libretto, as I had done for my first opera.

ANOTHER AMERICA: Earth is set in the Mississippi Delta in the year 1930, the same year that the planet Pluto was discovered from Arizona. The opera tells of Ruth and Marcus Yellow's struggle to survive against the US government's systematic attempt to take away their recently granted land (forty acres and a mule) and Marcus's quest to find his son, Buck, whom he has driven away by his cruelty.

The North–South divide, religion and racism form the backdrop to the action, which is based loosely on historical fact.

I followed convention and started to write the story and libretto with the intention of getting that into shape before composing the music. Here's how I started:

ANOTHER AMERICA: Earth

Characters
Marcus Yellow
Ruth Yellow
Preacher
Star Woman
United States Government Official

Gelma
Chorus (SATB)

The year 1930. The Mississippi Delta.
The whole cast stands looking up to the sky. Some lick their fingers and hold them up to the air to sense the wind, while others stretch up their arms, palms outwards.

Preacher 'In the sweat of thy face shalt thou eat bread, till thou return unto the ground; for out of it wast thou taken; for dust thou art, and unto dust shalt thou return.' [Genesis 3:19]

Marcus (*rests his hoe in a field*) I hear a train coming. I hear the sky singing.

Ruth (*comes out of the house*) Why you want to leave this land, Marcus, when in your hands there is a new future? Here. (*Picks up a handful of dirt.*) This is our dirt now. Not theirs. Let our sweat run into it.

Marcus In the South, the dirt will always belong to them. The North calls me, baby. In the North we can be free. We can forget that we were tied to this land in chains. We can forget that our blood ran into the earth. It's too hard to make a living from this land. I can't make it breathe no more.

Marcus (*alone*) **and Chorus** (*looking up to the sky*) I hear a train coming.

I hear the sky singing.
I hear my son running.

Ruth This is my home,
I'm not going to where I don't hear the cock crow (*looking up to the sky*)
Where I can't hear the crickets,
Where I can't walk into the field to see the stars before I sleep
And feel the sun on my face before I wake.
We have lost our boy
But we have our home.
At last we have a home.
We have land. We have a purpose.
We own something. We are no longer slaves.
No one owns us.

Marcus I'm going to find my son.
Bring him home. Find the words to bring him back.

Ruth Let him be. Let him go. Stay with me.
Work with me.

Suddenly still. Everything black. We see the constellations.

Star Woman (*looking through the new Lawrence Lowell telescope in Arizona*) Black as coal, dense as iron. Where are you – new planet in the heavens? Neptune reveal. Throw back your cloak and reveal. Reveal.

Gelma (*running in*) Ruth! Ruth! Oh, Marcus! Didn't you all hear? There's a fire started up by Solomon Creek. Seven houses are still burning. You can smell it all the way down to Red Walk.

Preacher 'Be fruitful, and multiply and replenish the earth, and subdue it; and have dominion over the fish of the sea, and over the fowl of the air, and over every living thing that moveth upon the earth.' [Genesis 1:27–8]

Star Woman I guess you're hiding. Beyond Neptune.
I see the stars before I sleep
And feel the sun on my face before I wake.
But where are you?
Where are you?

Ruth Buck has left. Gone up north. Looking for a new life. Left home. Left our land.

Gelma When? Lord. When?

Marcus Last night. Says he's never coming back.

Gelma What did you do this time?

Ruth He took him, he beat him and flung him in a salt bath.

Marcus I took him, I beat him and flung him in a salt bath.

Hear a man's screams in the chorus.

Chorus He took him, he beat him, he flung him in a salt bath.

Ruth Like he always did.

Marcus Someone did set that fire.

Loud knock on the door.

US Government Official Open up! Is Marcus Yellow there? US Government County Land Official. Open up!

Ruth Gelma, go open the door.

US Government Official (*pushing roughly through the door*) Marcus Yellow? Mrs Yellow? I believe there's been an anomaly in proceedings for your land. I believe there's been a substantial anomaly in non-payment of your taxes. I believe there's been a transgression in the settling of your deeds. I believe you're in the wrong, Mr Yellow, Mrs Yellow.

Marcus We've paid our taxes. You know it.

US Government Official Your land ain't registered properly and I'm here to give you warning. Unless you pay the taxes due, the government will foreclose.

Marcus Forty acres and a mule. That is our rightful due.

Ruth We registered and we rightfully own this land. Why did you come here?

Gelma I hear you've been threatening farms up and down. I heard about the men who do your dirty work. There've been lynchings and families run off their land. I . . .

US Government Official You know nothing, girl. Illegally owned land is illegally owned land. I'll have you all off this farm, (*looking fixedly at Marcus*) boy.

US Government Official leaves. Cast turns towards Preacher.

Preacher 'While the earth remaineth, seedtime and harvest, and cold and heat, and summer and winter, and day and night shall not cease.' [Genesis 8:22]

Chorus Amen.

Preacher 'Sojourn in this land, and I will be with thee; for unto thee, and unto thy seed, I will give all these countries, and I will perform the oath which I swear unto Abraham thy father . . .'

Chorus Amen.

Preacher '. . . And I will make thy seed to multiply as the stars of the heaven, and will give unto thy seed all these countries; and in thy seed shall all the nations of the earth be blessed.' [Genesis 26:3–4]

Chorus Amen. Oh Lord, amen.

Preacher 'And God saw that the wickedness of man was great in the earth, and that every imagination of the thoughts of his heart was only evil continually.' [Genesis 6:5] Repent, therefore, sinners and let me baptise you in the blood of the Lamb.

Marcus I have nothing to repent. Someone did set fire to those farms and they will never be brought to justice. God won't help us. We must help ourselves. The meek will never inherit the earth. I say, let us move to the west or to the north where we can start anew. The government's going to run us off our farms, anyhow. Or the flood's going to get us.

Preacher and Chorus Step into God's water and sinner, repent! For He gave his only begotten Son . . .

Marcus I beat him. I twisted him, I flung him in a salt bath. I beat him to make him small. I twisted him to make him weak. I put his bloody body into salt water to make him scream. I am the father. He was my son.

Star Woman Black as coal, dense as iron. Where are you – new planet in the heavens? Neptune reveal. Throw back your cloak and reveal. Reveal.

Slowly each character joins in with Star Woman. Cast gradually looks up to the darkening sky.

Preacher and Chorus Step into the water.

Ruth Stay with me, work with me. This is our home.
Where my family is.
I'm not going to where I don't hear the cock crow (*looking up to the sky*)
Where I can't walk into the field to see the stars
Before I sleep

73

And feel the sun on my face before I wake.
We have lost our boy
But we have our home.
At last we have a home.
We have land. We have a purpose.
We own something. We are no longer slaves.
No one owns us any more.

Marcus I hear a train coming.
I hear the sky singing.
I hear my son running.

And that's where I got to before I realised that rather than continue to write the libretto and music separately and consecutively (which is the usual custom when libretto and music are by two different people) I could create both together at the same time. Words, music and I could go on the journey simultaneously, together. I never think twice about doing that in my songs where I sit at the piano and happily let the music and words chase each other. Might it really be possible to do this in a larger, dramatic form?

There is a general opinion that composers should leave libretto writing to others. But sometimes we composers just *have* to write our own words and shape drama without any initial intermediary, without travelling to meetings or making phone calls or sending messages – without having to negotiate or explain our vision in our choice of colours, movements, atmospheres, consonants and vowels.

The moment I sat down to write *ANOTHER AMERICA: Earth* in my Greenwich flat I had one of the best artistic adventures of my life. One thing triggered the other so that I went backwards and forwards between text and music and there wasn't the usual discussion, handover or linear sequence of tasks. I realised that I was in the fortunate position of being able to dive straight into the multilayering by working on story, words and music together. In an opera it is the music that drives the emotional narrative and shape, so I was able to dig into my subconscious immediately and sometimes found that the music came before the scene or words. At the piano the rest of the story unfolded rapidly, everything flowing from my imagination, sparked by two discrete events that happened in the United States in 1930.

Bill Bankes-Jones was directing *ANOTHER AMERICA: Earth* and before rehearsals started, he suggested I play through the vocal score to him in a small practice room at the Royal Opera House. So began our enduring friendship and I have borne in mind Bill's observations and advice with every subsequent piece I have composed.

Bill had noticed that in my playing I was adding lots of things that weren't actually written in the score – rhythmic and melodic nuances and inflections. So I went back and tried to capture those things in notation.

I compose music that often sounds free and even improvisatorial. Notating music to sound free means using complex notation, as the basic notation is set up to be rather crudely simple. Try annotating a Venezuelan folk song, or a blues song. Crotchets, minims, semibreves falling into a neat aural grid won't remotely represent what you have just heard.

Sometimes, in the early stages of composing a piece, you'd rather be *anywhere* than where you are. Your fear and stress tell you that you need a holiday, a phone call, a clear-out, an argument, a redecorating project – or a hunk of Battenberg cake.

In the case of composing *ANOTHER AMERICA: Earth*, I was the happiest I have ever been – holed up alone in my flat, watching invented situations surface and, best of all, witnessing vivid characters coming into view, complete strangers who lived, breathed, loved, hated and bore their regret through the conduit of my fingers at the piano.

It felt like being a child again. I was entranced and enchanted by simply 'making things up' and composed the vocal score in two weeks.

Bill Bankes-Jones was the ideal director for the opera and he accepted what I'd made without reserve. Staging it couldn't have been an easy task. The opera had a surreal quality to it and wasn't a straight-through plot; it also had several switches of time and place. I had decided that, given the time restraints, it was more fruitful for me to present a situation rather than to try to cram an entire story with a conventional plot into fifteen minutes.

Of all the operas I've composed *ANOTHER AMERICA: Earth* is particularly special to me because of the manner of its incubation. I felt absolutely free when creating it. I was also extremely lucky that Bill Bankes-Jones totally understood the complex emotional and dramatic structure. I've never written a stage work that sprang from me so easily and I was delighted that it was so immediately intelligible to Bill.

This little opera opened up a myriad of dramatic threads that demanded further exploration; I felt I had tapped into a new compositional pathway and I yearned to revisit the theme of 'America' – both the United States and Central America – and to examine the lives of black people there. The stories draw from my family's own experience of colonisation and emigration.

This opera became the first part in a cycle, subtitled by the names of the elements: *ANOTHER AMERICA: Earth, ANOTHER AMERICA: Fire, ANOTHER AMERICA: Air* and *ANOTHER AMERICA: Water*.

I recently asked Felix Cross about the background to this historic weekend:

'A Nitro at the Opera' sends me spinning back!

My initial idea for it was simply the notion that I believed that 'opera' was all about telling a story by singing the words; and that black artists, at some point, come from cultures where singing the words was the only way to tell a story. So we ought to be thriving at the heart of the world of opera – and clearly we are not.

. . . As to the event itself, we got over two thousand people attending on that day; around three-quarters were first time attendees to the ROH and a similar amount were black. Make of that what you will.

In one of the seminars we held on the day, I remember a woman standing up and saying (and I paraphrase): 'Back home (in the Caribbean) I went to the opera and to classical concerts all the time. It is only when I came here I felt these were places I couldn't go to, so thank you for organising this.'

There was a great amount of fanfare at the time. Sadly, apart from 'Revival!' the following year, the festival never happened again.

This was the first and last time Royal Opera House did anything on that scale to recognise the contribution black people have made to opera; there was also great nervousness that a black audience would not attend. In fact, so many were turned away that the two-day event would have easily filled the main stage of the Royal Opera House rather than being confined underground in the Linbury Theatre.

I pray for the day when our larger publicly funded opera houses represent the full range of creative talent in our midst – talent that is bursting with new stories to tell. Real change is taking too long.

The last new opera I attended on the main stage of the ROH was by a white male composer and I was the only black person I could see in the auditorium. 'A Nitro at the Opera' proved that when you represent black talent on stage a black audience will come.

There are always new and continuing challenges of creating musical works for the stage and the fact is that there are relatively few opportunities for composers of any background to get their operas onto the stage and that is why I have jumped at every opportunity, even if it comes when I already have a busy schedule. I have composed twenty-two operas, and counting. One was even about cake, courtesy of Tête à Tête Opera,* the company that is the Edinburgh Fringe of new opera and that has done so much to develop the form by giving opportunities to all.

I believe that we're living in a golden age of musical activity – when we creators, practitioners and scholars are realising that, for all the complexities, economic hardships and cutbacks to our resources, we do have a voice and that we can make a difference through telling the truth of what it is to be alive at this time. I believe we have a responsibility to tell the stories of our time. Because of the wonderful coming together of disciplines that is opera, I feel that there will always be a genuine curiosity and hunger for new music theatre.

*

PRINCIPIA was one of the works I composed for the opening ceremony of London 2012 Paralympic Games, performed by 430 amateur singers from across London and the London Symphony Orchestra. The brief was to encapsulate, in four minutes, the progress of physics from Isaac Newton to the Higgs boson via Stephen Hawking and the Big Bang; not

* Bill Bankes-Jones, artistic director of Tête à Tête, has given me countless opportunities to present and develop my stage work.

forgetting the Enlightenment and the Universal Declaration of Human Rights. The other work I was commissioned to compose for the occasion was *Spirit in Motion* for soprano (Denise Leigh) and full orchestra. The work was to be performed after all the athletes had assembled in the stadium and was to be a tribute to them. The stadium was a vast stage in which my two works formed part of a thrilling spectacle. I noticed how many of the artistic teams came from the world of opera – conductors, directors, designers, choreographers, lighting designers, production managers. It rained right up until one hour before the ceremony started. There was no roof on the Olympic Stadium.

As a small child it crossed my mind to be an opera singer before I knew what an opera even was. I wonder if I was motivated by the family's vivid place mats with scenes from *Carmen*, which I looked at at every mealtime. Years and years later, when I came to write my first opera, I realised that, as a listener, what I perceived to be the hysteria of grand opera no longer spoke to me in quite the same way as when I was eight.

The first opera I ever saw staged, when I was a schoolgirl, was Cavalli's *La Calisto*, which was first performed in Venice in 1651. I loved the stripped-away sound and austere textures. As a music student my favourite periods of music were definitely the baroque and the music of my own time. In my early formal training as a composer I was trained to deny the freely expressive in favour of music that was more based in numbers and set theory. I enjoyed this approach as I was a curious student, keen to learn new techniques. That early training taught me that you can make music and powerful atmospheres through restrictions and constraint, and it was how you shaped phrases through rhythm, tempo and interval that revealed what invention you possessed. As a child, I had grown up with the sound of soul, reggae and Ella Fitzgerald, so I already had a smorgasbord of sounds to play with, even though, as a student composer, I was steeped exclusively in contemporary avant-garde music.

When I am writing the music for an opera, the characters come first. Though the libretto can take a long time to get right, I regard it as something of a magical skeleton and once it's in shape, it's as if I have to start again from the beginning. I feel that I must then live with the characters and absorb their hidden secrets, possibilities and motivations, sometimes only hinted at by words on the page. I must be patient and wait until the characters become 3D – until they speak to me. I imagine their facial gestures and nervous tics before I write a note. In the opera *YES*, which premiered at the Linbury Theatre in 2011, though Bonnie Greer's libretto doesn't specify the character Joan's precise location, I imagined her in a particular London square with the sound of bells coming from a nearby church. That became a motif in the score.

I start by composing the vocal score, which I regard as a map in which the voice and text are fixed, accompanied by a piano part that serves to outline the harmonies and important instrumental lines. It is only when the vocal score is finalised that I move on to orchestration and the full score. There, the orchestra's or ensemble's job is not only to flesh out the characters but to place them in an environment where that environment is itself also a character. Both what the singers sing and the music that they sing over are important for the storytelling. The opera composer's job, then, is twofold: we have to tell the story, through putting breath into character, and also step outside it to comment on it, subvert it, plant the seed of what's going to happen later, and sometimes reveal the opposite of what's going on. We lie, cheat, steal, murder and live to tell the tale.

For those composers who have a writing background and a strong dramatic sensibility, I believe that there are times when the work simply requires them to write their own libretti. I really enjoy composing works for a wide audience – it pushes me to think about the fundamentals of communication. In 2012 I worked on three public commissions: my cantata *Diamond Greenwich* – commissioned for the Queen's Diamond Jubilee, the re-opening of the *Cutty Sark* and Greenwich becoming a Royal Borough – and two works (*PRINCIPIA* and *Spirit in Motion*) for the opening ceremony of the Paralympic Games. I wrote both the text and the music so that my response to the demands of the brief would be direct and unfiltered, and I could shape everything to my requirements. This all-in-one process is very different from the situation when a composer collaborates with a writer. In the best collaborations, new worlds of expression open to both artists and, in the mediation between the two, an opera results that is unique to that team. In each experience I grow in my understanding of the wide range of approaches to the shaping of words and dramatic scenarios as well as realising that different writing encourages me to compose music I wouldn't otherwise contemplate.

A year after composing *ANOTHER AMERICA: Earth* I went on to write *ANOTHER AMERICA: Fire*, produced by PUSH* at Sadler's Wells. The opera, again to my own story and libretto, is about an astronaut, Asante, who is preparing to travel to Mars. Astronaut Steve MacLean's insights in our hours-long telephone conversations helped enormously. There is biographical information in each of the *ANOTHER AMERICA* quartet of operas – *ANOTHER AMERICA: Air* is about my Uncle Edwin who was a navigator in the RAF during World War II, flying Mosquitoes and Beauforts, and who was shot down twice in the Atlantic. In *ANOTHER AMERICA: Fire* I include a scene with Asante's mother and father arguing on the phone with each other while speaking to her, which is exactly what my parents always did with me. I weave continuity between the four operas by bringing back characters. In *ANOTHER AMERICA: Fire*, we see the reappearance of Ruth and Gelma who we first got to know in *ANOTHER AMERICA: Earth* and also an ancient African ancestor. Star Woman's theme appears in each opera.

I always encourage the librettist I work with to feel liberated while writing so that their distinct characteristics are there for me to respond to. A libretto is very different from a play and

---

* PUSH, a Black-led theatre festival with the Young Vic Theatre, was founded by Josette Bushell-Mingo, who was also artistic director.

what can look quite sparse on the page is actually perfect for a composer. Opera doesn't need many words, just the right words to help trigger the action that is conveyed through the music. There needs to be plenty of space for the music.

What is interesting about the libretto for *Sabina Spielrein*, no doubt because he is a highly experienced opera director, is just how much space David Pountney has consciously made for the music, thinking out possible timings for the various sections, and has staged it in his mind's eye very clearly as he wrote the text.

*

Composing *The Silent Twins* marked a turning point for me in my attitude towards writing opera. Jennifer and June Gibbons were complex, highly creative, obsessive characters and I learned that every interval, every rhythmic nuance had to be right in order to show their inner and outer lives. Writer April de Angelis and I had struggled for a few years to get the work commissioned and staged but, nevertheless, we would meet every week to discuss how we would make *The Silent Twins*. We felt the story was crying out to be told – and in opera. When the call eventually came from Almeida Theatre to discuss ideas I might have for operas, I ran down a list (every self-respecting, hustling composer has got a list) and Patrick Dickie, producer for Almeida Opera, stopped me when I started telling him about *The Silent Twins* idea. He could immediately imagine it on stage. The year and a half we spent working on this opera, greatly helped by Marjorie Wallace, author of the book *The Silent Twins*, changed forever my way of approaching opera. April brought wit and humour to what is essentially a heartbreaking tragedy. Michael Attenborough, then artistic director of Almeida Theatre, really pushed us to go further with our exploration of the twins' inner world and provided us with invaluable workshop time.

Of course everyone asked us why write an opera about two girls who don't speak? I usually reply that it is always best to start a project with a challenge!

Earlier I mentioned that at the start of my opera-composing career I was less influenced by nineteenth-century opera than by baroque opera. I am also hugely influenced by film and the way it can cut in on scenes, cross-fade and show different scenes simultaneously. But when I was composing the oratorio *Carbon 12: A Choral Symphony*, it was being at a performance of Puccini's *Tosca* one evening that had a profound effect on my orchestration of the oratorio. *Tosca* is a perfect opera where not a note is wasted yet it's brimming with passion and atmosphere, much of that to do with the orchestration, which never gets in the way of the voices but which shimmers with colour and foreboding. In 2022 I saw a production of Benjamin Britten's *Peter Grimes* at the Royal Opera House and it was strikingly clear how much Puccini had influenced Britten in this regard.

John Binias wrote the libretto for my oratorio *Carbon 12: A Choral Symphony*, which was commissioned by Welsh National Opera. The libretto is a masterpiece. We had to tell the story of coal mining in South Wales in fifty minutes with over three hundred people including the men's chorus of WNO, Risca Male Voice Choir, a community choir, a brass band, soloists and full orchestra. Like April de Angelis, John Binias produced a libretto that combined rigorous research with spine-chilling drama and poetry. There was a lot of text but every sentence was packed with information and we knew that people in the auditorium would understand the meaning of everything. We had surtitles, which made it easier for the audience too. Before I composed the climactic section I had to stop composing on this project – just for one day – to take stock of the words related to the mining disasters that had taken place in South Wales. I had to find a way of setting the words within an orchestral texture that wasn't melodramatic. There were to be many ex-miners and relatives of miners in that audience at Cardiff's Millennium Centre as well as in the cast for whom Aberfan had stark, personal meaning. The brothers of the principal soloist, Jason Howard, had helped in the rescue attempt in 1966. When the name 'Aberfan' was sung, just once, unaccompanied, by Jason, you could have heard a pin drop.

*

I was joking the other day that I'm going to throttle the next person who comes up to me saying 'Wow! I've got a great idea for an opera!' without the least idea of what all-consuming work it is to create one. The most recent suggestion was from someone in a maximum-security prison serving a life sentence, so a set-to could be a little difficult. It can take years to write the music for an opera. You have to have a strong stomach when diving into such a big undertaking with a crew of people who might be largely unknown to you, all with strong ideas as to how it should go. But it is interesting to ask the question: what subjects *do* make for good opera?

The truth is any subject can make for opera but I believe that it must be a matter of life-or-death importance, ultimately, for the librettist and composer to tell that story. What was interesting and moving about the letter I received from the prisoner was that until he heard about *YES*, he didn't realise that an opera could be about one's own life or situation.

Personally, I believe that we opera-makers must remember the obvious – that opera is a dramatic form and so, for me, I am always interested in finding a situation that is full of dramatic possibilities, able to unfold in several directions. I can usually smell whether it's the right subject for me from very little information. Of course, this is a personal matter and different composers have different predilections. I think about where and when the story is set, and can I really live with these characters for years on end? What can I bring to it that's not already there? I ask myself why the story needs to be told as an opera and not a play or a film, or a novel or a poem – all forms where the words are more easily intelligible.

With my collaborators I ask, 'What do we need to show and how do we show it?' Some of the most powerful moments on stage involve no words or physical action.

Since composing *Carbon 12* and *The Silent Twins* I feel a strong desire and a responsibility to write about the world around me. I believe that opera should have a universal reach. Opera is a form that can endlessly adapt – combining, as it always has done, text, music, movement, costume, visual spectacle. We take the form forward because of the emotional demands of the content. It is this emotional force that should make singing inevitable, the voice being the final frontier of emotion.

As a performer it is also important for me to put my own stage works together. I made *Jordan Town* for the Edinburgh Festival Fringe. There was no narrative in that show and while it isn't an opera, it is an integrated stage work with song at its centre. I invited the film-makers the honey brothers (Mark and Dan Goddard) and dancer Tom Sapsford to respond to my songs and together we created a new form combining film, music and dance. The director Daniele Guerra also made a show around my songs called *My Feet May Take a Little While*, which was put on at the Arcola Theatre in London. It is my songwriting experience, and love of singing, dance, visual art, theatre and film that have led me to opera and to all my musical adventures. Song is at the centre of it all.

*

YES, the opera, was performed at the Linbury Theatre in November 2011.

I was approached by John Lloyd Davies and ROH2 to collaborate with Bonnie Greer on an opera that was based on a real-life event. John explained that it was a state-of-the-nation opera about the reflections and thoughts of Bonnie Greer and the general public before she appeared on the BBC Television programme *Question Time* in 2009. Here was a story of our time and it has been revelatory working on it – trying to give voice to people who would otherwise go unheard. The riots that had originated in Tottenham the year before have made me reflect on the resonance of this aspect of the work. Bonnie Greer herself is at the centre of the story and the opera is composed in short scenes and vignettes, some of the words being verbatim, taken from blogs, newspapers, radio, television or tweets.

An opera is nothing without a talented, engaged, hardworking and emotionally intelligent team, from the rehearsal pianist, librarian, designers, director and conductor to the ushers. But at the cutting edge of it all are the singers. They are the inspiration for the composer and I try to have the sound of their voices in my mind as I compose. Each person's voice is unique and, ideally, I like to have cast them before composing the opera so that I can tailor the music to fit not only their range but also the timbre of their voices.

I have been extremely fortunate to have worked with some of the best singers and nothing gives me a greater thrill than to work with them in workshops and rehearsals where their suggestions generally make things better. There is no such thing as a score where everything is absolutely perfect before the singers get to it. Working with the singers, repetiteur and conductor, things can always be improved. The tiniest change registers strikingly in every voice. I try to learn new things about voices in each opera I write – where to write for them, in and out of their ranges, how to combine them for dramatic effect, how to vary the rhythm to suggest natural speech, chant or stylised flight. In *YES*, where there is a variety of textures employed – solos, duets, trios, chorus and spoken word – I can never forget baritone Omar Ebrahim's transfixing performance of 'Ed's Painting Aria'.

A lot of my operas have been on serious subjects, but I worked on Hilaire Belloc's *Cautionary Tales*, for children, in the same year as *YES*, and they both premiered in 2011. It was fascinating to discover just how brutally technical it is trying to be funny. Pia Furtado adapted the text and I added some text too. Pia also directed the opera and in workshops we were able to try things out, particularly to do with matters of timing and staging. The poems are all in reported action and we wanted to find a way of opening up a space so that the opera could engage the children (who were our main audience) with action too. We had four singers in the cast, each of whom played several characters. With just three musicians in the band the show was made so it could tour, which it did.

My father died in January 2011, at around the time that I finished the orchestration of *Cautionary Tales*. Throughout the composing process I had been going back and forth to New York to see him. My mother also had bouts of illness and was in another hospital way across town from my father.

I was to learn that nothing stops for bereavement. It turned out that on examining the full score, there was not the budget to accommodate the percussion I had chosen, even though this had not been discussed before. From Heathrow on my way to New York, where I was organising Dad's funeral (with the help of my father's childhood friend Liston Hall and my beloved US musician friends, Rita Porfiris and Jeff Robinson), I asked for a few days to be a heartbroken daughter. I was accidentally copied into an email that showed the producer's impatience with me. Afterwards, when the opportunity arose, I summoned all my determination and tenacity to make my own production with my own company, the Errollyn Wallen Company, and we took *Cautionary Tales* to Latitude Festival. Producing meant raising the money, casting and contracting the singers and musicians, choosing the creative team and crew, liaising with the festival, booking accommodation and transport, planning the rehearsal schedule, overseeing the budget, wangling passes, organising the publicity – and on and on. It was actually a lot of fun working on this with my friend Cathy Lewis, if at times hair-raising. On the final day of rehearsal (the day before going to Latitude) I learned we had got the funding. I didn't let on to anyone that it had all been on a knife edge before.

Producing an opera gave me invaluable insight into the entire process of putting on an opera and, moreover, I was able to reclaim this work for myself, adding happier memories.

*

I am committed to telling the stories of our time and *ANON*, my twelfth opera (the fourth to my own libretto), is no exception. Many of the stories I have set have been in order to give voice to those people whose stories have previously gone untold.

However, when I was asked by Welsh National Opera to compose an opera for young people on the theme of the exploitation of young women across the world, based on the Abbé Prévost novel *Manon Lescaut*, I was at first reluctant. In the novel, on which so many operas have been based, Manon has no voice – she is an object of desire, appearing to have few thoughts or feelings of her own.

After leading workshops with young girls from many different cultural backgrounds and exploring with them the themes of *Manon Lescaut* – young love, running away, the defiance of parental and social pressure, taking a wrong step and unwittingly falling into danger – I became excited about how I could adapt and contemporise the story. My thanks are forever extended to those girls from the RSA Academy in Tipton, West Midlands, and Newman University in Bartley Green, Birmingham. Later, having finished the first draft of the libretto, I also interviewed sex workers, five young women who were able to elucidate and enlighten me as to aspects of the story. I had written some things the director thought were improbable so I changed them. The young women told me how true my original words were. I put them back in.

ANON is made up of several short scenes where the audience is encouraged to consider the situation rather than the precise identity of the protagonists (who are simply called Girl 1, 2 and 3 and Actor 1 and 2) hence the title of the opera. We could all find ourselves in any of these situations. Furthermore, although it is possible to trace a narrative through-line, this too is deliberately disrupted and made opaque.

ANON is for three sopranos and two female actors. The scoring is for piano/keyboards, cello and percussion, and sound design. Another work made for touring.

What was interesting and challenging in equal measure in working on *ANON* was starting from the primary source of the novel and adapting that novel into pared-down language and creating a contemporary setting that tells a very modern story.

I hadn't adapted a novel before and, though my adaptation is very loose, my opera serves as a response to *Manon Lescaut*. Through workshops in Birmingham and in London, meetings, phone calls, Dropbox and a sing-through by Centre for Contemporary Opera in New York, our opera grew until it was ready for a tour, eventually premiering at Birmingham's Midlands Arts Centre.

I decided to work with director Wils Wilson, who specialises in site-specific work. We worked in 2012 on a play by Jackie Kay, designed by Amanda Stoodley. It was for Manchester Library Theatre Company and was called *Manchester Lines*. We converted an office space into a whole new environment. I wanted Wils as director for *ANON* as I believed she might be able to bring different qualities out in the singers, with the actors and singers working very closely together. I made use of speech and singing together as a feature of this opera.

I feel so privileged to have had many opportunities to write operas and stage works and since working on *ANON*, I am keen to continue to explore ideas from straight theatre – the use of actors and the collaboration with directors from outside the musical world.

In 2011 I was asked to write the music for a four-part BBC One drama, *One Night*, something I'd never done before. When I worked on this television drama with director David Evans, I appreciated how my experience of composing operas was invaluable for the scoring of the drama. I was able to explore the whole range of possibilities of incidental music, including music that held the screen without dialogue and sound design. And, always, the underlining of characters. The drama was first broadcast in 2012 and was broadcast around the world.

When I think of a work such as my Cello Concerto, composed for the cellist Matthew Sharp, I hear the same dramatic instinct I draw on when composing opera. Matthew plays the cello the way he sings – always with a heightened presence and always expressively. The form of a concerto is itself inherently dramatic and my opera writing continues to inform all my work.

COPING

The New Cross Train

onetwothreefourfivesixseven
eightnineteneleventwelvethirteen
fourteenfifteensixteenseventeen
eighteennineteentwentytwenty-
onetooscaredtostopincaseitallgoeswrong
wrongerthanitisnowitissoloudinmy
headthewhisperstellingmetodoittwenty-
twotwenty-threetwenty-fourtwenty-five
twenty-sixtwenty-seventwenty-eight
twenty-ninethat'swhymumdiditshewasn't
countingloudenoughnotconcentratingor
maybesheranoutofnumbersthirtythirty-one
thirty-twothirty-threeatthecentrethey're
sayingthatI'mdoingsowellbutnowthey're
screamingatmetodoitandIcan'thearwhat
anyone'ssayinganymorethirty-fourthirty-
fivestopthirty-sixthirty-sevenI'mscaredwhy
couldn'tyouholdonmum?thirty-eight
thirty-ninefortyforty-oneforty-twoforty-
threewhydidn'tyoushoutoutthenumbers?
forty-fourfightbackforty-fivethey're
louderandlouderthanmefifty-onebeachyhead

*

I knew a wonderful boy, in his late teens; I met him every week at the Sunnyside Centre in Deptford. It was a day centre for people with mental health problems. He and his fellow patients, young and old, found it almost impossible to hear the songs I was playing on the piano because of the competing voices in their heads. They found it difficult to mimic the movements being taught them by the dance instructor, herself struggling with premature osteoporosis. However, the boy was the one who put the brightest face on things, cracking jokes and encouraging his fellow sufferers. He was very kind. And then one week he was not there. Two weeks after his mother jumped to her death from Beachy Head, he threw himself beneath a train in South London – at New Cross station.

Decades later, in July 2021, a dear composer friend jumped in front of a train at New Cross Gate station.

Carrying on is easier for some than others. Putting one step in front of another is not always the inevitable course of action. Not every day opens possibilities or is even welcome. Not every night has an end. One becomes in thrall to the melancholy of life aware that each day we are all moving at different speeds towards death. After the loss of friends, family or lovers we grow more connected to the reverse side of life. Where *do* the dead go? Part of us has already gone with them and we sense that beneath the order we so frenetically try to create in the living world is a limbo land where there is another, tranquil and very sane reality. I am walking down a familiar street. I take this street for granted. But before these buildings, neon lights, zebra crossings, advertising hoardings, clanking factories was mud. Mud and rats. Why not then live like a nomad, a tramp, a gypsy, a travelling musician, a troubadour or trouvère, and *connect* to the fundamentals of humanness, of the body's bounds – uncertainty, loss, emptiness, smallness, *mess*. We find it very hard to own up to these feelings in our search for power (often over others) and our almost pathological need for control. But what would happen if we, particularly those of us living in the Western world, were to embrace the fragility of our state without feeling impelled to quash it or compensate for it? What would happen if we just . . . listened?

Music, in the end, is not *for* anything. It just is. It was a fact of the physical, material world before we ever got here. Where there is movement there is sound. Music is motion, the movement of air and energy. We live in it and, as with air and energy, we are surrounded by it. Our particular brand of humanness makes us love patterns and pattern-making and making patterns in sound greatly appeals to all our senses. The fact that sounds are invisible, yet we can *hear* shapes, patterns and textures that we can almost touch, moving right there in front of us, in the air that we are breathing, lends music its greatest force. It is a mystery. It is a disappearing act. It is like magic. And in the practice of music as in the practice of magic, we can, through the use of ritualised pattern-making, attempt to keep ourselves safe. I have written music to cast spells, to charm, to woo, to plead, to curse, to frighten, to call, to summon, to retaliate, to keep intact, to transform, to remember, to keep harm away.

Music, before I discovered a secret hollowed-out tree trunk, covered with dead branches, was my only escape. But it was total escape. The life of a child can be one of tyranny, mindless cruelty and claustrophobia. I coped with my own by fleeing into the corridors of my imagination. Endless corridors turned into labyrinths, caves, dungeons, sparkling palaces and queendoms. I had everything I wanted to eat there: squelchy, glistening plums, many-tiered iced, cherry-topped cakes, quivering, multicoloured blancmanges, purple nectar. Falling asleep in the real world I would have a recurring dream about playing a magic piano. As I played it with my still stubby fingers, I could feel the black and white keys move beneath my entire hand. While I played, I could mould the piano like bread dough, and it was a texture and sensation that I had never felt before. The keys moved and undulated in waves beneath the palms of my hands. I loved this dream because not only could I play anything – and I think that I was dreaming my own, swirling sounds – but playing the piano was an even more tactile experience than it was in real life. The piano was literally responding to my touch, to my hands, like another living being. My hands were holding the paws of a wild creature, a friend. We were attached to each other in happy pursuit of sound and motion.

Some children need to get as far as possible away from their homes before they are ground down, with no hope of getting up again. I sometimes meet these children and I want to tell them, 'Get out!' Home for some children is no sanctuary. I never felt completely safe in my childhood home. It was partly because nothing about our situation was secure or explained yet the stress of the situation most certainly also had an effect on Kene and Uncle Arthur. I grew up feeling worthless, neglected, intimidated and confused. All four parents seemed to be actively promoting this sense in all their children and, indeed, had little idea of what children were *for*. My mother had been raised in a culture where children were born in order to help their parents; my uncle and father believed children should live in fear and be regularly beaten (as they had been) so that the dominance of the parent would be felt at all times. My aunt was there as the martyr, the one who had sacrificed her life to look after these cast-aside children. All four presented a united front.

The late-teenage years were the worst. Aged seventeen I tried to kill myself. I had run away from school just as I was about to go into the final sixth-form year. I had become deeply depressed and unhappy that the school I loved so much was coming apart at the hinges. It really was. The younger girls weren't being looked after properly and rules were being bent by the staff in favour of their favourites. There was an air of quiet chaos and neglect, and I missed my friends who had left.

Unfortunately, I was jumping out of the frying pan into the fire by returning to live at home in Tottenham, the place whose effects I'd managed to escape by going to boarding school in the first place. I should have gone to another school or sixth-form college in London but we couldn't find anywhere that did the A level syllabus (I think it was the Oxford syllabus) that Holly Park did. It was decided that I would have tutors at home in my subjects: English, Latin, French (later dropped) and Music. We couldn't find a tutor for music so I had to do that by correspondence course. I had only one lesson each week in each subject and I was at home the rest of the time, left to my own devices with no schoolmates around.

No more playing the piano and composing throughout the night, no more walks in the sixty acres where I had done so much hugging of trees, no more dreaming in Trish's and my den, 'Hatters' Retreat'. Never one to exert unnecessary effort academically, I had even less incentive with no teachers around. I was coming adrift and, almost without noticing it, gradually began a long yet utterly calm walk down a pitch-dark tunnel. It had become obvious to me that I would never amount to anything and that I was a thorough disappointment to myself and all around me – my intense struggle to get through even one day was proof of that. One night I decided to take the bottle of Valium that had been prescribed for a muscle condition. I hadn't actually taken any, so the bottle was full. At around 1 a.m. I wrote a short note to my sister, Karen, then swallowed the tablets. I was surprised to wake up a few hours later, so went downstairs to the drinks cabinet and slugged some alcohol. That didn't seem to work either. I went back to bed.

Later that morning, when Kene came back from taking my brother Byron to school, I told her what I had done. She called the ambulance, though I was fully compos mentis. Kene told me that if I had tried this in the past I would be imprisoned. Not quite the sympathy or understanding I would have liked at that time but I imagine she was very frightened. I stayed in hospital for a couple of days but my stomach didn't need pumping out and I found myself thinking about how my Latin A level exam was soon and that I needed my books for revision while also thinking that the human race could do with being just a little kinder. Kene told the hospital I had not taken the whole bottle, even though I had. If there had been two hundred pills in the bottle I would have taken all two hundred and searched around for more. I worked out later that those pills I swallowed must have been placebos – or else I had witnessed a miracle. I kept thinking about that. The hospital sent me to see a psychiatrist who asked if I heard voices in my head. When I said I didn't, I was discharged without any therapy.

That was that.

So began the next new chapter in my life. I was jolted out of the depression that had been covering me like a metal blanket and to which I had paid no attention. I had had to work it out for myself, but the biggest lesson for me was that the only way to live is with kindness. An invigilator came to our house and I sat my A levels in the front room. My family didn't mention what happened and there was no counselling of any sort, but for the next few years they slightly tiptoed round me.

After my suicide attempt, I knew I needed to get back on track, lose weight and get back to dancing. Ballet had been my very first love since I was aged about six or seven, before I started piano lessons. The flame was ignited when I heard Chopin for the first time, played in ballet class at Maureen Lyons School of Dancing. It led me to search for this music and music like this on the radio; this is how I discovered BBC Radio 3. In the years at Hollington Park, knowing that I wouldn't be able to be a ballet dancer because my parents refused to send me to a ballet school on account of the fact that they had never seen a black ballet dancer, I had found it unbearable to watch ballet on TV or even to look at dancers in magazines or newspapers – it was just too painful. Now it was time to go back to my passion: dance. I enrolled at the Urdang Academy in Golders Green and remember Leonie Urdang saying that she could see the bones in my chest. It was fantastic to be back taking proper ballet class again since those at Maureen Lyons School of Dancing which I had left behind at thirteen to go to Hollington Park School. Leonie was a wonderful teacher. I had sprung back to life.

I continued to get back in shape and that summer in New York I attended the course at the Dance Theatre of Harlem. I had decided that I would throw myself into contemporary dance – it wasn't too late for that. That was it: I would be a dancer and a choreographer. All the while I was playing the piano and composing. That never ever stopped. When I received my A level exam results, I got a D for Latin, a B for English (quite fortunate, considering the night before I realised I hadn't read one of the books on the syllabus) and a B for Music. I had been offered an unconditional place to study Music at Leeds University (with Alexander Goehr) but then found a course at Goldsmiths College, University of London, which had just started a degree in Dance and Music – it was perfect. I had already taken my ATCL Diploma in Piano Performance as an external student. The exam was on a hot summer's day in London and I had eaten an orange on the way to Trinity College of Music; when I started to play my fingers were sticky. Duh. Nevertheless, afterwards one of the examiners seemed impressed, by both my playing and my youth, and wanted to know more about me.

My last couple of years in the upper fifth and lower sixth at Hollington Park School for Girls saw a turbulent inner life of soul-searching as I tried to work out what my path might be. Through my close friendship with Trish, who had arrived at the school in my second year there as a devout Christian, I too, at the age of fourteen, became a fervent Christian. I prayed constantly, read the Bible, and meditated on our sorry world – though by the time I was sixteen I was questioning what I saw as the restrictions and misogyny towards women in the Church. I knew I wanted to be free, and I knew that forgoing my religious beliefs meant I could go straight to hell but nonetheless decided I had to strike out alone. I had even wanted to be a nun – an organ-playing nun, a nun working as a missionary bringing with me the gifts of music. I flicked through the Yellow Pages in the hall at home in Tottenham, searching for a Methodist nunnery. No luck there, but I was still deadly serious about my religious vocation.

One day I overheard the worried whispering of my aunt and uncle saying, 'She'll grow out of it.' Ironically, despite the Victorian values they passed down to us, in these circumstances, they would have preferred me to be a bit more like my younger sisters, who blithely climbed out of windows to go to parties that started after midnight. After all their efforts to keep me away from boys, and the dangers of the street, I, the very embodiment of their rules, only caused them the same anxiety they had been trying to avoid. I was not a typical teenager, and in rather similar ways I hadn't been a typical child. My inner world, the world of imagination and possibilities, fed by words, imagery and music, was still more exciting than anything I had encountered outside it. My sisters must have found me unsufferable at times. I had always written poetry and won some competitions. I would go on to win an Amnesty International Competition judged by Ted Hughes and Philip Larkin. I had to read out my poem (with the sound of trains rumbling overhead unfortunately) to the assembled greats at a reception after a gala concert at the Southbank Centre and then present it to Yehudi Menuhin. I had been too shy to tell Yehudi Menuhin that I was a pianist and a composer. My poem was printed in the *Sunday Times* with the line breaks in the wrong place.

I was passionate about reading, writing, dancing, playing the piano, composing, art. How would I fit it all in as an adult? I suddenly had a flash, a glimmer of myself sitting at a grand piano in the music room at Holly Park, in the future, somehow doing it all. The suicide attempt was in part because I had lost that glimmer and with it any faith in myself. I had barely enough energy to get washed and dressed and felt completely cut off from the world. The thought of continuing like that, of shuffling through life in a near-comatose haze was unbearable. I was very calm in my decision to end my life, as I could see clearly that I was a waste of space. I was not hysterical or even sad. After all, I lived in a house where feelings were not allowed; or rather they were the sole domain of my aunt, who could sit for hours 'worrying' and smoking. She found life difficult and took her frustrations out on me. I was both her confidante and her punching bag. But I loved and believed her when she said, 'My life is hard, so yours can be too.' I believed her when she said, 'You're nothing special.' And I nearly believed her when she said, 'No, you didn't come first in the poetry competition. You came second, or was it third?' Of all the children, it was me whose achievements she felt the need to minimise.

I began to do it too: minimise my achievements, minimise my feelings, minimise my very self to the point of disappearing. Too many teenagers suffer this way. That first bout of major depression is so treacherous because you can't see a way out of the dark tunnel – it is absolute and final, and it is your learned self-loathing that tells you it is your own fault that firstly you feel that way and secondly you can't get out of it. But, as I sit here, decades later, looking out at the sea, I am here to say that if you can get through that tunnel, you can get through anything.

After I had tried to kill myself, I dwelled on the fact of how a kind word or a cup of tea can be enough to bring you back from the brink. That was the overwhelming message I wanted to shout out. To the outside world, all that youth, beauty and vibrancy should have absolutely no connection to the fervent wish for death. But so many young people, caught in a trap of insecurity and despair, incarcerated by their surroundings or by a community in which they simply don't belong, are unable to see their loveliness, their divine potential or a better life ahead for themselves. That a good night's sleep and someone to talk to can fix most things. I certainly did not have the insight or the audacity to tell myself that my misery was caused by simply being in the wrong place at the wrong time.

If I could have reached out my hand to my younger self, to the New Cross boy, to my New Cross Gate friend; if I could have hugged us all across the years and told us that each one of us would somehow find the strength to walk away from our anguish to a pathway of hope, safety, imagination, wild dreams and ambitions . . . There could be a horizon for us, too.

I was lucky to survive my suicide attempt. I was lucky to have survived the nadir of my teenage years. I was lucky to survive my family. Not everyone does.

But I knew that was not enough. I would have to reinvent myself.

HOMELAND

Waking up early in Ladyville in Ernesto's house I listen to the call of the 'Island Blackbird', which tells me I am in my birthplace. It's already hot in the village and the lonely dogs mooch at their chains in the yards at the front of each house, occasionally barking at each other. The dog across the street at the panades shop echoes the dog outside this house.

I get up – it's way too early – make coffee, eat cake, compose, write a bit then slope back to bed.

Because of Cambridge and my MPhil studies, I was able to afford to return to Belize in 1999 on a research travel grant from King's College. Back to my birthplace since being carried away, aged two.

I was researching the influence of colonialism on the music of Belize for a possible PhD. I felt that time was running out for the people of my father's age and older, who had grown up in Belize in the forties and fifties, decades before Belize gained its independence in 1981. I spent time in the library, perusing copies of newspapers, which, I noticed, even included the court circular from Buckingham Palace. I spoke to people who had sung or led choirs at around the time my father was growing up, including Gerald 'Lord' Rhaburn, Sir Colville Young, my father's cousin Laurene Pook (who was the same age as my Uncle Arthur) and I got to know and befriend the musicologist and piano teacher Gina Scott and her family.

I met Ernesto Kerr who was ten years old. I was staying with my stern-faced, softly spoken godmother, Aunt Catherine, and Ernesto was helping her with her chores. His mother had died only months before and his father could not take care of his family. Wherever I went in Belize, Ernesto with his chubby cheeks would somehow find me and we would have adventures – the biggest adventure just being together.

Now I am back again, the first time since the pandemic. Ernesto has been married for six years to Kishana and we are all getting ready for a long-awaited trip tomorrow to Placencia with Gina and her mother Marjorie.

*

Ernesto, my beautiful son.

A YEAR AT CAMBRIDGE

In 1999 I attended two artists' colonies in the USA: Djerassi Resident Artists Program in California and MacDowell in New Hampshire. How I came to be at either of these wonderful places was due to a work I'd composed in 1990 titled *In Our Lifetime* to mark the release of Nelson Mandela from prison. It was performed shortly after he had been freed. I had heard from fellow musicians in South Africa that he was to be released several weeks before it was publicly announced. I had been commissioned by Black Cultural Archives to compose a work celebrating Marcus Garvey. When I heard this news, I immediately switched gear. I felt compelled to compose a work that reacted to such an important event in my own lifetime. We had all expected Nelson Mandela to die in prison. Margaret Thatcher's government considered Nelson Mandela to be a terrorist and the apartheid system seemed to be at its height.

I only had two weeks. What could I compose that could be realised and performed with minimum forces yet maximum impact? My clever friend Kate Holland suggested using just one performer and electronics; I would record and mix at my studio in Camden. So the work I made to celebrate the release of Nelson Mandela was for solo baritone and tape.

I composed for the unique Mike Henry, whose voice I had heard on a cassette recording given to me by a friend. I was so taken by the sound, the warmth and flexibility – a voice that could sing anything, from soul to opera. At the emotionally charged premiere at the Commonwealth Institute, just weeks after Nelson Mandela's release, Mike sang live over the tape, which had his voice multitracked. I had asked that he be lit by a blue spotlight. A few years later Christopher Bruce made a ballet, *Waiting*, for London Contemporary Dance Theatre using *In Our Lifetime*. Christopher Bruce, who had not been at any of the live original music performances, spoke of having the character of Mandela bathed in blue light . . .

In Our Lifetime was on the first issue of Unknown Public, a CD box of new music released quarterly, founded by John L. Walters and Laurence Aston. It was also played on the Radio 3 programme *Mixing It*, presented by Robert Sandall and Mark Russell, and somehow got to the ears of composer Charles Amirkhanian, who ran a radio station in San Francisco, the Other Minds Festival, and Djerassi, an artists' retreat in Woodside on the San Francisco peninsular. On the strength of listening to *In Our Lifetime* and recordings of my songs from *Meet Me at Harold Moores*, Charles invited me to California to take part in the Other Minds Festival in March 1999, where I would perform my songs and also have other works of mine programmed, including the premiere of *Louis' Loops*, specially commissioned for Margaret Leng Tan.

Before the performances, all the composers spent time together at Djerassi discussing their work and then went into San

Francisco for the three-day festival.* I quickly made fast friends with Alvin Lucier, the American experimental composer. From this point in my life, mainly through being part of this festival, and also through being in America and absorbing the fresh air of optimism and energy, I feel my life changed irrevocably. Charles had arranged that after the festival I should stay on for several weeks at Djerassi's 583 acres. I had never been in such an expanse of space before. I wrote the song 'About Here', describing the unforgettable experience of being there.

While I was at Djerassi I came across a a copy of *New Notes*, a British new music magazine published by The Society for the Promotion of New Music. It contained an announcement of a Radcliffe Trust award for the study for an MPhil at Cambridge University. I had no commission for a large-scale piece and was itching to compose an orchestral work. I saw that this could provide the opportunity to achieve this ambition. I applied, and after an intriguing interview with Robin Holloway – the composer, professor and Fellow of Caius College – and filling in a mountain of administrative forms, I was accepted into the Faculty of Music and King's College for Michaelmas term 1999. Thus began another life-changing year. I met new friends whose fascination for their subjects continues to inspire me. It was at Cambridge I met and began my friendship with the Butt family, of which

* Composers featured 25–27 March 1999 at Other Minds Festival 5 at Cowell Theatre in Fort Mason, San Francisco: Luc Ferrari, Mary Ellen Childs, Linda Bouchard, Julian Priester, Sam Rivers, Alvin Lucier, António Pinho Vargas, Errollyn Wallen.

I have now become a member, joining John and Sally Butt and their five children. In this same year I was asked by Siân Ede to keep a diary for a Calouste Gulbenkian publication called *Art, Not Chance*. The book was published in 2001 and documents my experience of combining professional commissions and performances with a return to academic life for a year – a most happy year. The orchestral work I composed for my MPhil was *The World's Weather*.

From *Art, Not Chance*

22 January 2000

Greenwich. I'm longing to get down to work on *The World's Weather* but I have to fix my fax machine and do post-officey things. I listen to the fax repairer's warnings of Armageddon: I am wary of angels. Shopping in Deptford High Street – a totally different experience from Cambridge Market Square, no yams or plantains *there*. A wisp of a Creole accent reminds me, with a sudden pang, of Belize. I say a quick prayer for Ernesto, the ten-year-old friend I made there at Christmas.

There's always a sense of trepidation before I begin, like last year in Florida when a group of young girls taught me to jump wildly into the bay from the landing stage. It's Saturday. I'd like to reach bar 50 by Monday and I'm at bar 34. The trombones have just made their first entrance . . .

23 January

I am discovering in minute detail the difference between

solitude and loneliness. When work is going well, I am absorbed in a 'stream' and feel utterly connected. It is when I am anxious about it that I feel loneliest. I sometimes feel as if I've been lumbered with an anachronistic gift: compelled to sit alone in a room without sound, at perhaps the busiest, noisiest and most troubled time in earth's history, and write music for – a symphony orchestra. Yet this is what I must do; I must watch the little black ants creep across the page over minutes, days, weeks, years.

24 January

Cambridge. I show the beginnings of *The World's Weather* to Robin Holloway and he shows me his 'Finellium Marmalade'. We peer and poke at the oranges bobbing in the steaming pan. He has good and useful things to say about writing for the harp (the piece begins with harp and double basses) and advises me not to question my 'flow', just to be grateful – and to keep going.

25 January

So many practicalities: tapes to send off to a publisher (we're beginning negotiations), a programme of my works to plan for the Chard Festival in May, decisions about which of my songs the Eikanger-Bjørsvik brass band will play (with me singing at the piano) at the Aperitifo Festival in Bergen, also in May. Musical director Ray Farr has asked to arrange them. Meanwhile I've mislaid the notepad with scribbled ideas and texts for *God's Penny* to be performed by the children of

Islington Music Centre on 3 April. I haven't written too much of earth-shattering proportions yet.

Having a sound system with decent radio reception in my room is re-revolutionising my life. Everything I hear gives me countless ideas for pieces. I've lived for years in relative silence.

30 January

Urrrrrrgh. Still can't find the notebook for *God's Penny*; will have to get on without it. Today, for the first time since I began thinking about this piece (last October) I feel the shape of it. Work on it at home in Greenwich, and it flows, words happily presenting themselves with the music. Maybe the Benylin cough medicine *is* working!

31 January

The World's Weather. In the end you just sit down and *do* it. You make it easy for yourself. By doing it. No more torment. Just you and the paper. Blessed relief. Shaping your very own world.

Out of mud. Out of imagination. Why question it?

2 February

I love what I do. When I'm doing it I feel out of harm's way.

4 February

In composing I am trying to understand the fundamentals of music and the patterns of motion in sound. I crave essentials.

7 February

When considering all I have to do, I feel beleaguered. Still, *God's Penny* is finding its own swing. It helps so much to know exactly who I'm writing for.

A visit to the doctor: I don't have a chest infection, so to Boots straight away for more cough medicine, inhalants, lemon, ginger, vapour rub, tissues . . . It's Monday, and I've got to kick this thing by Thursday's concert.

8 February

I wake up and phone singer and conductor Madeleine Lovell for her singerly advice, then inhale, cancel tomorrow's rowing on the river and – relatively speaking – chill out.

9 February

Still struggling. I realise I've been dragging myself around for some time. Practise for tomorrow. May have to cancel if my voice doesn't return sufficiently. Although the virus is oppressive, I feel grimly determined. It's just past midnight. Helen Tunstall thinks she can play (the harp) in *God's Penny* on 3 April.

10 February

After a day feeling gruesome the gig is *tremendous*. Right up to the sound check (when my bass player Tim Harries nervously asks just how much of my voice I am saving) I think I'll have to quit. Keynes Hall in King's is small and there are about a hundred Fellows and students in it. The feeling of warmth from them is delicious and intoxicating. Everyone seems to dig the songs from *Meet Me at Harold Moores* and half of them buy CDs afterwards. Man, I love performing when it's this good. The fact is, my voice is barely there and I have to adjust the contours of songs to take account of its frailty, but something magical is happening, electric communication on stage and the enthusiasm of the audience. My heart is full.

11 February
Bask in some glory. Delightful concert in evening at Caius, Jeremy Bines directing and conducting his ensemble from the piano. All Ravel apart from Stravinsky's *Three Japanese Lyrics*. Excellent playing and such wonderful music.

12 February
Go rowing in the afternoon and am feeling shivery by evening. Rally to 'sing' in King's Voices concert in the chapel (Beethoven *Mass in C*) although I haven't had a voice for a month. However, put on red lipstick and Patrick Cox houndstooth shoes and there's a good party afterwards – with marshmallows.

13 February
Very shivery. Little Evie phones to ask if I am coming to Yorkshire. I am lying collapsed on my bed, still with my coat on. Force myself to do the three-hour drive. Crazy, but I love my precious friends Trish, Caroline, Evie and Maya.

14 February

In bed most of the day. Can't even play properly with Evie. Trish and I go to the Grand Theatre, Leeds, to the premiere of Northern Ballet's *Great Expectations* choreographed by Stef – Stefano Giannetti, then artistic director. I am sitting behind Stef, or so I imagine, and keep slapping him heartily on the back to congratulate him until I realise it's his twin brother Maurizio. Party afterwards. Lovely to see James (Bailey, ballet master) again. Whole evening is a fantastic tonic.

15 February

Always feel better in Yorkshire. Able to go with Caroline to collect Evie from the school crouched beneath dark crags. Suddenly a boy runs out ringing the school bell, through the crowd of parents, round the whole circumference of the school, all his force and energy concentrated on ringing *that* bell. Back to Cambridge at around midnight. Find I've received a Valentine email from 'ew.gush', a fan of my album.

17 February

Greenwich. Decide to stay in and hunker down, cosy amid all my clutter, my piano close to hand, river swirling outside. I want *God's Penny* drafted in rough by Monday (21 February) – so I read *Harry Potter and the Philosopher's Stone*. Chard Festival in May is making me composer of the month.

18 February

Mark-Anthony Turnage's opera *The Silver Tassie* is inspiring. Reminds me how big things grow from small, as with Stef's ballet. A good night in the theatre is a *good* night. Have a few breakthroughs with *God's Penny*.

Elgar Howarth (composer, conductor, trumpeter and champion of music for brass) calls to say how I wouldn't believe the way *Chrome* will sound with the Eikanger-Bjørsvik band in the Bergen Festival.

Ray Farr has finished arranging my song 'What Shall I Sing?' And I faxed it to him only yesterday afternoon! Finish my Harry Potter book – truly excellent. I'll send a copy to Ernesto.

19 February

I can see the children of the Islington Music Centre in their bright red sweatshirts in my mind's eye as I work. I'm so enjoying writing *God's Penny*. I feel as though I'm unearthing a new London just when I am discovering the delights of living away from it, my home for most of my life.

20 February

I nearly always work at the piano but much of *The World's Weather* has been written away from it. Today I brave trying bits of it out. I feel a shiver of excitement and have the tiniest glimpse of worlds beyond this.

21 February

Back to King's and this pretty town (the ivory-towered bit). A wonderful letter from Ernesto: he has sent me his spelling test (he got 98%) and says I am 'very much missed'. Think I'll go with Dad next September.

22 February

Finish the mud song from *God's Penny*. It turns out to be about a rat's-eye view. Get the 'poo' word in several times – for the children's sake.

24 February

Conductor Jeremy Bines comes to look at the score of *Hunger* (for 19 instruments). We're going to do it in Emmanuel College next term. Walk around all day with a tea towel in my coat-sleeve lining, without noticing.

25 February

Delicious cross-country drive in the setting sun to St Mary's Church in Kidlington near Oxford to hear the first performance of *Romeo Turn* (for viola, cello and double bass). Goes well, although the church is freezing, not ideal for the fingers of the Adderbury Ensemble. A member of the audience tells me she loves my piece and loves my hair. David Hopkins, who commissioned it, seems very pleased. It's being performed again at the Holywell Music Room in Oxford on Sunday.

28 February
Bright, sunny day. Sing lovely Stravinsky *Ave Maria* at Evensong.

29 February
Dangerous pursuits . . .

1 March
If I call this Mad March and keep saying it to myself, I can get through the enormous amount of work I've got. Have started sending off chunks of *God's Penny* to Richard Frostick (director of the Islington Music Centre). Being commissioned, as distinct from happily and gratuitously banging out notes from the piano onto the page, gives me an association with homework. As I've hardly ever done any, there's a dread of being found out. Sometimes I have to remind myself that I'm doing what I love and know. I am dedicating the piece to Ernesto Kerr in Belize and the children of the Islington Music Centre. I know he'd love to be friends with some of them. Deliriously happy to be well again; composing is such a physical activity and I hadn't realised how weak I had become.

3 March
The premiere of *God's Penny* is in a month, Although the shape and structure are clear, in music it is the detail that makes all the difference between a clearly executed and a scrappy piece. It doesn't matter how good the *idea* is, the details – the housework – bear the task of illuminating it. I'm writing a paper about Michael Tippett and his use of

spirituals in *A Child of Our Time*. It is extremely painful delving back into the history of slavery. Did he know what he was taking on? These are more than simple folk ditties – they are cries and wails of survival. Am also thinking about a ballet with Stef, *Macbeth*. I'd like to try combining electronics with the orchestra. James thinks Stef will go for it.

7 March

Post more music to Richard Frostick. Always a surge of relief and release when that brown envelope slips away into the darkness of the large box in Trinity Street.

14 March

Jeremy Bines now has the instrumental parts for *Hunger*.

16 March

Vic Gatrell, a Fellow of Caius, is finding out what day of the week 3 April 1500 was – so I can find out the chant specific to that day for the opening procession of *God's Penny*. Stephen Cleobury (King's College music director) will give me a copy of the original chant to fiddle with.

21 March

That missing notepad with ideas and words for *God's Penny* has finally turned up as I'm in the final throes of it, in a folder of music left in the porters' lodge. Please, *please*, let it hurry up and finish. It's a far bigger work than I'd anticipated, or indeed than was commissioned. Ideas kept coming so I've kept going. Just when I think I've finished, I read about 126 species of wildflowers found on London bomb sites after World War II. *Have* to include another song. It will include the audience whispering their names: 'Ragwort, Gallant Soldiers, Greater Plantain, Penny Cress . . .'

22 March

Finish all the vocal parts. Put songs in order. Photocopy and post off the new bits. Have to finish the harp and percussion parts now.

24 March

The British premiere of my setting of Ted Hughes's poem 'The Warm and the Cold', for baritone (Peter Savidge) and piano (David Owen Norris), in Abingdon. (The first performance given by the commissioner, baritone Thomas Buckner, and me was in New York and coincidentally on the day Hughes died.) Just make concert. Friday evening traffic.

27 March

Spend some hours with harpist Laurette Pope in Christ's [College] seeing what does and doesn't work.

29 March

Meeting at the South Bank in London to discuss an opera commission for Broomhill Opera next year. Start to organise my birthday party at the Oyster Bar in New York.

30 March

Four days to the premiere of *God's Penny*, two to the first rehearsal I attend. Feeling good but the thousand other things clamouring for my attention are like water closing over my head. Water. I've decided I must live by the sea. I can't go back to noise.

31 March

Speak with Margaret Leng Tan, who I've affectionately nicknamed the 'Kinky Dinky Diva of the Toy Piano'. She's been performing my *Louis' Loops* at the Beethoven-Haus in Bonn and the Smithsonian in Washington.

1 April

Islington rehearsal. The children are just great, but 'first composer rehearsals' are overwhelming. The impact of hearing music one has spent months beavering over in a new acoustic environment – the real world, the intended space, not my head – is high-octane. I'm immediately made aware of the magnificence, magic and alchemy of music – and of my failures and miscalculations.

3 April

Premiere of *God's Penny* at St Giles Cripplegate. Only time to perform 15 minutes of the 45, so it is a taster. It goes really, really well. Part of the 500th anniversary celebration of the Cripplegate Foundation, which sponsors Islington Music Centre. Amusing sermon by the thespy Bishop of London.

4 April

Send Ernesto the programme with his dedication.

10 April

Birthday in New York. Drinks with American friends at the Oyster Bar beneath Grand Central Station. On to Haveli's in the East Village for dinner. A motley crew of struggling artists and writers.

13 April

From the beauteous Grand Central Station with its blue, fishy ceiling to New Haven and Wesleyan University for talk and performance, with my friend Zinovy Zinik, the writer in residence. Our discussion on 'Emigration as an Artistic Device' is so-so. We're coming at it in different ways. It is better when I just sing and play. Great to see Alvin Lucier again. I adore his humorous wit and twinkling eyes.

29 April

Cambridge. Have been looking at the score of *Hunger* and listening to a recording. Was too close to it before. Now I can see the things that need improving. Think my inner ear has got sharper. Remembering the circumstances in which the piece was written is painful: it was a year after Rory Allam, friend, lover and muse, had died and I'd just finished writing my chamber opera *Look! No Hands!* I was exhausted. I think, however, that we can make something of *Hunger* in performance.

Hot, hot day; Jeremy and I spend four hours wheeling timps across town. Loads of comments ('Drum 'n' bass, man') and people thrumming their fingertips on the skins.

30 April

Spend morning sorting out more percussion. Borrow a thunder sheet. That's the last time I casually mark a dot on a page that turns out to break my back.

Haunted by memory – *Hunger* is dedicated to Rory.

1 May

Very good rehearsal tonight. Jeremy is very relaxed and clear with the players. The learning curve of these young musicians has been extraordinarily high. *Hunger* is beginning to sound gutsy.

3 May

Great concert. *Hunger* goes excellently as does Stravinsky's *Dumbarton Oaks*. In the final rehearsal I decide to end *Hunger* with the quiet rumbling of the thunder sheet. Jeremy conducts superbly.

13 May

At around eleven on Saturday night, go over to King's for a quick burst of piano practice and get locked in – all night. Faulty lock, disco overhead. No one hears me screaming and banging until the next morning when a choral scholar comes to practise next door. There is no way out and no window in that room. I am more furious than scared as I'd reported the lock as faulty several days before. I sleep in the velvet curtains, which I wrench from the walls – and put thoughts of peeing from my mind.

18–22 May

Bergen, Norway. Have fallen in love with this place and its air. Feel impelled to travel as far north as possible through water. No time on this trip. Great to see Elgar Howarth again – big hug. The Eikanger Band is a crack team. I've never heard *Chrome* sound so sleek and powerful. It is performed on three successive days, starting in a huge warehouse on Friday. Singing some of my songs from *Meet Me at Harold Moores* with the band (and Ray Farr's arrangements) makes me feel like a 1940s American star. The concert on Saturday is in the Grieghallen and includes Elgar Howarth's *Ascendit in Coeli*; on Sunday it doesn't rain and *Chrome* has a fine outing in the town square. I video it. A man shouts: 'Hallelujah!' Back to Cambridge just in time to sing at Evensong.

28 May

Chard Festival in Somerset. Drive there and back from Cambridge in a day. One of my best gigs ever, although I am shattered. Relaxed, happy atmosphere on stage, great musicians, everything gels, the audience stamps and cheers. Realise it is the tenth anniversary of my band Ensemble X.

Drive home with Ray Charles and James Brown. Get to Cambridge at 3.30 a.m. in a glow.

8 June

My feet are wedged in mud; eyes are in the firmament.

10 June

Am about halfway through *Tiger* (a piece for organ). This is inspired by thoughts of the poet Veronica Rospigliosi as she lay dying on Christmas Day 1999, gently repeating the words, 'I am thinking about the shape of a tiger.' My first attempt was jotted down on two pages of A4 manuscript paper. Most of that was jettisoned. I kept the opening statement and a couple of ideas, which I've sharpened and expanded in this new draft.

Once I've started a piece I feel really tense until I've completed it, and then it's immediately on to the next. Ten weeks to complete *The World's Weather*.

Walking past King's Chapel, I feel so glad that *Tiger* is going to receive its first performance there, by John Butt. It encourages me to think big. I like to imagine that the dusty, trumpeting angels on the organ screen will hear it. From small things . . . Margaret Leng Tan is going to perform *Louis' Loops* (my toy piano piece) in a Wigmore Hall concert with Evelyn Glennie and Emanuel Ax next spring.

Singing in the choir has really strengthened my voice.

16 June

Spend fifteen minutes with organist Ben Bayl (King's senior organ scholar) playing through *Tiger*, really just going through sounds and stops. Hope this piece will work; it's quite strange.

17 June

Write the first two bars of *Aries* for unaccompanied chamber choir. Setting of part of a larger poem by W. S. Merwin, 'Runes for a Round Table', given to me at my birthday party in New York.

19 June

Tiger is done, written slowly in small chunks, never more than six hours a day. I am conscious throughout of four briefs: remembering Veronica; thinking about her thinking about 'the shape of a tiger'; meeting Faber's commission deadline for a piece lasting between two and four minutes, and filling King's College Chapel on 24 June.

My feelings when I composed this were dispassionate, as they often are these days. I know myself and am more interested in pushing beyond what I can already do. Ben is a terrific sight reader. He seems to grasp the nature of the piece quickly.

20 June

Mornings can be difficult. A golden moon at night.

21 June

Still need a second violinist for the King's 2000 concert in the Chapel in three days.

Sorting, faxing, photocopying, phoning, writing messages. Practising my songs is the easy bit, though there's endless work to be done on interpretation, improvisation and *attitude*.

22 June

Sally Butt (John Butt's wife) is going to play second violin. She knows the CD of *Meet Me at Harold Moores* well so that's excellent news. Ben's girlfriend will pull the organ stops to avoid hiatus in the music. I have changed a few registrations. I've now run the compositional gamut of keyboard extremes, from toy piano to organ.

23 June

Have a go on the Steinway installed in the Chapel. Sounds much clearer than I would have expected in those acoustics.

24 June

Painless photo session in the Chapel. Rehearsal of my Second String Quartet and songs, including *Tiger*. Not a great sound check. Good concert. I feel more nervous than usual. Very formal audience, though some are reduced to tears. I love King's Chapel and performing my music there is a moving, if awe-inspiring, experience. All the music that has gone before . . .

28 June

Singing with King's Voices in Ely Cathedral. According to

fellow singer Rosemary Curtin, there's a music theatre piece that I should write based on Etheldreda, one of the founders. Hmmm . . .

2 July

Turning pages for John Butt, director of studies in music at King's College, university lecturer and director of King's Voices. He is recording Elgar's organ works in the chapel. As night draws in, I watch the stained-glass windows slowly fade into dark luminous crystal.

5 July

Administration. I really need to improve my technology skills. Possible recital in Leicester in November. Complete performance of *God's Penny* postponed until the autumn.

8 July

The World's Weather should have a storm raging round a point of calm. Will attempt to maintain a child's-eye view.

9 July

I make great headway with *The World's Weather* by talking it through with anthropologist Catherine Bolten. She helps me find a less daunting way in than the title would suggest. The story of a single raindrop will contain the story of the world's weather, and am mesmerised by this idea. Want to get *Aries* out of the way now but it's going slowly. Fiddly and fugal.

3 August

Stopping for dinner with a mixture of curious frustration and mild excitement. Have been working in minute detail on some string figuration for *The World's Weather*. Slow work, and I haven't got as far as I'd like. Will *have* to work more quickly.

6 August

Sunday. I am preparing my score for the day's work, ruling the staves and drawing in the clefs for the instruments: flutes, oboes, clarinets, bassoons, horns, trumpets, trombones, tuba, harp, percussion and strings. This alone takes hours. Getting through a pencil a day. The bells are ringing in St Edward's Church opposite. A door slams. An overcast day. Good for working. Yesterday was a 'blind' day, barely inching along.

As I'm scoring I can sometimes see imaginary individual musicians – a good sign. The quotation at the head of my score is from E. B. White: 'The glory of everything.' Finally, *The World's Weather* is a celebratory piece. I am thrilled to be alive and to be able to summon up sounds from all sorts of exotic instruments.

16 August

Working well in the bowels of King's, can work through the night. At this stage I lose the power of intelligible speech and must seem distracted, 'away with the fairies'. I am. Catherine has brought me back a little silver bird from Greece to help with inspiration.

Ah, 99's a lovely number; means I'm nearly halfway through my orchestrating. Writing in the staccatos, staccatissimos, slurs and accents in the woodwind section. Brain's getting weary and I'm feeling queasy. Too many notes? Play the same brass passage over and over to determine how to place the accents correctly.

18 August

Trying to sustain a sense of enjoyment through this last slog. Writing about the process has helped. I've been building a shell to protect myself at a sensitive time. However, I must be like a warrior as well as a turtle to get through.

Looks like I'll be visiting Belize in September with my father, the paradise where I started *The World's Weather*. Will surprise Ernesto.

Meanwhile, somewhere in my compositional recess lurks an embryo Christmas carol. The digital metronome I bought in New York in the spring is proving very useful in calculating the subdivision of beats.

20 August

Ten days until I have to hand in *WW*. Must remember to leave room for the horns to breathe. Working on the 'benevolent sea' section.

25 August

The final push and I'm feeling afraid. Thirty more bars to orchestrate. As soon as I finish I have to write a carol and a set of variations for the piano. I feel physically ill and have lost my appetite. Don't want to disappoint myself.

Some of yesterday was lost as I had to go to London to record a voiceover for a TV programme on the composer Coleridge-Taylor that I'm presenting. At last I've booked my ticket for Belize. Every day I think about how I need green and quiet to compose well.

The sun is setting and King's is resplendent against the sky and grass. I am feeling much calmer and quietly satisfied that I'm writing the piece I've been dreaming about for years. It's not very long and I'm surprised at how much of it becomes joyous and dancelike after the dark asymmetrical rhythms of nature in the first part. I am enjoying letting my instinct guide me in quite technical considerations.

Gosh. Writing the high lines above the stave for the flute is giving me vertigo.

Party. Walk back through King's in my *Wizard of Oz* shoes, which hurt a bit, chatting all the while with Catherine whose wisdom I'm acknowledging in the dedication of *The World's Weather*. Do another hour's work and crack a contrapuntal puzzle in *Aries*. Though first thing in the morning is usually best for composing, sometimes doing a little bit just before I go to sleep gives me a sense of well-being and often, in this wound-down state, ideas flow freely. I've noticed that if there's a particularly thorny problem to solve, I will look at it briefly before sleep and will have solved it by the morning.

27 August

Emblazoned on my mind in gigantic theatre lights is the word FINISH. I must. There's a palpable fear in my belly and I wake up in the middle of the night sweating music. Seven or eight bars to go. Up against the deadline but I'll do it. *The World's Weather* was started nine months ago, put to one side for months and finally sprinted through in the last six weeks. Must remember to go back and put some *divisi* markings in the strings.

Later. Bar 218, two to go. Was feeling forlorn, as I sometimes do when I'm coming to the end of a big piece. Then I get a 'hit' as I come up with a new idea. This must be what is meant by a 'gift'; the brainwave felt genuinely bestowed. *The World's Weather* is about a new kind of spring.

28 August

Stride across Silver Street Bridge and deliver the last fragments to Martin Iddon, my copyist. Trying to keep calm and not drink too much coffee. I have to accept that every time I look at it there are improvements and changes to be made. That the finishing process is itself without end.

30 August

Binders. West Road. Granta pub. Sleep.

DIDO: PART I

Time is where we live.

We are born and from the time of our awareness of the possibility of our limits – of our mortality – we begin the hopeless fight to remain here. Plan B is to be, at the very least, remembered. But remembered for what? For what we have done? For what we are? For what we have become?

If you ask me what I have done I will not be able to tell you in a way that would make much sense. I do not know, nor overly care, what I am. Of the greatest concern is what I have yet to do. Therefore, I have not the time nor the patience to admit death. Yet. Yet there she looms every day, beckoning like the arms of a lover. And every day we die a little more – in biological terms and also when we put off, give in or give up going beyond the limits of ourselves and of what we know.

Is it possible that we can be remembered, like Dido, for the quality of our passion? For the flame that drives us to connect, to explain, to discover? Is the manner of how we do things, make things, as important as the resulting end? Do the questions we ask make us into the people we are – or is it only what we eat, how we dress, the possessions we acquire or the company we keep? My companion is music and I have eaten it alive. For music I have made myself lonely and it has eaten *me* alive. Do I want to be remembered or do I just want to forget? Music sometimes limps beside me like a wounded dog, yet it is part of me. My companion is sometimes a jealous wolf that tolerates no competition for my soul. I can call to a god, but only through music's jaws.

Every day, the sulky mermaid visits the invisible labyrinths, subterranean water worlds; then returns, transformed like Aeneas, warrior of the seas, to the shore where someone awaits, holding a cloak they are making that she may never wear.

In music we are transformed; we are man/woman, Hera, hermaphrodite, beyond bounds. We fly over the earth.

When I began, which is to say, before I knew of my existence, it was enough to respond to the vibrations of music through curly-stubby infant toes and fingers, to be terrified by the sound of a bow rasping on a string, to feel unexpected tears fall at the lowing sound of a trumpet, or the unpredictability of an off-key lullaby. I had little thought of myself beyond addressing the urgent physical needs but it was through sound that I could connect to the looming giant, adult faces that peered into my crib. It was through sound that I could bend various events to my will.

As soon as I knew myself, I longed to know where I had come from, and I burned to remember the state of unselfconsciousness from which I had so recently emerged. I would lie on my bed, aged four, just thinking. Thinking. Where was my babyhood? What preceded it? Was I some other, totally different being before this current one? Might I have even been some other creature – not a human at all? I asked all the adults I knew about it. Of course I did not have the language, let alone the vocabulary, to make my finer points of argument understood but the grown-ups seemed little interested in this fundamental question, which so mightily obsessed me. They couldn't even tell me about their own sense of being thinking selves.

I watched the shadows on my dolls' faces and willed *them* to speak of their secrets. Perhaps they were the ones who might have the knowledge of 'being'. Their silence certainly spoke of another wisdom and their stiff little bodies and transfixed expressions suggested a connection with a dimension of time that I so needed to understand. How could it be that nobody, no one at all, knew? But my beloved doll, Jenny, didn't speak in my presence, though she cried when I did and shared all my thoughts. How was I to proceed through life if I did not know where I had come from? Who could help me? And why, for adults, was straightening a pair of socks, yanking my hair to comb it, lighting the stove or gossiping with the neighbours *so* much more important than answering this question? *Where the hell did I come from?* Was it hell? Was it that burny place that Granny said I, a three-year-old toddler, was surely destined to leap into because of my sins and misdemeanours? Actually, it sounded quite jolly there. Had I come from fire, then?

Fire was certainly in my tempestuous little body. I burned like I still burn. Every single day I had a tantrum and frustration seemed to mark my hours. I was bound by the punishing limits of short legs and not enough words. Not the right words. Never fast enough. Hell. There were occasional giddy moments of bliss and odd glimpses of perception when I just 'knew'. Moments when I could tell you the secret connection of everything: the way a violin sounded like a human voice, like a woman singing to herself; a shell, when you held it close, sounded just like the sea. How could that be? But the fact that these things *were* was a mighty revelation to a young child. It seemed to be a miraculous concatenation of object and subject. Let me listen again.

First-hand discoveries like these were a treat of childhood but many others – like my origin – well, those I had to make up. Working with fragments and scraps thrown to me by distracted adults, I wove a secret night-time story for my sisters that kept them enthralled for years:

You were in Mummy's tummy and everything was very, very dark. You were all curled up. You were all cosy. You were eating your favourite sweets. Yes, sugared almonds. All curled up and cosy as can be. Then, one day, you heard a strange sound. 'Blumpum, blumpum, blumpum . . .' You were really scared when you heard that sound. It was coming nearer and nearer. You couldn't escape. You couldn't move. You were all curled up and started to cry. 'Blumpum, blumpum, blumpum, blumpum.' What could it be? You couldn't run away. I was outside, in this world, so I couldn't help you. I was already born. 'Blumpum, blumpum.' I could hear a little squeaking sound coming from Mummy's tummy. Oh no! Little baby's going to die. Little baby is in danger from the big monster coming to eat her all up! What should I do? Mummy was fast asleep. Nobody was anywhere. It was the war and everyone had run away. 'Blumpum, blumpum, blumpum, blumpum, blumpum, blumpum . . .' Nearer and nearer. 'Blumpum.' Monster coming to bite your head off, coming to strangle you – your little neck, like this. Oh. Sorry. Ouch! Then, little baby – that's you – then, little baby suddenly a sound: 'Bish! Bish! Bish!' Another special friendly monster, hiding in Mummy's chest, suddenly burst out and beat the horrible monster and he vanished out of her mouth in a puff of smoke. So, the next time you see smoke coming out of her mouth . . .

Entertain. Tell stories. Hold an audience. Well, why *do* we composers write music? All we really have is the now and in the now we can draw a simultaneous hushed breath from a crowd. Who wouldn't want to do *that*?

A guiding principle in my work has been to try to put as much devotion as possible into what I do – from the tiniest miniature to a symphony. I learned the quest for perfection in musical performance from my music teacher at Hollington Park, Miss Pearse. Music is just noise without love. Love resides in our concentration, energy, effort, thinking and feeling, being alive to the blistering moment and to the performers and to the audience.

The more I devote myself, the more easy it is not only to put myself to one side but, as Corinthians enjoins, to make myself someone that 'beareth all things, believeth all things, hopeth all things, endureth all things'.

My working life is comprised of balancing commissions with my own initiated projects, mile-high mountains of admin and trying to please too many people. Over time, I have created a catalogue of works in which may be discerned patterns of thought and characteristic traits but day-to-day life can somewhat fracture the vision as one moves from task to task, from one work to another, from one email or interview to another. The bigger picture is not always clear as I concern myself with the deadlines and details at hand. What preoccupies me is the here and now. *Now* is where I choose to make my reputation and to be remembered. I can do nothing about it once I am dead. (I was spooked recently when I spotted in a music dictionary the blank space waiting for the date of my demise.)

Dido's Lament from Henry Purcell's opera *Dido and Aeneas* is a miracle of memorability. Built over a repeated bass sequence winding downwards in semitones, the melody languidly explores every crevice, through its chromatic search for expression of the imagination of death: 'When I am laid, am laid in earth'. I have sung this myself and was struck, at every performance, by the freshness and timelessness of its sentiment. The words and music sound spontaneous, as if Dido is using her last breath, imploring us, in that frozen moment, frozen for centuries, to remember her essence, her living, breathing, sweating humanness, and not her fate — an accident of birth wrung from worldly, ephemeral circumstance and bickering gods.

Who decides who will be remembered anyway? The history of Western classical music as documented by non-composers has been the history of white, middle-class men with much music outside that bracket, though treasured in its time, eventually lost or simply dismissed. As more contemporary classical composers who originate outside a hitherto narrow sphere of practitioners widen their concerns to include a genuine respect towards the vernacular and towards non-Western techniques and document this music themselves, we shall uncover more and more music from the past that for a variety of reasons we find relevant today. Living composers have no control over what will remain, of what future generations will find of use or of interest. We do what we do and take what we can get. We give what we must.

A new costume, a new cloak, is being made for me by my extraordinary friend, Anda Winters,* for when I next sing Dido's song in my multimedia show, *Jordan Town*. I shall relearn Purcell's music and, through the mind of a pale, dead Englishman, will clutch a fragment of Carthage and remember the plight of a queen.

---

* Anda Winters is the artistic director and CEO of the Coronet Theatre.

HITCHHIKING

After finishing my A levels I decided to take a year off before going on to higher education. I didn't always spend it productively. I would dearly like some of those days now – free whole days which I spent wandering around Leeds, walking in the deserted city in the middle of the night just a few months before we learned that the Yorkshire Ripper was on the prowl in the same street; learning Italian; discovering Thornton's chocolates for the first time; practising the piano; hanging out with old and new friends and, mostly, being completely skint.

My friend Trish was a wild spirit and she was doing a lot of wild travelling. It was she who had persuaded me to become a Christian at school (which had had its apotheosis in my big nun ambition) and now she persuaded me to go hitchhiking with her for six weeks around Europe, after my A levels that summer. We had £50 between us.

We set off from my home in Linley Road, Tottenham, in the cheapest way we knew how. We took the 171 bus all the way to New Cross (that would have taken a couple of hours), and then we caught a bus or a train to Dover – or did we even hitch to Dover? We caught the ferry to Calais, then hitched our way around. There was no Internet and no mobile phones. I think I sent one postcard back home during the entire time I was away. Anything could have happened to us – and everything did.

Trish was a dab hand at hitchhiking and I, too, got to learn the ways of the road.

We probably looked like hippies – we were certainly semi-feral, Trish with her long brown plaits and me with very short hair and a long blue cheesecloth dress. We had a tent and lived off a diet of half a baguette and a single triangle of La Vache qui rit (soft processed cheese) a day. If we were unexpectedly flush (if we had been fed by someone else, such as the kind Frenchman who took us to a restaurant, and who was forever known as 'Meal'), we could afford half a tomato to go with the half baguette and the single triangle of La Vache qui rit.

Having thrown myself back into dancing, I did try to keep up my daily barre exercises at the roadside while we waited for a lift. Pliés, tendus and ports de bras every morning, in full view of passersby, after a night spent sleeping in a hedge or on the stony ground.

Trish and I developed telepathic communication, almost becoming the same person. This protected us in many dangerous situations, although we had no real sense of danger. The world was ours to explore.

We nearly got murdered three times.

Having crossed into France one of the first people to pick us up was a lorry driver who we nicknamed 'Matelas' as that is the word he repeated constantly. His real name was Flaminio. We didn't have an extraordinarily wide French vocabulary but we eventually learned that '*matelas*' translated to 'mattress' in English. Flaminio was Italian and had a mattress at the back of his lorry, which was otherwise filled with peaches. We ate a lot of peaches and avoided the mattress. We spent a couple of weeks with Flaminio who spoke no English at all. His lack of English didn't prevent him from negotiating my price with a bulky, leather-clad German in an underground bar in Venice, or with a wizened and wiry old Italian vineyard owner in Italy, or inviting a married couple who we'd met at a mountain-top club, into the bedroom where Trish and I were sleeping, so they could choose how they wanted us.

Flaminio had seemed like a decent enough man compared to the previous narrow escape.

We had got into the car which already had several men in it. We gave them details of where we were headed but after a while grew concerned when we saw that we were being driven down a very long, narrow path lined by trees. It was pitch black. Everyone got out of the car and we were told to get out too. There were at least five men surrounding us. But we were young and felt invincible. Suddenly I clutched my head and started groaning that I had the most terrible headache. The men suddenly disappeared. It was too dark to pitch the tent properly so we did the best we could and in the morning woke up to find ourselves in a cornfield miles from anywhere and anyone.

Another time Trish and I were sleeping on the beach at Antibes. I awoke at around 2 a.m. to find myself looking into the eyes of a man dressed in a suit lying alongside me in the sand. Trish had almost identical besuited company too. There followed a bit of a skirmish (I remember Trish hopping in her sleeping bag towards the sea as I drifted back to sleep), which resulted in us eventually losing the unwanted attention of the men in suits. However, when we woke up in the morning, my glasses had been stolen along with some other things. Luckily, we still had our passports. We decided to report the robbery to the local police and walked to the police station. A couple of guys were in the police station too and when they heard of our predicament, they offered to drive us to our next destination, which was into Italy via the Alps. We set off but when we reached what seemed to be the sharpest, most hazardous stretch of a bend, one of the men drove off the road and stopped the car. The car was a two-door car. I was sitting in the back with one guy and Trish was in front with the meaner-looking of the two men, the man who had stopped the car. Our rucksacks with our passports and all our belongings were in the boot. I was trapped at the back and watched as the man took out a knife, got out of the car and took Trish with him to the edge of the cliff and spat over it. Then he cut off some of her hair. I could tell that the man sitting beside me in the car was not mean like the knife man. I don't know how I did it, but I persuaded him to let me out of the car. I kept saying that I was engaged to be married and that I was awaiting the results of my A level exams. I ran to the roadside and tried to wave down cars but they were hurtling by so fast.

The two men let us take our rucksacks out of the boot, then sped off, leaving us on the treacherous bend. We walked and walked and, because we were in shock, we treated ourselves to the first proper meal we had had in the four days we'd been travelling.

We pitched our tent in the nearby forest and fell into a deep sleep. When we awoke and set off again, we saw a sign saying, 'Beware, Wild Boars'. We knew we had already had several lucky escapes after being on holiday for only a few days and, while we could have done nothing about reading important signs in the dark, we vowed at least to never *ever* get into a car with more than one man. The next car that stopped had three men. We got into it and were driven, unscathed, into Italy.

The truth was that every man we met was an opportunist for sex.

On the streets of Rome a man pulled open his overcoat and flashed us while thrusting a magazine depicting various body parts towards us. In a car on a motorway in Italy, I was sitting in the front seat and Trish was in the back. I murmured to her that the man had his willy out and that we needed to stop. We were dropped on the hard shoulder, cars whizzing by, and almost immediately a couple of policemen apprehended us, pushing us down a grass verge at the side and harshly interrogating us, their guns clearly visible, insisting that I was either '*una americana*' or from Uganda. They too had a leering glint in their eye.

Two young girls travelling with no money across Europe

were fair game. We were told by a Frenchman that a young American couple had been murdered recently and that the authorities had little sympathy, regarding hitchhikers as bringing misfortune onto themselves. We had been warned.

I would like to say that we learned to trust nobody but we had such exuberance for life and such *interest* in people and places; moreover we were too naive to realise how we were perceived.

We travelled around France and Italy and drove through Switzerland. We stayed a few days in Milan with a youngish man from Nigeria who played Jim Reeves records all day long and with whom we watched John Wayne films projected onto his wall.

The last night of our trip we were back in France – Rouen. In the middle of that night I awoke in time to rescue Trish, who was in great danger from our host. We hurriedly grabbed our belongings, ran out of the house and slept below a bridge in the pouring rain.

LOVE SONGS

To be in love is to be caught out. You are torn from yourself
and are rent by flame. You wear your heart on your brow
and the heart's breath causes you to sing a new song. You
no longer belong to yourself and start to see yourself as the
beloved does – a wingèd angel brought to defeat sadness,
boredom, old age, loneliness and death. All the things you
are or ever will be are suddenly held in the palm of your
hand like a jovial, bejewelled Buddha. You suddenly have
the secret of life and you are holy. See how that oak tree,
nodding at you – look – is so green; that solitary leaf in the
kerb is gold-plated by the sky's nectar. Even the traffic is on
your side. And they're playing your tune . . .

Then. You fall out of love, nearly as quickly as you fell
into it. You are consigned to watch the world wither in whispers about you. The adoring leaves, skipping out of park
gates, now grate in cackled laughter at your feet. It's gone
wrong. No one loves you. No gold anywhere. And you're not
supposed to care. That's for teenagers – the wallowing, the
staying in bed all day, snuffling into already damp tissues,
the intoxicating enthusiasm for grief. But the very last thing
I want now is to listen to a love song. I want to get on and
live – give me a prelude and fugue or a new dress. Do *not*
give me a *chanson*.

Well, I suppose finding a way *not* to write a love song can make for a more reasoned song – that and the experience of knowing and loving Rory Allam, who became my muse. We were introduced to each other at a mutual friend's flat in Stoke Newington and we became fast friends. If anyone wanted to get hold of me on the phone, they would try Rory. If he was similarly engaged, they knew that they should probably try ringing again in a few hours' time. We once spoke on the phone for over four hours. Rory had a distinctive, soft, high-pitched Scottish accent and laughed, like me, a *lot*. We loved staying in, smoking, drinking coffee, joking, joshing, gossiping, talking about music. We shared an utter contempt for exercise, fresh air and 'healthy living'.

Rory was born to Nancy and Michael in Haig Maternity Hospital, Hawick, and was taken home to Ashkirk on the borders of Scotland. He went to London for the first time to study clarinet with Alan Hacker at the Royal Academy of Music. Annie Lennox matriculated at the same time as Rory, studying flute. Nancy told me that Annie Lennox was extremely shy and would always wait for Rory to accompany her into the cafeteria. Rory was not shy and was very kind. From the moment he hit London he was in absolute heaven. His wild heart could soar in London. Countless times he recounted his stories of parties, clubs, bright lights, his adventures touring with theatre companies, chatting up girls (especially Japanese girls) with his one-liner: 'Do you live alone?'

I sometimes think that if you could just hollow the important words deeply enough into yourself so that they become part of your connective tissue, part of your brain and sinews, part of your tongue even, you could master the art of living. I see that these good and true words that can guide you are actually everywhere. Even the bottle of fancy handwash in my bathroom contains a philosophical lesson for the day: 'Celebrate each day as a new beginning.' Somehow, Rory had the ability to do that – he could celebrate each day as a new beginning. Life for him was an adventure – a riot of experience and sensation. I know that up to the very moment of his death he would have been fascinated by the process of what was happening to him. Rory inspired so many of my songs, including 'Rain' and 'Meet Me at Harold Moores' (the title song of the album) and his speaking voice is embedded in my work *I Hate Waiting*, composed for Ensemble X. The words of 'Meet Me at Harold Moores' came about by asking Rory what, when he was well, would be his perfect day.

Rory was there at the time in my life when I formed Ensemble X, when I was running my recording studio in Camden, working as a freelance keyboard player and pianist – and when I was just beginning to write the songs that form the core of my catalogue.

When the multiple sclerosis took hold to the point where Rory had to move back to Scotland to be cared for by his parents, he was still the one to whom his friends turned to share their secrets and their troubles. He urged me to get rid of my commercial studio and just compose. Every so often I still hear him saying, 'Just compose, Errollyn.' So here I am in Scotland, composing and, for the moment, until I've finished this book, this other opera, staying the hell in.

*

As Kene and Arthur's marriage disintegrated (Uncle Arthur was having an affair that went on for several years before they lived separately and eventually divorced), I, as the eldest, still had a sense of trying to hold things together. Somehow.

So, my final school years and first few years at university were troubled. I see that now as I look back. I needed to make sure my aunt, who was emotionally broken, would be all right. At Goldsmiths, I remember summoning up all my courage to call Uncle Arthur and ask him to promise that Kene would not be left destitute, that he would do right by her.

Both my aunt and my mother grew up with different love songs to sing – and, unlike me, they didn't write their own, though my father sang his beautiful songs to my mother at their wedding. I saw how they lived, like so many women in the fifties, in thrall to their husbands and with little power of their own. Throw in the added ingredients of their men being made to feel unwelcome in England, and it is easy to see how husbands and fathers would need to muster dignity and dominance at home.

The cognitive dissonance between the chivalrous fairy-tale princes and the reality of the short-tempered men around them didn't stifle Kene and Barbara's compulsion to pass down to me and my sisters the dream of one day meeting our very own chivalrous fairy-tale princes, who would sweep us off our feet, who would be the very pinnacle of our worldly achievement. These Mrs Wallens were conditioned to be subservient in their marriages and I was raised to understand my own subservience to men. It didn't help that, despite being ordered to do chores at home, I clearly was *not* devoted to housework. By the time I was eleven or twelve, it became obvious to them that I was a lost cause. What, after all, was the point of a girl who didn't know her place, her domestic duties?

When my mother and aunt were together I was fair game for ridicule, taunts and put-downs. This seemed most pronounced from when I turned thirteen for the rest of my life. Why did I put up with it? Why didn't I stand up for myself? When my mother first heard me sing at one of my very first professional concerts, all she could say, immediately after I came off stage, was that I didn't sound like Barbra Streisand. Much later, when I was taking meetings with orchestras and agents in New York, she suddenly burst out in an angry tirade at me, that I was wasting my time, and why couldn't I be like Oprah Winfrey? OK, failing that, a doctor, or a lawyer . . .

Once I had to give a talk at Lincoln Center about my music and my friend Michèle, who was staying with my mother, father and me in New York, was going to turn pages when I played the piano. My mother ran up to her in a panic, just before the talk started and said, 'How is she doing?' Michèle replied that I was a pro (or something along those lines). My mother replied, 'No, really, tell me the truth.' My own mother.

My mother, Barbara Wallen, died some years ago. The last time I heard her voice was when I was on the platform of Glasgow Central Station on my way home after Christmas with the Butts. She loved hearing me practise my song 'My Feet May Take a Little While', so I dedicated it to her in *The Errollyn Wallen Songbook*. The tenderest moment was one morning in Brooklyn when she kissed the back of my neck while I was practising and said, 'I should have done that a long time ago.'

Despite most of her life being blighted by respiratory problems, being rushed in and out of hospitals with asthma attacks, my mother was a great deal stronger than she appeared. She had so much potential but such little self-esteem. She found it impossible to imagine that her eldest daughter could possibly be gifted, let alone belong to her. On the rare occasions that the whole family was together, I would catch her looking at us askance, as if we'd landed from outer space. I loved my mother as did all her children – she was so cuddly and funny – but I believe she would abandon us all over again if she were to come back. My mother seemed to have little understanding of the impact her leaving had on us. In fact, any slight feeling of guilt or irritation she might feel at the knowledge was meant to be assuaged by us, certainly by me. Today she might have had help for whatever it was that traumatised her own childhood but, in every sense, my mother not only made me who I am but gave me a profound insight into the many kinds of mothers there are.

Despite the fact that I still don't sound like Barbra Streisand, these days I am having some of the best times of my life in music. My work is performed all over the world and my wish has come true that nearly every day someone somewhere is performing my music. Friends and music-lovers are forever texting and emailing me to say that they have just heard my music on the radio. I am overwhelmed with requests for commissions, scores, talks and appearances. I love my students and my students love me. Yet, every single day, I carry the doubting, critical glance of my mother within me, even though she hardly knew me. I will always know that the people who gave me life were of the opinion that I wasn't worth coming back for.

I have made my own family from people I have met all over the world and through them have learned to love and to accept love simply.

Did the fact that we were 'hand-me-down' children affect my uncle and aunt's attitude towards us? When you know that a child isn't loved, do you think that child is less worthy of love? All I know is that there seemed to be no pleasing Kene. Whatever I did, it was never enough. For most of my life she took out her bitterness and resentment on me. Yet I knew she loved and depended on me. I knew she would help me as much as she could if I were in trouble. I was by Kene's side all through her last remaining sibling's illness but, just months after Auntie Joyce's death, when I told her my Rory had died, Kene said tersely (probably miffed that I'd called my parents in New York first as they would have been awake when I heard the news), 'Well, you knew he was ill.' My blind, unswerving loyalty to her evaporated in that instant.

*

Love can be complicated.

TOP OF THE POPS

It started when I sent my boyfriend out to Selfridges to buy what amounted to lumps of gelatin to put in my bra for my forthcoming television appearances with Eternal, the all-girl pop group. This mission must have embarrassed him but was at the firm behest of Eternal's stylists and, in the weeks to come, I was further educated into the various techniques and subtleties of uplift, squeeze and pout. One of Eternal's former members, Louise (now Redknapp), had left the band in order to go solo, leaving the remaining three members – Easther and Vernie Bennett and Kéllé Bryan, three young black women – to relaunch the reconfigured band with a new album.

So it was that one day I received a call from a musicians' agent to go for an interview in West London with Eternal's management company. There was no need for me to clutch my degree certificates or conservatoire diploma in my hand as there was to be no playing live – which was just as well, as not all the band, made up entirely of young black women, were even musicians and had not come within a bow's throw of a living, breathing instrument. The single being launched was 'Power of a Woman', a mixture of elements of old R & B and rock hits – catchy. I listened to the recording and practised miming the keyboard part to it. We then embarked on a six-week tour of television programmes such as *Blue Peter, Richard and Judy, Pebble Mill at One* and *Top of the Pops*. Eternal's stylists gave us more intriguing tips on how to arrange our breasts for maximum impact, lent us various items of clothing, and I checked before each performance that the piano was a dummy one. No one wanted to hear Schoenbergian chords drifting out over the grooving track . . .

Our *Blue Peter* appearance was memorable for the fact that in rehearsal the *Blue Peter* logo fell off the wall and my years of illusion were shattered when it was perfunctorily banged on again by a chirpy chippie with a hammer. The set was tiny. I was sorely disappointed. At the end we were all given badges and I noticed that they were plastic. It didn't stop me bragging about being on *Blue Peter* to this day.

The *Top of the Pops* rehearsal was long and arduous, but the director was tall and warm, flamboyantly dressed in sparkling evening wear with diamanté, dangly earrings: 'I always believe in dressing up for a shoot.' I was to meet her a couple of years later when taking part in a concert from Alexandra Palace she was filming, to mark the anniversary of Windrush. The *Top of the Pops* slot was clearly a big deal for Eternal's two managers (as it would be for any band) and they hovered throughout, making sure that the image of their three girls was just right. I suddenly felt glad that I had no manager; in that studio was the faint whiff of sleaziness and the glare of sharp, calculating, money-tinted eyes. We rehearsed with the track in the dark studio and on this occasion the Eternals sang live into a mic while the rest of us mimed to a pre-recorded backing track, as was *Top of the Pops* policy at that time.

We learned that Cher was going to be on the show that night – we were all keen to meet her and decided to check out her rehearsal, but we were told that it would be delayed. It was – by four hours – while the hair of Cher was being dressed. When we did finally meet her, when she came into our dressing room, I noticed that she was in fact wearing a long glossy wig (black on one side and white on the other). I inwardly marvelled that a wig really can take four hours to place on the head of Cher. Everything about Cher looked perfect and she was tiny and appeared almost doll-like. She admired my leopard-spot waistcoat, acquired by me before I had ever heard of Eternal and before the TV tour. Later that night, when I got home to my council estate flat, my neighbours were enchanted with me – I'd finally made it. I, on the other hand, felt sick and uneasy. I had been miming to someone else's performance on the recording – so very little skill was involved. That TV tour was the last job I did as someone else's keyboard player – I didn't want that phoney feeling. I wanted to play music, *be* in music, for real and on my own terms.

At the same time as working with Eternal I was developing an opera with a fascinating but obsessive/possessive librettist who was rather jealous of the attention I was giving my new boyfriend – the one who bought the silicone gel 'chicken fillets' for my bra. This boyfriend sweetly understood the situation and would offer to include my librettist on dates with us.

Through working on pop and classical projects at the same time I came to realise that being a composer of classical music would give me greater artistic freedom – even though there was less dressing up.

Nonetheless, I had some terrific adventures as a keyboard player and the experience of working with a wide variety of musicians – heavy metal, rock, punk, jazz, indie, funk, soul – has helped shape my musical personality and taught me so much about people, collaboration, adapting to different musical situations, songwriting and *show time*. I would be a very different composer today without this experience.

I had begun to write my own songs. They were pouring out of me and, though I didn't yet have the confidence to call myself a singer, I was singing them. I sent demos out to everyone I could think of. One resulted in a meeting with Midge Ure, who was very interested in my South African protest song, 'When the Bough Breaks'. I received a lovely letter from Enya's manager to say I was a major artist but it eventually became clear to me that no one was serious about signing me. I faced up to the fact that whatever talent I might possess, being a black singer-songwriter, I was far less likely to receive commercial support than if I were white. To this day I think of the range of exceptional talent that I worked with whose careers were stifled simply because they were black.

Working as a keyboard player opened my eyes to the stranglehold of the mainstream popular record labels. I also saw how major black talent was not supported and how most black musicians had to struggle, being encouraged to stay in their

R & B, jazz or soul boxes. I didn't fit in any of these boxes.

My studio had worked on the recording for television of *The Secret Policeman's Ball* from the London Palladium. It was headlined by the reggae band Aswad. The head of the major record company who was releasing the accompanying album had wanted to cut them out, and was heard to say, 'Black acts don't sell.' At that time, Michael Jackson's *BAD* was one of the most anticipated albums of its time, entering at number one on the Billboard Top Pop Albums chart, selling over two million copies in its first week in the US. The album also reached number one in twenty-four other countries, including the UK, where it sold 500,000 copies in its first five days and became the country's best-selling album of 1987. It was the best-selling album worldwide of 1987 and 1988. Black acts don't sell . . .

The acts I'd worked with included Courtney Pine, Juliet Roberts, Claudia Brücken and I mimed playing the piano for Des'ree live on TV on the *Wogan* show.

When I worked with Courtney Pine, the saxophonist, he had just brought out a new album that fused jazz with reggae and was touring it nationwide. His regular keyboard player had broken his arm so Courtney, impressed by my classical chops, asked if I would step in for concerts in the UK and concerts in Trinidad as part of the Steel Pan Festival over there. I tried to talk us both out of it as, though I loved jazz, I had not, like my brother Byron, had a thorough grounding in it – I wasn't completely fluent in following jazz charts and felt that rhythmically I had spent too long practising solo classical music (without a metronome) to play brilliantly with a rhythm section. But Courtney persuaded me and I got a trial by fire and a roasting in modern jazz – and reggae. At one point, playing at a club in Manchester, Courtney suddenly stopped the band and pointed to me, saying, 'Play Scarlatschki!' Before rehearsals he had heard me warming up by playing a Scarlatti sonata and suddenly I had to play it there and then on my plastic keyboard.

When I later played for singer Juliet Roberts, who had guested with Courtney on his album and on tour, she had me open the show at Brixton Academy with 'Scarlatschki'. I came on stage in pitch darkness with dry ice billowing all around. It was so dark that I couldn't see the buttons for the sounds and the sound of a high-pitched whistle was discharged. The perils of opening a show in the dark. Juliet's song 'Caught in the Middle' reached number four in the charts, which meant that Juliet frequently got invited to premieres and openings. She asked me to accompany her to a film premiere and a stretch limo was sent for us. I took the limo back home alone, and again my neighbours in Greenwich thought I had made the big time.

We were young, gifted and Black British – Courtney Pine, Juliet Roberts, Steve Lewinson, Pete Lewinson, Gary Crosby, Angie Brown, Raiso, Jason Yarde, my brother Byron, to name but a few. Courtney with his mantle of famous Young Turk of British modern jazz magnanimously looked out for other black talent around him and drew us all into his net by inviting us to play in his band. We are all still connected spiritually, even as our work has taken us across the globe, and the music industry ever so slightly began to register its homegrown, second-generation black talent.

Working in the pop and jazz world meant that I was working with musicians who worked primarily from chord charts rather than notation. Some bands didn't even have chord charts. I would usually have to make up my own parts or transcribe them from recordings, listening to the songs again and again. My aural and improvisational skills greatly improved, not to mention my memory.

My silent-keyboard-playing skills had landed me the part of featured extra in Stephen Frears's *Sammy and Rosie Get Laid* with a screenplay by Hanif Kureishi. I had to sit on a bed while my screen boyfriend, Roland Gift of the band Fine Young Cannibals, spoke with legendary Indian actor Shashi Kapoor. Stephen Frears gave me not one note of direction but as I played silently away I grew concerned about who would dub my fingers' rapid scales, arpeggios and twiddles. I had a word with the sound recordist, who didn't seem fussed, and it was only months later that Charlie Gillett, who had the job of matching sound to my flying fingers, gave me an earful for improvising so flamboyantly asymmetrically. I've never seen the film but years later when I was briefly a chauffeur for Hanif Kureishi, I forgot to tell him that I was in his film.

I did like playing keyboards with Claudia Brücken. Claudia had previously been in the German band Propaganda and she had just made a solo album, co-written with John Uriel. Also in the band were drummer Ged Ryan and John Murphy, who at the time was writing the music for the film *Leon the Pig Farmer*. Lindsay Crisp (then partner, now wife, of Glenn Gregory – who kept asking me to compose an opera for him) was able to jump up and down through the entire set while also singing backing vocals. We all had so much fun on stage. All our gigs had pop glitterati in the audience and Steve Jansen, drummer with Japan, played drums with us for the pop video 'Kiss Like Ether', directed by Anton Corbijn. Before the gig at Subterania Jim Moir (aka Vic Reeves) and Bob Mortimer came into the dressing room to kiss us and wish us well. The album had been released only that day, yet the audience in the front row could already sing along to the words.

Then there was my stint as a TV game-show hostess. I had been working on my first large-scale theatre job at the Contact Theatre in Manchester. It was a new play by Charlotte Keatley, an adaptation of *The Singing Ringing Tree*, for Contact's Christmas show, directed by Brigid Larmour. The play had a lot of music, all of which I composed – both songs and incidental music – and after my first visit to go to a rehearsal, I unexpectedly ended up staying as music director. For weeks. While I was there I got a call from fellow Greenwich inhabitant, comedian and comedy entrepreneur Malcolm Hardee, who I knew from doing one of the first gigs at his Tunnel Club near the Blackwall Tunnel with my band PULSE. Malcolm later ran Up the Creek. He called to say that Channel 4 was looking for a keyboard player to appear on a game show with Tony Wilson and a bunch of comedians being filmed at Granada. I went down to Granada Studios and the producers (who had produced *Stars in Their Eyes*) looked me up and down and the job was mine.

I was awestruck to think we would be working on the original *Coronation Street* set. I might have looked television-worthy but that job involved composing for and performing in two programmes a day, the scripts only being delivered to me at 10 p.m. each evening. Every day for six weeks, I had to programme the keyboards so that each category of question chosen (the categories changed every day) had its own special musical moniker. I also had to compose the music for 'The Wheel of Death' a one-minute interlude where a contestant was spun around on a big wheel. I wrote, arranged and rehearsed music with a different comedian each day as they took it in turns to have their own 'spot'. With Caroline Aherne I played 'All Things Bright and Beautiful' before she did her sketch. One day someone had gone sick and I was asked if I'd do a tap dance to fill the slot (it had been rumoured that I tap-danced). I hadn't tap-danced for years but my protestations went for nothing. Tap shoes were presented to me and I had to choreograph my own dance as well as compose and pre-record the music for it. I drew the line at dressing up in a grass skirt at the suggestion of Frank Sidebottom. At the end of each show I had to jump up and down in abandon with my keyboard guitar, the rest of the cast and members of the audience and lots of hand-held cameras, as the credits rolled. I got up at 6 a.m. every morning and

Left: Henry Wallen seeing his daughter Errollyn off to Hollington Park School for Girls
Right: Barbara Wallen taking leave of her daughters, Karen, Judith and Errollyn,
at Heathrow Airport

Arthur Horatio Douglas Wallen in Paris

The wedding of
Renee (Kene)
Richardson and
Arthur Wallen
in London

Karen, Errollyn and
Judith Wallen outside
74 Seymour Avenue

Edwin Ewart Lincoln Wallen,
Winnipeg, 1943

Barbara Wallen with baby Byron and
Errollyn, Judith and Karen in costume

Errollyn, Arthur, Judith, Karen, Kene and cousin Stephanie

Family with cousins
Michael and Lincoln,
sons of Molly (*pictured*)
and Edwin Wallen
(*taking the photograph*)
and family friend,
Kaye McCoy.
Lancing, West Sussex

Rory Allam on tour with the
Royal Shakespeare Company

Errollyn and Trish in Italy

Hollington Park School Choir performing at White Rock Pavilion,
Hastings. Errollyn at the piano, Miss Pearse conducting

Ernesto and Kishana's
wedding in Belize

Recording *Meet Me at Harold Moores*, pictured
with Nell Catchpole and Matthew Sharp

Tim Harries at Edinburgh
Festival in rehearsals for
Scottish premiere of *Dido's
Ghost*, August 2021

With Anthony Parnther,
Tai Murray, Isata Kanneh-
Mason and Chi-chi
Nwanoku after recording
Concerto Grosso

Mrs H's 103rd birthday party, London

Grace notes: Portrait of Errollyn Wallen, composer. Oil painting by Gill Robinson

Left: Errollyn in dress rehearsal for *Jordan Town*, Royal Opera House

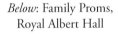

Below: Family Proms, Royal Albert Hall

Errollyn Wallen at The
Ivor Novello Awards at
Grosvenor House,
London, 2013.
Errollyn was the first
woman to receive the
award for Classical Music

Investiture at
Buckingham Palace

Rehearsing for premiere of Magnificat and Nunc dimittis at Evensong, Westminster Abbey, November 2022. Choir of Westminster Abbey, James O'Donnell, conductor, Peter Holder, organist

Above: Errollyn on Kilimanjaro with a roll-up piano

Right: Backstage at Symphony Space, New York

ERROLLYN floating near the pilot's seat on the shuttle STS-115. The CD travelled 7.84 million kilometres in space and completed 186 orbits around the Earth

Errollyn, 2022, Sonia Boyce. Digital pigment print on paper

World premiere of *This Frame is Part of the Painting* at BBC Proms, Royal Albert Hall. Errollyn Wallen, Catriona Morison, Elim Chan, BBC National Orchestra of Wales

Errollyn Wallen for Tête à Tête: The Opera Festival

The Butts, New Year's Day, Strathy Bay

after a breakfast of fruit went straight to the studio, rehearsed and programmed my keyboards before performing live for two shows back to back and went to bed at midnight after composing for the next two (in one case three) newly minted scripts. That is one way of learning how to be a composer.

The other comedians were Frank Sidebottom, Phil Cornwell and John Thomson. After six weeks of filming, during which we recorded twenty-one episodes, we went to The Haçienda with Tony Wilson (who founded the club – and who never once addressed me off set) and then went back to Curly's flat (Curly from *Coronation Street*, played by Kevin Kennedy). My memories of those six weeks of intense work are mostly rather hazy but I remember Leslie Crowther popping his head round the door one day, as Caroline and I were in make-up, and pronouncing to the room his aspersions on the new-fangled alternative comedy of which we were part. Simon Daniels was invaluable in helping me set up my keyboards, solving technical problems and lending moral support which extended to assuring Caroline Aherne that I really did want to drink my red wine without her adding lemonade to it.

I got on well with the costume supervisor after meeting her on our shopping trip in Manchester a couple of months before we started filming when she had sourced designer clothes in various boutiques for me. I still own some of the clothes and after the series I noticed how much I'd upped my style game. However, when I went for a proper fitting six weeks before the show it was clear that some clothes had been bought in much too small a size. Rather than returning the clothes and exchanging them for something nearer to my size, I was instructed to starve. So, I ate extremely little while making the show and what I *do* vividly remember is being both sleep-deprived and ravenously hungry.

A friend had been horrified that I had even contemplated doing the show as she felt it would damage my reputation. So I asked that I be put in the darkest sunglasses and got into trouble when a member of the live audience nicked the Ray-Bans from the top of my keyboard.

The experience of working on that game show proved invaluable for teaching me a wide variety of skills and has influenced my working practices to this day:

- I had to think on my feet and make decisions quickly.
- I had to work – and smile – even when exhausted and *hungry*.
- I had to work as part of a fast-paced team and deliver, deliver, deliver.
- Tap-dance when required.
- Wearing a Helmut Lang jacket is exciting.

I was hired because I looked glamorous, though there was nothing glamorous about the skillset required. Looking back, I should have got an agent to negotiate a proper fee but I guess doing that show went some way towards making up for my everlasting regret of not accepting the offer to play the organ for Billy Smart's Circus.

I had appeared on television before, and had made some music educational programmes for BBC for a series for which I had even made up the title: *Mad about Music*. For PULSE (who had the distinction of being invited on the *John Peel Show*) I had composed a song for the demise of the Greater London Council that went out on the national evening news. For *Mad about Music* I was commissioned to compose a short work, *Mondrian*, which was performed by an expanded Ensemble X, and for which I was interviewed discussing the compositional techniques involved in composing the work. I had asked my friend Nicholas Kok to conduct. In those days everything was handwritten, so Nick would have had to decipher not only my spidery hand but also several bars that didn't add up to the marked time signature. What Nicholas remembers most vividly now is waiting with the orchestra on set while I lingered in the dressing room putting on my lipstick *à la* Cher.

Another memorable television outing was when the BBC2 Windrush Gala Concert at Alexandra Palace, London, was broadcast on 21 July 1998. I had been asked to accompany Willard White, the world-renowned bass singer. I'd rehearsed at his house and then we did a film rehearsal at Ally Pally. The director of the show was the same ebullient woman with the dangly earrings who had directed *Top of the Pops* with Eternal. After the Eternal TV tour I had become quite depressed that I hadn't been able to use my real talents properly and in a fit of remorse blew all the money I'd earned on the outfit I call 'Fish'. I wear it to this day for performing. Designed by a Japanese designer, it reminds me of the sea and I wore it most recently to make a film of my song 'Daedalus'. When the Windrush director saw my outfit she decided to give me extra shots. It's that kind of coat.

In 2002 I was involved in the live televised celebrations for the Queen's Golden Jubilee. I had been commissioned by Bradley Hemmings, of Greenwich and Docklands International Festival, to compose *Rani, Queen of the Stars* (music and text) for the good people of Slough to sing in the presence of Queen Elizabeth II. The population of Slough had myriad nationalities living there and the plan was that as the Queen left Windsor Castle on her big day she would stop by Slough and hear the performance. I composed for the RAF Brass Band, two dhol drums and a choir of about a hundred people. I was sitting right behind the Queen and Prince Philip for the performance and was happy to see Her Majesty's foot tapping along. I had my camera with me and resisted the overwhelming compunction to film that world-renowned ankle at close quarters, the ankle with the prim black patent court shoe; unmistakably Queen Elizabeth II.

In 2012, for the Queen's Diamond Jubilee I was commissioned by Trinity Laban Conservatoire of Music and Dance and Greenwich Borough Council to compose the music and words for *Diamond Greenwich* for large orchestra and massed choirs which also marked the re-opening of the *Cutty Sark*. I was only given six weeks' notice but made it. It was pouring with rain but the performance, in the presence of the Queen and Prince Philip, conducted by

Gerry Cornelius, went well. I was happy until I was sent the recording and heard the sound of a single strangled violin bathed in cathedral-sized echo and the distant voices of a couple of children where there had been hundreds. I immediately took to my bed with what I thought was despair but which actually turned out to be an acute kidney infection. There I stayed for weeks – in a fever, exacerbated by my reaction to the recording and the lost memory of a special event. Greenwich Council had paid the sound engineer £4,000 to record *Diamond Greenwich*. Clearly he didn't know what he was doing, pressed the wrong button, and all was lost.

I had also been commissioned (again by Bradley Hemmings) to compose two songs for the opening ceremony of the Paralympic Games, *Spirit in Motion* and *PRINCIPIA*. Again they were also commissioned very late and there was no room to have so much as a cold, let alone be seriously ill. I would try every day to sit at the piano but I could not hold my body up for more than five minutes at a time. Every few days I would receive a call from the music supervisor asking if I was feeling any better but I was actually getting steadily worse. In the end my course of antibiotics was changed and I began to feel a bit better. Over a billion people watched the ceremony around the world; 86,000 were in the stadium. A genuine *Top of the Pops* moment.

CLIMBING KILIMANJARO WITH
A ROLL-UP PIANO

Monday, 25 January 2010

We leave on 20 February and these remaining weeks, now that I have finished *Clothesburger*, my children's opera, are to catch up with admin (look through a budget for an opera and write to George Steel to entice him with opera ideas for New York City Opera), do my taxes, and write *Park Slope*, a violin and piano piece being premiered in March in New York. Top of the list, of course, is getting my kit for the climb. My daily exercise has firmly taken hold of me and I rarely miss a day but I have no real way of being certain whether it's enough to get me up Kilimanjaro. I will try to get in a couple of really long walks before 20 February.

Today was a calm day after an emotionally turbulent last week and I aim to keep as calm as I can. I prayed a lot today.

Tuesday, 26 January

Takács Quartet playing Beethoven quartets at London's Southbank Centre. Had to walk up to the sixth floor and realised how unprepared I was for the highest mountain in Africa. The audience was amazing. Before the start of a movement the woman next to me squeezed her shoulders in anticipation.

Wednesday, 27 January

Practised Ivan's music for his memorial next Tuesday. Quite difficult. Ivan Reshetilov, my composition student at Trinity, drowned last August. More Beethoven quartets tonight. I sailed on the flow of the music.

Thursday, 28 January

Every day I try to do one thing in preparation for 'Manjaro. Today was the typhoid jab. All that's left now are the boosters. Andrew Brock has sent me a roll-up piano to take to Kilimanjaro.

Friday, 29 January

Went to Ned Bigham's party with Andrew Poppy and Julia Bardsley. We spent a lot of time talking about the hardships and sacrifices of being artists — but we do love the freedom.

Saturday, 30 January

I trudge up those hills in Greenwich Park. Quiet weekend practising, composing and writing about my favourite pieces of music for the British Academy of Songwriters, Composers and Authors newsletter. Booked flight to New York in March and am planning trip to Belize in May for Ernesto's graduation. What an achievement for that boy.

Sunday, 31 January

I want to do great things with my life and I want to make

a difference. I know these things are built on hour-to-hour, moment-to-moment industry and willpower. I am being tested at the moment but I am practising toughness, fortitude and resolve. I will be remembered.

Monday, 1 February

The delivery man turned out to be from the Ivory Coast and he said that Zanzibar was very dangerous and that Kilimanjaro was very cold. Now I'm warned.

Tuesday, 2 February

Ivan's memorial concert and I'm nearly on top of his piece. Still managed my three Greenwich Park hills. All this exercise isn't exactly making the weight drop off, I'm noticing . . .

Wednesday, 3 February

Dinner with Lucy's parents and Paul. She's so lucky. Fabulous parents.

Thursday, 4 February

Lucy's party. Was knackered and had hangover but party was so much fun. Spent ages with Tumbler and Aron discussing love lives and pianists. Scrambled on the floor for sweets that fell out of the piñata.

Friday, 5 February

Saw Peter Brook's *11 and 12* at the Barbican. Been out four nights in a row. Today was like spring and my walk was divine.

Saturday, 6 February

Walked with Del and Lucy. Del gave us a few useful pointers, including encouraging us to breathe through our noses.

Sunday, 7 February

Saw the second live football match of my entire life. Chelsea v. Arsenal. Christopher Allan explained the rules and told me to keep my voice down when speaking ill of the side whose supporters I was sitting among. I'll never forget the atmosphere. Walked past Frank Lampard's house.

Monday, 8 February

Jury service.

*

I can't find the rest of the diary entries but I can tell you that we eventually left for Kenya a few days later. When I was called for another case, I said that I had to go on holiday. Reflecting on that word, 'holiday', suggestive of rest and relaxation, causes me to think that I should have explained to the judge that it was my own captive self being led to the torture chamber that prevented me from continuing with jury service. I didn't buy my walking shoes until the late afternoon before I left. I was still in denial that the expedition was happening.

There were six of us – six women and a guide (a British doctor and mountaineer) who had made his name taking a group of celebrities up Kilimanjaro on a television programme. When we met our guide in Kenya, I could see that he had that worrying gleam of ambition in his eyes. He proclaimed that out of two hundred people he had taken up the mountain only three had not made it. I was fully expecting to be the fourth. If I'm honest, I was hoping to be the fourth. Two days into the walking trip, when I was already beginning to feel unwell (I had thought it was the altitude but I now think it was probably an adverse reaction to the malaria pills), I exhorted our guide to let Aki (a fellow musician and not particularly sporty) and me go back to base camp. Back to the comfortable hotel where we would sip cocktails and chat the days away. We had already been relegated to Team B and we took to calling ourselves Team B (we still do to this day). We took shorter, less arduous routes, as opposed to Team A who bounded off every morning with their colour-coordinated walking gear and toned muscles. An assistant guide carried our bags, so that we didn't hold up the rest of our group. In the early afternoon Aki and I had seen an ambulance come to collect some people and take them off the mountain. We questioned a woman waiting for the ambulance. It seemed clear to me that she and a few others were leaving the mountain because they were in a Team A/Team B situation, where Team B felt pretty demoralised and had lost all confidence. I worked out that that was our last chance as the next day it would have been impossible to get a vehicle further up the mountain. I told Aki that we ought to speak to our guide and tell him straight. My words to him were: 'I am a composer; that is challenge enough for me. I can always look at a postcard of Kilimanjaro. I don't need to climb it.'

It didn't do the trick. Aki and I had to keep on trudging, on course for our guide's ambitious statistics.

We got up and down Kilimanjaro in eight days. I was the last person down (way, way last) out of a few hundred people. Physically it was harder than anything I've done but mentally I drew on the ten hours' practice I did as a student, so I could push myself along, however slowly. My slow and steady progress certainly alarmed one intrepid climber who, on the final, gruesome ascent, just before Stella Point, came up to my guide and (he may have been speaking German) was outraged that I was still on the mountain, as he repeatedly jabbed a finger in my direction: 'Look at her! What is she doing here?!' It's true, I could barely walk more than an inch at a time over the course of several seconds. *'Pole, pole'** was now taken to an unprecedented extreme. In the end, our head guide fitted me with an oxygen tank and assigned several Tanzanian guides to me – some holding the tank, others going on ahead of me and the rest bringing up my sorry rear. As we passed the volcano ash pit not far from the summit, my escorts blithely told me that was where they played a football match each year – at an altitude of nearly 19,000 feet.

* *Pole, pole* is Swahili, meaning 'Slowly, slowly', and is what every Tanzanian guide tells the climbers in their charge on Kilimanjaro.

I asked my beautiful guides to sing to me in Tanzanian. And that is what got me up Mount Kilimanjaro. Not the roll-up piano.

HOME AND SCHOOL DAYS

My uncle and aunt wanted the best for us, educationally, and taught us to read and write before we went to school. Even though my mother and father were around at this point, it was Kene who did the majority of the childcare and Kene and Uncle Arthur who provided stability. My mother was working as a nurse at Middlesex Hospital, while training for her much-coveted SRN (State Registered Nurse) qualification. She often worked night shifts, so would need to sleep during the day. She suffered frequent asthma attacks all through her life and so it was, during those Tottenham days, that she was often admitted to hospital. She and Kene were as close as twin sisters, though Kene treated Barbara as a semi-invalid who couldn't cope easily with life – even though Barbara Wallen outlived them all.

Kene and Uncle Arthur's consistent care and attention to us meant that by the time we went to our infant school, as well as reading, we also knew how to do up our shoelaces, do simple arithmetic and tell the time. I remember in those first days of attending Parkhurst Infant School being bemused that the other children couldn't do these things. There was not a huge amount of books at the Seymour Avenue house but I remember that from the moment I learned to read I wanted to devour anything with printed words – I scoured the backs of cereal packets, gazing wonderingly at the names of the ingredients and place names of manufacturers. There was a book about Malcolm X at home and I started to read that before it was snatched out of my hands as being unsuitable for a small child; so then I moved to another book lying around, *Jane Eyre*. I read it from cover to cover, aged five, but I can't imagine what I could have absorbed.

I recently composed music for a short ballet film, *Bertha*, by choreographer Cathy Marston about one of the characters from *Jane Eyre* (Rochester's wife), and as I looked again at Charlotte Brontë's novel, I wondered what thoughts could have crossed the mind of my child self as she read about the complexities of human relationships and class in nineteenth-century Yorkshire. I was intrigued by words, numbers and certainly letters and signs on shop hoardings – the shapes and colours of them. One day, aged around three, I was sitting elatedly on a bus with my beloved Kene and, as we rode by the shop in Tottenham High Road that had pink, white and black pointy bras and corsets, I asked how to pronounce the large word above the shop window. When Kene told me, I shouted, 'Brassiere! Brassiere! Brassiere! Brassiere! Brassiere!!' at the top of my piercing voice for the remainder of the journey, much to Kene's embarrassment. The 'Janet and John' books still being read in school must have seemed a bit tame as I was now already completely hooked by the glory of grown-up words, incomprehensible yet thrilling in their (yelled) effect.

My memories of infant school are of having tantrums every single morning as my sister and friends left without me.

I could never ever find one or both of my socks. The school was only at the end of the road yet I was late every single morning. I have a mental snapshot of us bewildered toddlers, confused at all the lining up we had to do, but I think I was happy enough. We sang hymns (though from the moment I heard 'All Things Bright and Beautiful', I despised the tune and harmonies), had daily bottles of milk in sweet, clinking little bottles and, shod in plimsolls and wearing navy knickers and white vests, we did exercises to *Music and Movement* on the BBC Home Service and sometimes hit percussion instruments. I never got any star parts in the Nativity play, though I did narrate Daniel in the Lions' Den.

Seymour Avenue, the street we lived in, had families from many backgrounds, including Irish, Sikh, Jamaican, Cockney, Welsh, Scottish, Liverpudlian. The children grew up happily together and played out in the street most days after school and all during the summer holidays, roaring up and down on our roller skates, bikes and scooters, playing rounders, skipping, singing nursery rhymes, sharing jokes ('When is a door not a door . . .'), playing clapping games and shrieking with laughter. One year we children even canvassed for the Labour Party during elections. On one side of our house was 'Uncle' George and 'Auntie' Florrie and on the other 'Aunt' Cissie, mother of Jean, married to Albert Ryder, who had two boys near our own age. Uncle George and Aunt Florrie had a motorbike with a sidecar that could accommodate only one very excited little girl at a time, so we would have to take it in turns to go with them when they went to Chingford to buy bread rolls crowned with what looked like a smaller roll shaped like a bun on someone's head. It is likely they were going to Chingford to do other things too but the little cottage loaf roll, which we ate with jam when we came home, was such an incredible treat we believed that was the whole purpose of the trip. We three girls were often dressed identically and Aunt Cissie knitted us each red cardigans with a pair of white poodles on the front. We must have been quite cute.

Every week, the mothers of Seymour Avenue would gather in Kene's house on wash day, and I very much regretted missing it once I started going to school. The women would be laughing, smoking, chatting and whispering, drinking their tea from the teapot and coffee from the percolator, as one by one they turned the handle of the mangle and squeezed the moisture from the damp washing. I was too small to understand what they were saying but I felt blissful in the cosy glow of their conspiratorial conversations and couldn't wait to grow up so that I could join in the jokes properly.

I also loved the years before I went to school for the time it gave me to *think* and *be*. I would lie on my bed for ages, dreaming and imagining, listening to the street sounds, hearing the rag-and-bone man's cart and cry getting closer, then moving off again into the distance. In the bedroom I shared with my sisters I would often hear a man's strange, deep, slow voice coming from behind the wallpaper on the left-hand side of my bed, slightly taunting me. It was worse when I was sick. Was it real or imagined? No one else heard it. In any case, it was proximate to my babyhood with its soft down of fantastical images and sounds. I certainly believed in magic and believed that my doll Jenny and my furry lamb, Lamby, were alive. When I cried, Jenny cried. Lamby was my constant companion in every undertaking until, reduced to tatters, he was quietly consigned by an adult to the bin, not long after my stay in hospital with pneumonia when I was four.

In hospital all four parents came to visit. I wasn't sure what was going on but would race after them, screaming, when they had to leave. A nurse would yank me back. It was distressing and I just couldn't make myself understood. The one delicious moment before going to hospital was waiting for the ambulance to take me there; my sisters were in bed and there was I, watching the strictly out-of-bounds television with the adults! Unfortunately, it was a western, a genre I never liked. Kene swore ever afterwards I wasn't really ill (worried I'm sure that she would be blamed for not looking after me properly) but I was in hospital for ten days.

When I came out of hospital, I was very happy to see my sisters, who hadn't been allowed to visit me. Bunting and streamers greeted me. There was also something new in the living room – a piano! It was for my father to write his songs on. He had been away a lot studying agriculture (or was it design?) in Newcastle and, in a sparkly jacket, performed with his own band in working men's clubs. He made a seven-inch record of his own songs with them, 'If You Let Me Have My Way' and 'The Night Is Young'.

I was deeply attached to Kene and would follow her everywhere, wailing sorrowful tears if she threatened to leave me behind because of my naughty behaviour when she went off on one of her trips 'up the road'. I still remember the smell of her and the sound of her breathing as we lay down on my bed in the afternoons and she told me stories, the sound of her resonant voice, the mole on her upper lip, her lovely voice as she sang snippets of Vera Lynn – though she wasn't particularly musical and regarded the music we made in the house as 'noise'. We three little girls loved nothing more than our picnics by the River Lea, eating our cheese and pickle and sandwich-paste sandwiches, listening to Kene's invented stories of three little girls just like us, 'Una, Puna and Duna'.

By the time I went to Coleraine Park Primary School, our parents were on their way to their new life without us. It was just a matter of carrying on living in the house as we had always done, so the disruption was not as great as it could have been. But we were never told what was going on. We were left to live in limbo, which caused its own kind of disturbance, distinctly different for each of us. Kene and Uncle Arthur told us not to mention anything about our home life to the teachers or to the authorities. They were terrified we would be taken away from them. It was hugely important to them that they owned their own home and Kene told me how they had saved and saved to buy 74 Seymour Avenue. They had no children of their own.

Kene gave up work to look after us and Uncle Arthur had two jobs: as the deputy pharmacist in a hospital and then as a chiropodist in the evening. He worked extremely hard. And he made his own yoghurt.

Boxing was a big thing in our house and when a match was on the house would fill with Belize family and friends, all shouting at the television. I loved it too and Muhammad Ali was our hero. I recently found a photograph of my father, aged about seventeen, in boxing pose outside in Belize. Our grandfather (Albert Percival 'A. P.' Wallen, who died before I was born) did some boxing promotion in Belize and at one point was doing so well that he considered taking the family to settle in New Orleans. Either way, his granddaughter would have encountered and fallen in love with the blues.

On a recent trip to Belize I stayed at my cousin Barbara Hall's A Belizean Nirvana hotel in Placencia, at the same time as old schoolfriends of my father, twin brothers Clifton and Liston Hall. A big boxing match was on late at night and I sat with them, the sea splashing outside, conjuring up the lively spirit of my father through the shouts and remonstrations of Clifton and Liston.

Uncle Arthur would make the family's skin cream, toothpaste and hair pomade and made sure we took our spoonful of Radio Malt every morning. We ate a good breakfast and a cooked meal every evening, unlike many of my schoolmates, who would just have bread and jam after school. Early Sunday evenings were for polishing our shoes with our Uncle Arthur, and he would sometimes also do our feet, digging out the little corns as we sat enjoying the smell of the alcohol swabs. He always made sure we wore sensible shoes.

Uncle Arthur kept himself extremely fit, decades before it was fashionable, training at a boxing gym in Kilburn, swimming, running in the park and exercising after break-fast before we went to school. One of us little girls would sit on his ankles and act as weights as he did his sit-ups. That was a lot easier than having our hair brushed, yanked and combed for school. Kene would have been confused by the texture of our hair and not have known how to brush and comb our hair so that it didn't hurt.

Shortly after Kene died, one of her close friends, June, who had lived near us when we were small said that once she had been round at our house and Uncle Arthur had pro-nounced, 'See, they don't need their parents. They have us.' That sentence astounded me, revealing as it did not only his love for us but also his shared anxiety with Kene that we could, at any time, be taken away from them. June also told me that Kene idolised me. I was even more astounded.

Our education continued after school when Uncle Arthur came home. We would have to recite chunks of poetry aloud standing in the hall so that our voices learned to project: Tennyson, Wordsworth and Dylan Thomas. We would be asked at random to recite the times table. I once got into dire trouble for stumbling over my twelve times table, which led to my being whipped with a rope by my appalled uncle. This was the Belize way of ensuring educational standards. To this day I am still hopeless at arithmetic, despite that constant, overhanging threat of physical punishment.

Uncle Arthur also educated Kene, who had left school, like so many at that time, aged fourteen in order to take up employment. She was born Renee Richardson in Bethnal

Green into a working-class family that had moved to the East End of London from Newcastle and away from the coal mines. Her father had died on Christmas Day when she was quite young and I never found out what he actually did. Kene was the youngest of four children. Her siblings were Tommy, Joyce and Doris, who died of tuberculosis when she was twenty-five.

Kene had worked as a seamstress and absolutely hated it. From as early as I can remember she would tell me how on Sundays she would dread the next day. Despite hating machining, as a pretty young woman she loved clothes and would on occasion spend a month's wages on a dress or a pair of shoes. She adored dancing and had plentiful suitors. She went on to work in the registry of the same hospital Uncle Arthur worked at, which is how they met. Kene would never have met someone like Arthur Horatio Douglas Wallen before. Dark, proud, straight-backed, well spoken and handsome. She would have been in awe of him but she would also have relished hearing the stories of the beautiful country, Belize, from which he came, his veneration of Shakespeare and Dylan Thomas and his own aspirations to be a writer. His deep appreciation of all music and his great respect for the arts in general would have been instilled in him through his education at Wesley College in Belize City.

Maybe Arthur told Renee about his journey with his brother Edwin and fellow Belizean young men from lustrous, tropical Belize to the harsh cold of Canada in order to train for the RAF. Perhaps he told her about the discrimination he faced – such a proud patrician man from a proud, influential family, imbued with loyalty to the mother country, and who was prepared to lay down his own life for her. When people crossed the road – or spat as they walked down the street, arm in arm together – she would have been educated into a wholly different world.

Kene learned to cook Belize food and would combine English fare with Central American dishes. We had rice with everything: steak and kidney pudding with potatoes and rice; bangers and mash . . . and rice; roast dinner . . . with rice. Kene perfected the Belize way of seasoning and cooking chicken accompanied by rice and beans, plantain and potato salad. Then there were the buns, cakes and dumplings . . . To the many Belizeans passing through London, she was a warm and welcoming new friend who could cook and bake the taste of home. It was only late in her life that Kene stopped off for a few hours in Belize, on a cruise with Barbara, our mother. Neither of them seemed to like it much.

If you looked below the stairs in our home in London you would find enough tinned food and bags of rice, sugar, beans and salt to last several years. The war rationing was still having its effect.

When accompanying me to Victoria Station, laden down with school trunk and bags, headed for Warrior Square for the new term at Hollington Park School, Uncle Arthur would say things like 'Work hard, play hard' and 'Apply yourself' – advice that it is only now I fully understand and that, looking back, would probably have been his own advice to himself. He also told all us children that we needed to aim to be twice as good as anyone else because, being black, life would be that much harder for us.

I don't believe Kene, having been born in England, fully understood this imperative from our perspective – just what a difference it made being an immigrant, and an immigrant from the colonies, an immigrant of colour. I think Kene was more preoccupied, and always haunted by the fact that she had grown up so poor. When she responded to my aspirations by saying, 'My life was hard, so yours can be too', it was without any appreciation that my life was always going to have difficulties she would never encounter, simply because of the colour of my skin. Uncle Arthur, brought up with middle-class values, saw a good education as our birthright, whereas to Kene, education above a certain level would take me away from her. Once, when a guest to the house asked what I wanted to be, Kene replied, 'A history teacher.' To her, that was far enough and, it's true, I loved history, but my aspirations even then had no limit. For Kene, 'getting above your station' was to be frowned on. Decades later she came across mention of me in an actual book – *The Pandora Guide to Women Composers* by Sophie Fuller. She told me it was only then that she realised my achievement had been recognised. My love of reading and writing did have its practical uses. Kene was always very nervous of officialdom, doctors, clerks, policemen and teachers and she was unconfident about writing any kind of official letter. From a young age I was often called on to help write letters for her.

Despite my love of books, school and I didn't make the best of each other: I can't add up, and my knowledge of geography and the sciences is slim. Notwithstanding my inattentiveness as a school pupil, being a composer is a continuing education in all the ways of the world and even the outer reaches of other worlds. As a composer I can ask the questions I felt I couldn't ask at school and, in most cases, in trying to find an answer, conceive of a new work of music. The questions go on and on, both practical – 'What is the range of a theorbo?' 'Is that harmonic possible on that string?' 'How should I order the instruments in the score?' – and metaphysical – 'Was this music always there before I wrote it down?' 'How does this music relate to quantum physics?'

When I left Miss Beale's class and was in the final year of Coleraine Park Junior School, I was barely paying attention in class and would sit reading my own books throughout the lessons rather than pay a scrap of attention to the actual subject being taught. My desk in Mr Hassanali's class was stuffed with these books, to the point where it couldn't close. All I wanted to do was read and play the piano. It was as if I wanted to be out of it, out of the 'real' world and buried in my own absorbing world. I remember going daily to the school library and the teacher telling me that I should try to read books other than those by Enid Blyton. As well as loving the 'Famous Five' series I had also fallen deeply in love with the 'Malory Towers' series, which, without doubt, sharpened my yearning to go to a boarding school. I had wanted to go to a mixed school for my senior school but

Kene and Uncle Arthur were adamant that they should restrict any contact with boys for as long as possible. Around this time my baby brother Byron was born and the household dynamic radically changed. My mother's pregnancy was unplanned and it was decided that she would come to London to give birth and return to New York, leaving the baby behind once he was weaned. So Barbara Wallen, our mother, now the mother of four children, was back living with us for three months before she went away again.

All four adults came up with schemes to accommodate my mother and father's neglect of their children with little thought for those children's understanding of their situation. Sentences were somehow put together and told to us by way of plausible explanation – sentences that we children then repeated brightly, parrot fashion, to ourselves and to others without having the faintest understanding what we were really saying.

So, after my mixed junior school I went to High Cross Girls' School in High Cross Road. It meant walking further along a busy road but it also meant I could pass by the library and pull down from the shelves as many music books as I could lay my hands on. I remember taking home the vocal score of Humperdinck's *Hansel and Gretel* and playing it through – the first opera I learned.

Once I started learning piano at the age of nine, my playing out in the street was severely curtailed. Friends would knock on the door but I often said I was too busy practising. Once I was at my piano, it was very hard to prise me away from it. That habit continued. I remember my two years at High Cross only hazily but it was during those years that the desire to be a ballet dancer grew and grew, the more I read about the pathway to being a ballerina. *Prima ballerina assoluta* is what Kene and Uncle Arthur told me was the title for Margot Fonteyn. A ballet dancer is the one thing I wanted to be so very badly that I didn't care if I wasn't the best; I didn't care if I was right at the back of the corps de ballet, just so long as I was on stage, dancing. I was desperate. Janice Kent, also a student at Maureen Lyons School of Dancing, and I would discuss our favourite dancers and ballets. I had not yet seen a ballet live in the theatre but lived in my ballet books, in which I had also started to read about contemporary companies all over the world – the Joffrey Ballet and Martha Graham in the USA, Maurice Béjart in Brussels.

When I think about it now, I wonder how much my tuning out was to do with the situation at home. Whatever the cause, it meant that from a young age I learned that my inner life was both a sanctuary and a resource for me.

After High Cross School came the place that saved me. The thing about Hollington Park School for Girls was that, despite the surface appearance of micro-control over every aspect of the pupils' day-to-day lives, it was pretty unregulated – and never inspected. I fell between all the cracks of a conventional school life through shining at music. I was allowed to give up Geography and Biology in order to give me more time for music, which explains my difficulty reading maps – or, for that matter, my own body.

Hollington Park was known as the school Princess Anne *nearly* went to. Its best years were over as I joined but they were crucial, liberating years for me. I was away from a repressive household and my eyes were opened to a much wider world than I would have encountered at High Cross; at 'Holly Park' I made friends with girls from every part of the world. It was there that I was, for the first time, able to immerse myself fully in music and where not only was my talent recognised and nurtured but my true character could blossom. Being at that school massively expanded my knowledge of the multiplicity of customs, languages and religions of the world and my belief in the inherent goodness of others.

One of my very best friends and dorm mate, Aishatu ('Tish') Modibbo, whose father was the Nigerian High Commissioner to the UK (at one point living next door to Tony Curtis!), was Muslim and for the month of Ramadan she would fast and rise early to pray. The school made no provision for her eating outside the fixed mealtimes; she had to stock up on sweets and biscuits from the tuck shop, which was out of bounds. Tish barely spoke English and there were no extra English classes provided for the many girls arriving from abroad. The kindly 'Saddlebags' (Mr Sadler), who didn't want her to feel completely left out in Latin classes, made sure that Tish was the only one to answer with the one word she knew: *cum*, which means 'with'. She didn't go on to learn any others.

We passed happy days of teacher-baiting, chatting, singing hymns and laughing.

As time rolled on, I (but not Tish, who was a sporting superstar) increasingly tried to dodge the hour a day we had of lacrosse and netball. It was when I started the cake diet that I realised the true relevance, nay *urgency*, of trying to get into a team, if only on the reserves. Being part of a team that played in matches against other schools in the area, such as Benenden, Bedgebury Park or Roedean, meant getting a slap-up tea afterwards – with a huge variety of cakes. Most girls would want to be part of a team for the kudos of being officially recognised as sporty. I didn't care about that. Evidently I had started out quite promisingly in lacrosse according to Mrs Gorrie, who I could tell was now disappointed in me. Mrs Gorrie had one green eye and one blue eye and was a redoubtably flinty woman. You couldn't mess with Mrs Gorrie.

I enjoyed the excitement and adrenalin of running up and down on the lax pitch, even with its vicious slope, where you would see girls disappear and sometimes not come back, but by the first couple of weeks I had witnessed first hand the injury a lax stick could cause – teeth flying out, broken limbs, swellings, contusions and agony. I decided it would be safer to be in goal. I was wrong. Despite the lacrosse tradition of being padded out more comprehensively than any American-football player, empirical experience instructed me that a hard lacrosse ball travelling at eighty miles an hour towards the goalkeeper's body (especially when delivered by a banshee) will always cause excruciating pain to the rare unpadded inch of that girl in goal. Sensibly, that was when I decided to forgo my aspirations in procuring extra cakes via lacrosse.

I switched my attention to netball. I was quick and liked running around. My position was wing defence. However, I didn't have the essential killer instinct and didn't take any pleasure in the harsh physical contact and combat required. Tish, Lucinda (Lucy) Smith and I were a trio of best friends. Tish was like a black gazelle, beautiful with long legs, and should have represented Nigeria at the Olympics. Lucy was perhaps less obviously gifted at sport but was tenacious, red-haired and determined and was my competitor for a place on the reserves; she was the final frontier between me and cake. Lucy seemed to possess the innate killer instinct that I lacked and I gave in. So, I never made it onto the reserves. My one sporting regret.

Eventually, my new friend Patricia (Trish), who arrived at the school the year after me, and I took to hiding under the dormitory beds to avoid sports lessons. We occasionally slipped out of school for day-long walks to Battle or wherever else took our fancy. We would have been expelled if anyone had bothered to check up on us. Our walking jaunts prepared us for our hitchhiking adventures around Europe.

Tennis was another matter. Holly Park had fairly dilapidated courts and I can't remember ever having a tennis lesson but the moment I hit a ball across the net I was addicted. I never learned to serve properly but I loved the running around, trying to get to the ball in time. I would offer my services to girls who could really play and would be their warm-up partner. I could play for hours on end and my sister Karen and I promised ourselves a proper tennis holiday one day. During the summer holidays at home in Tottenham, Karen and I would go over to Bruce Castle Park, just minutes from the family home in Linley Road, and hang out with the young Rastafarians, a few of whom would play tennis with us. If they weren't around, we would wait for any other strangers to have a match with. We would play for hours and I remember being exhausted, dehydrated, vomiting behind a tree, and then carrying on with the match. Because I had never been taught to hold a tennis racquet properly, I noticed that my squeezing of it was somewhat incompatible with playing the piano and it hurt to practise after a day in the park playing tennis. Tennis absorbed me nearly as much as playing the piano and I would still like to learn how to play it properly.

At Holly Park I could have real adventures. I could roam. There were sixty acres of land, comprising lawns with the copious rhododendron bushes where we performed our summer play on Parents' Day, woodland, 'the Alps' where a rope had been improvised making it possible to swing among the bushes and trees, hidden pathways, the tennis courts and the lax pitch. I often hugged and spoke with trees. Trish and I had our own den made of shrubs and a tree trunk that we called 'Hatters' Retreat'.

Midnight feasts featured prominently and I took it on myself to spearhead several expeditions to the kitchens, once returning – after dodging mice, prefects and matrons with my hard-won spoils – to find everyone had fallen asleep. The best time to have midnight feasts was after half-term when we were all stocked up from home visits. We each had large hessian sacks (our book bags) full of cakes, biscuits, cheese, Caramacs, Old Jamaica, Aztec and Mars bars, marshmallows, crisps. It was astonishing to think how much we could all eat in the middle of the night, still bleary-eyed from sleep.

Holly Park provided me with the best grounding for getting on with people. It was there I made my friends for life, friends who forever hold my childhood as I hold theirs. Being with young human beings for twenty-four hours a day, you get to know someone's essence, to see into their core before the pressures of adulthood change their outer layers and defences. This shared growing-up with a school of 180 'sisters' from all over the world was the making of me.

I remember one afternoon coming back to Holly Park from White Rock Pavilion after winning a piano competition. It seemed as though the entire school of 180 girls was draped down the winding banisters all the way to the school entrance to welcome me back and find out how I'd done. I couldn't quite believe such outpouring of love and pride.

I have made close friends throughout my adult life but the friendships I made in childhood at Hollington Park provided me with joy, adventure and a level of emotional support that brought and still brings deep happiness to my life. Kene and Uncle Arthur also thoroughly enjoyed the company of my schoolfriends, who would visit our Tottenham home: Aishatu, Lucy, Trish, Meta (Metsy), Tina, Ali, Jan. I would also go to stay with these friends in their homes too and got to know and love my friends' parents. It was Lucy Smith's father who told Lucy that I was musically gifted, and I would often play the piano for them. Lucy's father drove with Lucy and all his family from Ingrave, Essex, to Tottenham, London, to pick me up and take us on to Smith Square – I was impressed that a Smith actually lived in Smith Square! – to collect a cousin before having dinner at Wheeler's fish restaurant and then going to the Royal Albert Hall where we sat in a box for the Last Night of the Proms.

Decades later, when I came to be involved in my own Last Night of the Proms with my re-imagining of *Jerusalem: our clouded hills*, it was of Lucy Smith and her family that I first thought. There could be no audience in the hall, however, as it was broadcast during the Covid pandemic. An eerie concert experience with only the BBC Symphony Orchestra and film crew for company. But when I received my first proper BBC Proms commission[*] in 2019 for *This Frame Is Part of the Painting*, it meant everything that my dear friend, Lucy Smith, could be there, sitting beside me in the audience.

[*] The third movement of my Concerto for Percussion and Orchestra had been performed previously at the Proms – the first time since the Proms began in 1895 that a black woman had music performed.

REJECTION

I am reduced to nothing every single day. Aren't we all –
unless we manage to persuade ourselves, like Nelson, that we
are utterly invincible? I become a cavity where all hope has
drained away except for the tiniest glimmer, which proves
often to be nothing more than sentimentality. Personal histories and stories can tell us much about our reactions to
defeat but that is no armour for the dark times.

I have nothing. Nothing I am become. Did my parents
abandon me? Was I tossed upon the tide of sound instead of
my mother's voice? Is there no physical comfort to rescue me
from absolutes? Am I worthless? Am I dirty? Am I undone?
Besieged by doubt, confusion and adverse criticism, where
do I go? There is an aching pit in my belly and the world
is striding along without me, oblivious to my impediment.

Yet. Yet. Yet I must do what I do. I must do what I *must*
do. I am committed to my life and to a life of driving purpose. That purpose is to create music. Without question, I
cannot just look down into the snake pit but, just as when I
was a small child, I will walk to the light.

When I was about seven years old I had a dream that I
immediately understood as foretelling my future in some
way. It was the dead of night and I was outside the house.
The streets were empty and the large metal bins stood like

sentinels outside our window. I began to walk up Seymour Avenue in my nightdress. Then my eyes were suddenly drawn up to the sky. There was a man, looking not unlike the Jesus in my Sunday school drawings pinned up on the wall, with his long golden hair. He was swathed in white rays and said quite simply, 'You must follow the light.' When I woke up I knew that my life would be different from the mores of my family, and I slowly set about thinking my way out of the trouble that was my home.

Reader, I followed the light. Now that I am firmly on my path, I am a lot less fanciful. Now that I forged my path, I have to get on with the pressures of composing music to a deadline every single day and find ways, like all of us in adult life, of juggling my dreamworld with the practicalities of staying alive. But I still carry the yearning seven-year-old Errollyn with me.

To enter the arena of possible success is to be occasionally traduced. I got used to that in childhood, from the moment I showed promise, when I was told by my aunt most days to stop practising, and when I was dissuaded from the thought that the music I loved so much might, in any way, belong to me – or that I might possibly one day live in its embracing light.

You put your pencil to paper and you make a mark. The mark turns to sound that means something. If you are lucky. You put a face to the sound and make a family.

Our mother doesn't possess motherly feelings and was unable to bring her children up. There were various reasons why – asthma, a quixotic and domineering husband, the need to make money. Mostly I think it was the need to be as far away from us as possible. The result has been that she has spent a life racked with guilt, which on the telephone tips over to sentimentality but which can quickly turn to spite when we are near. Her expectations of what we should have are so low so that when we children as adults informed her that we felt abandoned, she replied that we should consider ourselves very lucky not to have been running barefoot in the streets of New York.

The streets of New York. The streets of London.

Big cities are where so many musicians go to try to make a career. I was brought up in London with ties to New York. When I was at university and saw the freshers arrive from out of town, I found it difficult to imagine what it felt like for them. What was their sense of London like in comparison with mine? Everyone seems to have strong opinions of these cities. For me, they are the cities I know best and are the places where I have had the most memorable artistic experiences. As a student at Goldsmiths I was out practically every night attending concerts and was at nearly every important premiere – Ferneyhough, Maxwell Davies, Birtwistle, Boulez, Reich, LeFanu – mostly male composers, it is true. So very many concerts by London Sinfonietta. But how did I make the transition from concert-goer to concert-giver? Not long after leaving King's College, London, where I did my master's under the supervision of Nicola LeFanu and David Lumsdaine, I met the then artistic director of

London Sinfonietta, Michael Vyner, who sniggered half-jokingly, '*Are* there any women composers?! Why don't you come up to my office with your scores – I'll look over them and have a good laugh.' Joking or not, that was the prevailing attitude. Nicola LeFanu did so much to promote her mother Elizabeth Maconchy's music and I remember her saying how difficult it had been for her mother to be taken seriously as a composer. Nicola, along with several of us fellow women composers, musicians and administrators, founded the organisation Women in Music in 1987 to help address the woeful situation.

Wherever I turned there was rejection. Nothing about me fitted the picture of a composer. I didn't even fit the image to myself – I wasn't white, male, dead, in a wig or on a wall. I applied to all the major composing courses, including Tanglewood, Banff and Dartington, and entered many competitions with no success. I also applied to the brilliant Gulbenkian Course for Choreographers and Composers, finally getting admitted on my third attempt. I wasn't going to be recognised as the young superstar composer. My ambitions for my music seemed out of step with the prevailing classical-music structures. But there came a day when I realised in a flash that no one was ever going to play my music unless I did something about it myself.

I had started to have a vision of contemporary classical music that was fun and joyous. I loved going to concerts of new music but they were so resolutely serious and seemed to be mostly for the benefit of the already initiated. Most of the composers were male. There were a lot of brown jumpers. My years performing more widely – from care homes to stadiums – reinforced my desire to connect with a larger world. I decided to put on a concert with my friends based around repertoire I had already composed. This was Ensemble X's first gig. The line-up for that first concert was: Fiona Baines (soprano), Ron Briefel (sound mixing), Emily Burridge (cello), Faye Clinton (cello), Jonathan Cooper (clarinets), Mike Henry (baritone), Sally Herbert (violin), Jocelyn Pook (viola), Stephanie Power (percussion), Martin Robertson (clarinet and saxophone), Stephen Roe (baritone), Sonia Slany (violin), John Tilbury, my piano teacher at Goldsmiths (piano), and me (voice and piano).

In that concert, which took place at the Purcell Room on London's South Bank in 1990, the audience was greeted with a bite-sized Mars bar each. I had always wanted to go to a concert that involved chocolate. I had written the press releases and posted them by hand to music journalists and newspapers. I came up with a motto for the band: 'We don't break down barriers in music . . . we don't see any.' While I was concerned about the use of the negative twice in that motto, it did genuinely speak to my own musical aesthetic. The first concert earned us a three-column rave review in the *Independent* by Robert Maycock.

*

Not that long before, in my dealings with *New Note* magazine, the newsletter for SPNM (the Society for the Promotion of New Music), I had met Jonathan Cooper, who was the editor of the newsletter. He turned out to be a kindred spirit with a dapper sense of dress. As he reminisces:

Dog of The ESNW,*

Memories:

The ubiquitous black leather jacket and bright red lipstick! In fact, I remember you wearing quite a lot of black. You have become much more colourful with age! I also remember you always being laden down with bags. Bags full of stuff . . .

The Camden Studio and trying to keep it afloat while it ate up money. Lots of cups of tea on those sofas. Rehearsals there. My friend Debbie Licorish and her sister Vicky were just around the corner. So was Lucian Freud, wasn't he, in one of his studios? I remember spending a lot of time there – God knows how because I had a full-time job I think . . .

Claudia Brücken and Steve Jansen! I was starstruck.

Doing our first Ensemble X gig at the Purcell Room. Doing the publicity. I was then the editor of *New Notes* (remember that?).

'We don't break down barriers in music. We don't see any.' (Or words to that effect.)

You being a beacon of light for me while I was working at dreary old hidebound SPNM in that hideous basement in

* East, South, North and West.

Stratford Place below the BMIC* . . . You being one of the few people in the classical world to think that pop wasn't an evil word.

Travelling together to perform for the Women in Music Festival in Atlanta. Going to Florida to see your sister and being asked by Dwight (Dwighty!), her then partner, 'Jonathaaaaan. Do you carry a weapon?' The implication being that we were so weedy we should . . . Then we visited your parents in Brooklyn, I think it was. Anyway, it was all fun.

Later gigs with Byron and Tim doing more of your songs rather than your chamber music.

Recording several times for children's TV shows – I kept getting repeat fees from the Metropolitan Orchestra for a few years, which was welcome!

So many things. I loved our time together.

Jonathan xxxx

And when pressed to recall just how nutty I was, Jonathan goes on to recall:

Your Royal Dogness,

Well, you definitely were quite barmy at times. We were quite manic.

I do vaguely remember a rocking, singing madwoman in Atlanta. I think Eleanor Alberga was there as well from the UK. Anyway, we played your two-piano music . . .

* The British Music Information Centre.

Yes, everyone in the audience got a mini Mars bar at the Purcell Room! I'd forgotten that. I do remember designing the programme, which I might have somewhere.

I also remember . . .

. . . your little old car [a 1955 Austin A30]. You often used to drop me off near home after a concert or whatever despite the fact that it would be in the *opposite* direction to Greenwich. And no one else ran a car in London that I knew at the time. I was forever on a night bus otherwise.

. . . giving a birthday party for you at Wilberforce Road.* I have photos of you with a lot of people I don't recognise in that lovely dining room with the mural above the picture rail.

. . . Claudia [Brücken] was very briefly at a party I think in the studio once (with Paul Morley?) but I never did get to meet Steve Jansen, no. Boo.

. . . last-minute checking over with you the orchestration of your Percussion Concerto (was that for Young Musician?).

. . . *Having Gathered His Cohorts, it all depends on you*, arrangements of songs like 'Jesus on a Train', lots of your early nineties stuff is indelibly there in my aural memory. And 'In Our Lifetime', of course, and Mike Henry.

Hope this helps! I am now feeling very nostalgic!

Love

Jonathan

*

* James's house in Finsbury Park where Jonathan lived.

In 2019 I was commissioned by David Jackson, the producer of *Cardiff Singer of the World* to compose an orchestral and vocal work for the winner of the 2018 competition, mezzo-soprano Catriona Morison. That work turned out to be *This Frame Is Part of the Painting*, a work celebrating the paintings of Howard Hodgkin.

I was invited by the BBC Proms to write an article for the Proms Guide that year, looking back at the previous fifty years of the Proms. In writing this article, I came to understand the shifts in attitudes that, in part, had made it hard for me to become established:

Historicity

The world which I inhabit involves negligible commercial gain but gives the creator the greatest opportunity for freedom of artistic expression.

An individual's life is short, puny and full of humdrum. Most people have little opportunity to create but those of us who do have intermittently seen the mountain top – especially when our work reaches and moves an audience.

I remember attending a concert of new music as an undergraduate in London (including the premiere of Brian Ferneyhough's *Transit*) in which a man in the audience suddenly stood up and shouted, 'Music has taken the wrong turn!' before stamping out of the Queen Elizabeth Hall in disgust. I can't now remember the work being performed but the passionate outrage of that man has stayed with me – listeners really *cared* about how things were going. Certainly, when I was studying composition there seemed to be a sense that the new music we were presented with, however dissonant and unfathomable to the average concert-goer, derived in a fairly orderly 'progression' from the lineage of Schoenberg, whose music was considered to belong in direct succession within the Germanic tradition going back to Bach, Haydn and Mozart. Indeed, my own teacher, Nicola LeFanu, had studied with Egon Wellesz, who, in turn, had been a pupil of Schoenberg.

Fifty years ago (the same year in which The Jackson 5 released their debut album) it was a given that contemporary classical 'serious' composers were white, middle-class men, educated at a university or conservatoire, and whose music was sustaining the progress of the unassailable lineage of the 'canon' and continuing it way beyond Schoenberg's serialism. Many composers viewed their practice in scientific terms, and in the heroic quest to be avant-garde, music could no longer obey the dictates of conventional Western harmony – tunes were still out. The composer Xenakis (also an architect who had worked under Le Corbusier) used set theory, game theory and stochastic processes in his compositions and for a time at IRCAM (founded by Boulez in the seventies) composers donned lab coats. I was very excited by all this and immersed my ears in these men's music; Berio, Berg, Cage, Boulez, Stockhausen were on constant cassette shuffle. Even though I was studying for a master's degree in composition, I was never fully encouraged to believe that I, too, could be considered a 'composer' because, well, a young black woman born in Belize, Central America, didn't *quite* fit in. However, I greatly enjoyed my postgraduate studies, relishing the playing with numbers and pre-compositional techniques derived from the Second Viennese School – all in the service of trying to avoid tonality. Until that day I sat down and wrote a pop song.

While I was a student the (modernist) world continued to turn on its axis until 'the veering winds shifted' (to quote Byron) and minimalism arrived on these shores, though it took nearly a decade for Great Britain to fully 'shift our sails'. Graduate composition students could be failed for forays into such radically different music, brought in on the breeze from the United States via Asia and Africa. As an undergraduate at Goldsmiths, University of London, I had already come across this music when fellow students, composers Andrew Poppy and Jeremy Peyton Jones, put on concerts of their minimalist music and in 1978 Andrew Poppy's band put on a performance in the refectory of Terry Riley's *In C* which starts on the chord of C major and uses short melodic fragments, aleatoric techniques and an indefinite number of performers. Andrew Poppy claimed that presenting this music in the refectory meant that everyone would hear it, not just music students. Later the work was performed in Goldsmiths' art department.

Though not a minimalist myself, on completing my master's at King's, I was asked to join a systems group called

PULSE. This invitation was extended largely on account of my owning a DX7 synthesiser – the first digital synthesiser of its kind, developed by composer John Chowning at Stanford University. PULSE was formed by ex-students of Middlesex University who quickly relegated me to the glockenspiel, while someone else played my DX7. Performing and eventually composing for this group, which mostly played on the comedy circuit of the eighties, was a revelation to me at the end of my studies. Contemporary music could go anywhere; it could even be funny – context was the thing.

On leaving PULSE, as well as composing I continued to work as a keyboard player with bands ranging from heavy metal to jazz (despite scant knowledge of popular music) and got a job in the nineties in Manchester, as the music hostess on a twenty-one-episode television game show presented by Tony Wilson – label boss of Factory Records and manager of the Haçienda club, which was associated with the rise of acid and rave music. The requirements were to compose and play for the live show, which featured comedians such as Caroline Aherne and Frank Sidebottom. I was working with samplers and programming keyboards with various sounds for the two shows that we filmed every day. This was possible only because of the rapid advances in music technology, some of which were made in places like IRCAM, Columbia University and Stanford University. These advances, together with the arrival of MIDI (Musical Instrument Digital Interface) had a transformative effect on popular-music production and performance. In turn, instruments such as the Hammond organ and electric guitar, invented in the twentieth century and strongly associated with popular music, were used in works by contemporary classical composers seeking new timbres.

On 21 August 1969 the BBC gave the Proms premiere of Stockhausen's *Mikrophonie II*, a work for choir, Hammond organ and ring modulator. On the other hand, the 1969 BBC Proms included not a single work by a woman composer, nor by any composer of colour. Fifty years ago the Afro-American Music Opportunities Association (AAMOA) was founded to support a range of activities related to black music and musicians. Its largest project was *The Black Composers Series 1974–1978*, released by Columbia Masterworks and re-issued by Sony this year. All the works are conducted by black conductor Paul Freeman, the architect of the project. The nine discs highlight two centuries of black composers (albeit solely male) performed by orchestras including the London Symphony Orchestra. The illustrious composers include William Grant Still (1895–1978), Pulitzer Prize-winning George Walker (1922–2018) and British composer Samuel Coleridge-Taylor (1875–1912). William Grant Still had studied with Edgard Varèse, and many had studied in Europe (including with Nadia Boulanger) only to return to the States with limited opportunities for performances of their music. For many of these composers, academia was the only place where they could subsidise their composing. A year before George Walker died Chineke! gave the Proms premiere of his moving *Lyric for Strings*. I had no idea of these composers' existence when I was studying contemporary music as a student and had little idea of the contribution of black women composers such as Florence Price (1887–1953), who was the first African-American woman to have a symphonic work performed.

Modern state global colonialism or imperialism began in the 1500s and has meant that for centuries classical composers have come from many parts of the world, not just from Europe. Significant composers include José Maurício Nunes Garcia (1767–1830) from Brazil, Fela Sowande (1905–87) from Nigeria and Tania León (born in 1943) from Cuba. The celebrated English superstar composer of the Edwardian age, Samuel Coleridge-Taylor (1875–1912), was half Sierra Leonean.

Composers have always composed for the performers around them – whether that be within a church, a school, a film sound stage or a university. Different genres and stylistic trends have had divergent histories. Many of these tributaries of music-making continue to be overlooked by academia and the establishment. It is clear that until a critical mass has formed around a particular trend, as in the case of minimalism, much music has been ignored and ultimately languished, especially if it has not been documented in recordings, scores or written about by musicologists, music commentators or critics.

However, today, with so much information at their fingertips (for a laptop computer can access scores, recordings and performances, both live and historical, literally at the press of a button) many composers and listeners have begun to question the received idea of a single Western classical-music narrative governed by progress and curated almost exclusively by white European middle-class men. As they come across new music, telling new stories, they ask: what methodologies and criteria have been used to create the received canon? Who are the gatekeepers of the canon? What was the vernacular music, the street music, which the 'greats' listened to?

While I was a student, the established British performing groups' repertoire didn't reflect the widest range of music being composed, yet some of these composers' works have now firmly entered the repertoire and can sell out any concert hall – Philip Glass, Steve Reich, Michael Nyman. In Europe the Hague school of minimalism, spearheaded by Louis Andriessen, who has a new work featured in this year's Proms, has had a significant and continuing effect on British composers, Steve Martland (who died in 2013) and Joe Cutler being among the most prominent. In their music, the influence of jazz, pop and rock music is especially significant.

Today, many composers, myself included, resist being part of any movement or 'ism' (or indeed 'wasm'), preferring to acknowledge that with the vast history behind us and the various cultures and ideas swirling around us, it is more productive to stay alert, ever questioning of the techniques we use in our work.

A pioneering curator such as Charles Amirkhanian,

who founded the Other Minds festival in San Francisco, acknowledges the deep curiosity of the listener (whether creator or audience) to cross boundaries and genres and, together with Jim Newman, has formed a global new-music community showcasing the work of composers from around the world.

*

The rejection I faced at the start of my career is common for most composers offering new ideas; many of us were rejected on the grounds of style and attitude. Trends come and go. But I was never going to stop composing the music I had been waiting to hear.

CLASSICAL COMMONWEALTH

A few years ago I was summoned to Buckingham Palace at very short notice while I was at the lighthouse. It was for a reception hosted by the Queen in honour of the Commonwealth nations.

I had two of my students staying with me, Andy and Ben, working hard on their big composition project for their finals. It was February and so cold that the farmer had to haul my car out of the ice on his tractor on the road from the lighthouse but I eventually drove off to catch the plane from Inverness to London where I spent the night before the reception.

On arrival at the palace I stood in line to be presented to the Queen who asked, 'Where have you come from?' I immediately replied, 'Strathy Point.'

*

As someone born in a Commonwealth country I have taken for granted that I have grown up with the richness of more than one culture. However, I have become increasingly aware that most people living in Britain are completely ignorant of the variety of life and customs in the colonies and former colonies and the reciprocal influences of empire. Even though Belize was formerly known as British Honduras, knowledge of its very existence by British people is patchy. Americans seem to know it better as a popular holiday destination.

I left Belize aged two and didn't return until I was an adult. The first thing I said when I stepped onto the shore of Belize again was 'Why would anyone want to leave this beautiful country?'

When I am in Britain I quite often ask myself, 'How did I get here?'

I was commissioned to make an arrangement of Hubert Parry's *Jerusalem* for the Last Night of the Proms 2020. The pandemic meant that there could not be the full orchestral forces, so I was making an arrangement for reduced forces to accommodate this. Now, every composer *loves* getting their hands on existing music and bringing a fresh ear – and fresh air – to it. I had grown up with *Jerusalem* and have had an abiding love of hymns ever since childhood (except, of course, for 'All Things Bright and Beautiful'). My job at Hollington Park was to play for assembly when our music teacher, Miss Pearse, couldn't be there and on Sundays, aged fifteen or so, I would confer with the vicar as to what were the most appropriate hymns for the morning service. We sang hymns every day from the *Songs of Praise* hymn book. 'Jerusalem' was considered a real treat among the girls, along with 'Dear Lord and Father of Mankind' and 'Let Us Now Praise Famous Men'. Hymns are in my blood. What inspired my Proms arrangement, which I titled *Jerusalem: our clouded hills*, was thinking about the Windrush generation who came to this country full of patriotism for the mother country. They would have grown up singing 'Jerusalem'. I also wanted to take a deeper look at Blake's poem, 'And Did Those Feet in Ancient Time', which Hubert Parry set. The words are much darker and more sardonic than Parry's setting and plead for a better humanity, a better England. I wanted to reflect this in *Jerusalem: our clouded hills*. However, nothing quite prepared me for the outrage levelled at my presuming to think I could even *touch* music that was not 'mine', let alone have an opinion about it.

*

As a Creole Belizean, that is, descended from slaves, my forebears being brought to Belize, which was colonised by the Spanish before Britain took over in 1798 – as opposed to the ancient indigenous people, the Mayans, in residence since 1500 BC – I am already a hybrid. Genetically I am a supermix – Abyssinian, German, Scottish, Jewish, Mayan. I will never know my true name. I grew up in London, with Belize–English traditions and with a primary link with the United States. I see this heritage as a source of strength – and an advantageous resource from which to draw artistically. It has given me a great sense of liberation. Thinking all the time about how people live in different places, in different ways, their language, their food, their culture, I know that nothing is what it seems at first sight. As a composer I am never worried about exploring ideas way outside my experience, partly because of the upbringing I've had. Where some might see a dichotomy,

I see artistic possibility. I think my journey through the world has made me open-minded – open to change and to different ways of doing things. I hope I can stay that way.

*

I grew up with a love of English literature, which was passed down to me from my Uncle Arthur. In Belize he was known as 'the Black Englishman'. Uncle Arthur was married to a white English woman, a true Cockney from the East End of London. My uncle, in a sense, educated her as much as he did us children into British artistic culture. It was my uncle who took me to my first piano recital at Wigmore Hall to hear the pianist Peter Katin, when I was very young. Uncle Arthur would have been responsible for us having piano lessons. It was his guidance that first lit my own musical aspirations. My aunt kept the programme from the Royal Opera House where Uncle Arthur had taken her to see Rudolf Nureyev and Margot Fonteyn dance with the Royal Ballet. I wish I could find that programme now.

*

I think the idea of 'Britishness' in music needs some careful examination. In the development of classical music, Great Britain has always been perceived to have rather lagged behind in its production of influential classical composers, which France, Germany and Italy have produced in greater abundance. In the late nineteenth and early twentieth centuries there was a long period of search for national identity when, in fact, that identity was already a hybrid one, given its geographical make-up. Parry, Coleridge-Taylor, Stanford, Elgar all drew their influence from German symphonic writing – and hymns. Coleridge-Taylor also incorporated spirituals into his music after hearing the Fisk Jubilee Singers in 1899. When later British composers such as Vaughan Williams, Britten and Tippett were trying to forge a uniquely British style, they went back centuries for their rejuvenation: to Byrd, Tallis and Purcell – and folk music. In the case of Tippett, it was the same spirituals of slaves of the United States, heard first by Coleridge-Taylor, that helped make Tippett's name in *A Child of Our Time*.

I have noticed that if a non-white musician blends influences, it is seen as somehow 'impure', whereas when white musicians copy, steal and appropriate from another culture without crediting the sources it is (in the words of Tippett on his inclusion of spirituals in *A Child of Our Time*) only seen to be 'elevating' it. The truth is that from the moment people of different cultures travel and trade with each other, music styles will do the same and merge to form new expressions, exactly what also happens to languages, food and customs. A pivotal point of cultural colonisation is through religion but no music can ever be completely colonised.

It is clear that one of the most significant hybridisations over the last few centuries is the fascinating journey of spirituals through to gospel, blues, rock, pop, jazz and classical music, all beginning with the combining of African chant with Protestant hymns on that first plantation. The past century has shown that the indomitable spirit and influence of Africa will never die.

Original forms will always coexist alongside new, constantly emerging hybrid ones.

*

Several years ago I was composing *Chrome*, a brass piece commissioned by the National Youth Brass Band of Great Britain. When I mentioned this to my father he told me about my great-uncle Rudolph Andrews and his Imperial Band of Belize. Rudolph was also head of the Belize Constabulary Band and oversaw all the bands in Belize. This snippet of family history excited and fascinated me. When I mentioned this to an eminent English conductor, he refused to believe it. Later I came across a nineteenth-century postcard of Creole Belizeans playing in a brass band. I sent it to the conductor!

When I returned to Belize in 1999 for the first time since leaving as a baby, I am so glad that I made a point of visiting Sir Colville Young, who is Belize's Governor-General. He is also a composer and conducted many choirs, some of which my father sang in. His eyes shone as he spoke at length about his love of John Rutter. My father was very proud of singing in the Adolphus Male Voice Choir. As a composer and performer, most of my visits to Belize have involved me performing and giving workshops. At a composition workshop at the Bliss Centre, a little girl ran up to me to say that she was learning my violin piece *Woogie-Boogie* (title courtesy of Roger*), which was in the ABRSM Grade 7 syllabus.

Classical music from Europe was a fundamental part of the colonisation of Belize.

The brass band incident had caught me up short and forced me to pause and think. For the first time, I fully realised the extent to which knowledge exchange (or even simple curiosity) seemed to go only one way. While the colonies compulsorily received not only news of Great Britain but also the court circulars and minutiae of British life, Britons had little interest in the cultural life and customs of the Commonwealth countries, of where their many doctors, nurses, scientists, engineers, servicemen and artists – the people responsible for the wealth of the empire – came from.

When I was asked to submit ideas for BBC radio programmes to producer Steven Rajam, I wanted to unravel how classical music fused with local musical traditions across the British Commonwealth. *Classical Commonwealth* Part 1 and Part 2 for BBC Radio 3's 'Sunday Feature' have been made so far; we have explored India, Belize, Nigeria, South Africa, Canada and Jamaica.

Music belongs to everyone. Any type of music belongs to anyone. Anyone can take part in making or performing it. Why even begin to try putting borders around the air, the air where music lives? The idea that classical music has not been

---

* Roger Deakin. *Woogie-Boogie* was composed at Walnut Tree Farm.

hugely influenced by non-Western music is absurd. The surprising human stories and new art forms that arise from cultural exchange are pure treasure. While making the programme I learned that the scottische (a partnered dance originating in Bohemia) is still danced in Belize. On a recent visit, Pen Cayetano, the painter, musician and founder of Punta Rock, promised to play scottische music for me on my return.

*

Today the children and grandchildren of people from the colonies who settled here are confident to give full voice to the richness of their experiences, the expression of which may have been more subdued in their parents, who simply wanted to fit in and be accepted in the mother country. These children and grandchildren, who are proud to call themselves not just British but English, Irish, Welsh, Scottish, want to be part of the documentation and celebration of their contribution to British history so that everyone can know the full story. Most people in the United Kingdom are ignorant of the extent of Britain's slave-trading and colonial history on which the wealth of this nation is built. They are also ignorant of the fact that even before empire, since Roman times, there has been a presence of black and white people here from all over the world.

The complex history of empire has produced composers, performers, writers and artists with new stories to tell about the past and present, the stories that are already reshaping our futures.

THIS FRAME IS PART OF
THE PAINTING

Inspiration can come from anywhere – the sound of traffic, a washing machine, the sea . . . or, as is most often the case, the notes are simply already there, waiting for me on the piano. But from the moment I saw the stamp marked 'This frame is part of the painting' on a table in Howard Hodgkin's studio in 2015, I was intrigued. I little knew then that these words (being a terse reminder to art galleries to refrain from removing the intentionally painted-over frame) would one day provide the title of a deeply personal musical work written in homage to a great British painter.

When I first came across Hodgkin's paintings I was instantly knocked sideways by their emotional force, conveyed through a superior technical mastery of colour, shape and form. These are paintings that move and dance with life, born as they are out of artistic necessity, delighting us with their range and depth, whether in eye-spinning colour (*Rain*, painted between 1984 and 1989) or in the distilled monochrome curves of a late work such as *Night Thoughts*. No verbal explanation is necessary for any of the paintings; every nuance of the works' actuality shines out in the conversation we make as we behold them. As Hodgkin said, and as I quote in the last bars of *This Frame Is Part of the Painting*:

'The picture tells you.'

My original intent for this twelve-minute work for mezzo-soprano and orchestra was to seek out and set one or more poems beloved by Hodgkin. He particularly admired the works of Stevie Smith and James Fenton and his paintings quote their titles ('Over to You', and 'In Paris with You') and he loved the lyrics of popular songs, similarly quoting those as titles ('La Vie en Rose' or 'You Are My Sunshine'). However, while mapping out the structure of the work in a notebook, I found that my own scribbled words most aptly expressed what I needed for the text. I have also included a few phrases from Hodgkin himself and have managed to include the tiniest snippets of music he was listening to while painting.

To have been provided not only with the endless possibilities of colours that an orchestra offers but also with the superlative voice of Catriona Morison meant that my own canvas became a fecund domain in which to contemplate every aspect of the painter's magnificent brushstrokes. After finishing, I was truly sorry to leave this world of creation and reflection. Achieving 'maximum feeling' in his work is what Hodgkin set out to do, in painting or in printmaking. Similarly, the performance instructions at the head of my score state 'with maximum feeling throughout' and every single instrument of the orchestra has as crucial a part to play as the voice in conveying this heightened state.

This Frame Is Part of the Painting can best be understood as one musician's paean to Howard Hodgkin's achievement together with the investigation – and framing – of the various stages of making any work of art. These stages are titled in the score: 'Innocence', 'Solitude', 'Certainty', 'Portrait of the Artist Listening to Music' and 'Sunrise over Hopkins'. Ideally, images of Hodgkin's paintings would be projected alongside the music and I have indicated my choice in the score.

My new work is cast in the span of a single movement. It journeys from the sound of the orchestra, shimmering and humming with innocence and 'unknowing' to the depths of 'dark memory', via the joyous humour and confident purpose in the section named after Hodgkin's painting *Portrait of the Artist Listening to Music*, right through to the apotheosis of achievement in a work's completion. *This Frame Is Part of the Painting* is, then, a journey from beginning to end; that end, with my summoning of Byrd's *Kyrie* from the *Mass for Four Voices* (over which the voice sings a list of the favourite paints Howard liked to use), alludes to an imaginary long procession of great British artists towards the mists of death – and towards another beginning, another birth perhaps, through the gifts they have left us. The last moments of the work attempt to capture the sensation of both sunrise and sunset, the sunrise being inspired by an unforgettable one I witnessed on Easter Day in Hopkins, Belize, the same year I met Howard Hodgkin. My musical sunset/sunrise is preceded by the great suns of India, a country the painter proclaimed he couldn't work without. Strains from the ancient Raag Ramkali, a morning raag, gently infuse the texture.

My intention has been to create a work that will stand on its own musical feet without any verbal explanation – the listener need only listen. Nevertheless, the composing of *This Frame Is Part of the Painting* has been informed at every level by my thinking about painting and the inspiration of Howard Hodgkin's work on my own life and music.[*]

*

Every composer is asked to write programme notes to accompany works when they are being performed or recorded. Personally, I am not particularly drawn to writing programme notes that detail every note or key transposition using florid description or quasi-scientific jargon. I never want to write words that merely describe the music but would rather draw attention to other aspects of the work and to my aims for the work. It can also be useful for an audience to learn about the external influences on the composer before commencing a work.

I want to be able to communicate my ideas so that they can be readily understood to someone coming along to a concert for the first time as well as being illuminating to a professional musician.

A programme note should be a way in. It can be helpful to give some background for certain works.

* The programme note I wrote for the BBC Proms premiere in 2019.

ONYX

I had already started composing *ONYX* when I heard that
my dear friend – and legendary filmmaker – Mike Hodges
had died. This short work is in memory of him.

I think that the unique directness and astringent
plaintiveness of brass instruments would have greatly
appealed to Mike and I focus on these qualities in my
attempt to capture the energy, drive and clarity of the man,
adding just the merest postscript to tell of my deep sadness
at his departure.

*

Many of my programme notes, like that for *ONYX*, are very
short and to the point:

Romeo Turn

Romeo Turn was written in the summer of 1999 in London
and New York. The inspiration came while sitting on a plane
waiting for it to leave Heathrow. I was in a reverie while the
plane was taxiing and, as I glanced down onto the runway, I
saw a white configuration with the words ROMEO TURN.
The work is in seven short movements and is dedicated to
my father, Henry Wallen.

*

When I have just composed a new piece of music, I can find it difficult to talk or write about it immediately afterwards in a way that anyone else would understand. It is sometimes much easier to compose a new work to reflect on the previous one. After completing the opera *Dido's Ghost*, I continued to think about aspects of the backstory of one of the characters that Wesley Stace (librettist) and I had researched. I felt I wasn't quite done with the character Lavinia. So, with ideas still spinning in my mind, I went on to compose a solo work for viola:

LAVINIA

My new work for solo viola was inspired by the character of Lavinia, daughter of Latinus and Amata and the last wife of Aeneas, the great Trojan hero. Lavinia appears as a minor character in Virgil's *The Aeneid*. In my most recent opera, *Dido's Ghost*, the sequel to Purcell's *Dido and Aeneas* (and which also folds the Purcell opera into my own), Lavinia is a central character.

Dido's Ghost begins with Anna, sister of Dido, saved narrowly from drowning after a shipwreck off Lavinium, where Aeneas and Lavinia live. Aeneas is fascinated and haunted by the resemblance of Anna to Dido but immediately the seeds of jealousy are sewn in Lavinia who plots Anna's death.

Composing this piece for Stephen Upshaw was a way of contemplating Lavinia in a different work. The viola perfectly captures the spirit of Lavinia, which is sung by a mezzo-soprano in my opera.

In *LAVINIA*, my music seeks to convey the overwhelming and consuming nature of jealousy, which most often grows out of pain at the prospect of loss. Towards the end of the piece we hear some notes from Lavinia's aria from my opera *Dido's Ghost*.

*

Greenwich Variations

I wrote this piano piece in 2000 to play myself. I was inspired by the River Thames, which flows outside my window in Greenwich, by a Ray Charles song and by the theme of Bach's *Goldberg Variations*. The work was commissioned by Leicester New Walk Museum in 1999.

This piece is dedicated to the memory of the great jazz pianist Michel Petrucciani.

*

Comfort Me with Apples

I have set passages from the first two chapters of 'The Song of Solomon' in this new work.

Comfort Me with Apples is in two sections of contrasting mood; the first sultry and 'perfumed', the second driving and urgent.

It has been a source of great pleasure to have been commissioned by my dear, admired friend John Butt and the Dunedin Consort.

*

Mighty River

Composing for the orchestra is my favourite challenge. This work is an especially important one for me. It was commissioned by the Rector and PCC of Holy Trinity, Clapham Common, and the Reverend John Wates to mark the bicentenary of the Abolition of the Slave Trade Act. It is an innate human instinct to be free, just as it is a law of nature that the river should rush headlong to the sea. That is the concept behind *Mighty River*, which is in a single movement.

In it I make reference to the hymn 'Amazing Grace' and the spirituals 'Deep River' and 'Go Down Moses'. It is as if the perpetual motion of the music, like water, like time, through its sheer momentum, carries with it the cries and echoes of human hearts and voices, that are singing out of suffering, repentance, humility and hope.

Each new piece I write is like an adventure and, in composing *Mighty River*, I reaffirmed my belief that history is a living thing of which we are all part.

It has been a joy to have got to know John and Carol Wates (Carol is a distant relative of William Wilberforce) and to have discussed with them the creation and meaning of this work. I feel honoured to have been chosen to commemorate this very special day.

Slavery claimed the lives of countless people, but somehow my ancestors found the grit and determination to persist in spite of the conditions in which they found themselves. I dedicate *Mighty River* to my great-great-great-great-great-great grandmother. Though I never knew her, I am driven on by her courage in the face of dreadful odds and am inspired by her example not merely to survive, but to thrive.

*

Loss

'Roundel' – a journey to loss and remembrance

From the moment I composed one of my first songs, 'Daedalus', a song inspired by the fall into the sea of Icarus, Daedalus' son, I knew that an important part of my life's work was to address what affects every creature on this earth – loss.

I have been fortunate enough to have composed for a large variety of forces and genres: orchestra, chamber works, ballets, film, theatre. But it is to song that I have turned time and time again for the expression of heightened emotion and atmosphere. The combination of words and music is, for me, a magical formula. Song, like dance, is at the heart of all cultures and in these forms we enshrine a collective memory and identity.

Being a composer is a particular way of being in the world, of thinking about the world around us and of finding out how music works and finding new ways of synthesising our ideas in sound. A musical work for me is a place where shapes, words, colours, theories, movement, atmospheres and dimensions of time are worked out together through the ear's imagination. By observing my process closely, I have now come to understand the various stages of work and to see the similarity of those processes in other disciplines. I find that I come closest to understanding the music of my time and other times by composing music myself. In this way the history of music I studied (sometimes rather drily as a student) becomes a living and evolving phenomenon.

I rely greatly on intuition in every stage of my composing. I was asked to write about it in the book *Navigating the Unknown*. Here is an excerpt:

> I am looking for something. Like a private detective or unwisely curious explorer, I have the faintest scent, a curling wisp on the air, a trill caught in the breeze as I bend to tie up a shoelace. I am looking for something I have neither seen nor smelled before. But how, in the myriad of possibilities of sound and combinations of sound, will I know when I have found it? And why am I looking for it in the first place? In these early stages of a work, when all I know is the timescale and date of

the first performance, it is as if I am inching my way down a long, misty road. Trees hang their frowsy heads in the wind, reaching out rheumy, breaking fingers to each other in order to keep safe. Tired and alone I am caught up in the limits of my body. Half blind I navigate the unknown. Eventually, after I have become accustomed to the overwhelming solitude and have surrendered hope of finding anything at all I begin to see patterns dancing in sparkles right ahead of me on the path. My heart leaps. I squint and they are gone. I rub my eyes. What can I do to bring them back? Did they go away or is it just that I can't see them anymore? Maybe I never saw them in the first place.

And so it was when composing my new work for Philadelphia Chamber Society. The poem, 'Roundel', spoke immediately to my intuition and chimed with my own experience of loss and thoughts about World War I. The words inspired a clear musical vision. I was also pleased to represent the words of a great woman writer, Vera Brittain (1893–1970) who is best known for her book *Testament of Youth* in which she tells of her harrowing experiences in World War I. So much more attention has been given to the experiences of men and Brittain herself reflected that the 'disadvantages of being a woman have eaten like iron into my soul'.

Vera Brittain was devastated by the death of both her fiancé Roland Leighton and her brother Edward Brittain in 1918. Her poem 'Roundel' conveys both heartbreak and the dull ache of bitterness and loss. Right from the start I knew that I wanted to set the poem for two voices so that we sense the presence of the lost person and, as reinforced in the music, realise that part of the living partner has also died as they look towards their dead.

Most of us are walking around in the company of ghosts. While it is memory that we summon every day in order to survive it is also memory that can cause the most profound emotional pain.

It was on a recent trip to London's Imperial War Museum that I stood among the tanks, cannons, aircraft and recreated trenches, and reflected on the scale of the theatre of war and the sheer numbers needed to engineer every aspect of it. I am still suffering my own loss of one of my dearest friends, who died last year and who was born in 1914, a few months before the outbreak of WWI. She told me that one of her earliest memories was the sound of a Zeppelin flying overhead. Her own father was deeply affected by his experiences in WWI and suffered mentally all his life because of it. My friend Ivy Gladys Hughesdon ('Mrs H' to me) still shed tears at the age of a hundred and three as she remembered her father's plight and her own loss after he died. I witnessed first hand that the death of a loved one will always leave its mark, however long the bereaved survivor lives on after them.

It has been a privilege to set the words of 'Roundel', written in France in 1918, and to accompany Vera Brittain on my own journey of loss and remembrance.

Roundel
(*'Died of Wounds'*)

Because you died, I shall not rest again,
  But wander ever through the lone world wide,
Seeking the shadow of a dream grown vain
          Because you died.

I shall spend brief and idle hours beside
  The many lesser loves that still remain,
But find in none my triumph and my pride;

And Disillusion's slow corroding stain
  Will creep upon each quest but newly tried,
For every striving now shall nothing gain
          Because you died.

*

Angel Waters

Titles are funny things.

When Ann Barkway, who approached me with this
wonderful commission, told me that this new work would
be premiered at St Michael and All Angels in Blackheath, I
immediately knew I wanted 'Angels' as part of the title.

A single word can open up several worlds of possibility for
me and it is the desire to drill down to discover the essential

nature of what can bind differences together that drives my curiosity. Words, meaning, association and human experience all find their way into my work.

The primary inspiration for *Angel Waters* started with hearing Liam Byrne (viola da gamba) and Jonas Nordberg (theorbo) playing the music of Marin Marais. I greatly admired their deep musicality and sensitivity and wanted to compose a work that would provide plenty of space for that to shine.

I composed *Angel Waters* in the most northerly coast of the Scottish Highlands.

Not far from where I live there is a favourite stream, which leads, via a magical path, to the sea.

*

Quamino's Map

It was in 2000 that I first read S. I. Martin's novel, *Incomparable World*.

Both the setting (in 1780s London) and the historical content made a huge impression on me and I was immediately inspired to make a work for the stage. I could picture the crowd street scenes in the cobbled environs of the London I know so well; I dreamed about the characters and the vivid musical contrasts and atmospheres I could convey in music and words. I have carried these images, sounds and smells in my heart for twenty-two years. When Lidiya Yankovskaya, musical director of Chicago Opera Theater, approached me to compose a new opera, it was shortly after I had finally acquired the rights to adapt the novel. COT introduced me to the librettist Deborah Brevoort and we began exploring a wide range of themes and stories we wanted to tell together.

I then suggested *Incomparable World*, which I had originally different plans for – a musical with my own words. Deborah and everyone at COT loved the idea so much that I decided to seize this opportunity and no longer delay in bringing this important story to the stage as an opera. It seemed that no one had encountered this corner of American-British history before. Moreover, I realised that so few people knew that there had been black wealthy people (not associated with slavery) in London centuries before our story begins. There is a multiplicity of histories of black people in the United States, Great Britain and Europe.

The stars seemed to align. *Quamino's Map* was born.

It was decided that for our opera, we would adapt and significantly change the story but keep the premise on which *Incomparable World* is based; namely, that black American slaves fought on the side of the British Army in the American War of Independence for which they were promised a passage to England and a pension. The British Army reneged on this promise and many ex-slaves were destitute on the streets, forced to beg or steal.

Quamino's Map is my twenty-second opera and, from the very first opera, it has been my mission to bring to the stage the stories of people whose voices have gone unheard.

I am profoundly honoured and fortunate to have received

this wonderful opportunity to work with Chicago Opera Theater, Deborah Brevoort and the whole team involved in this production.

*

black apostrophe

Robert McFall's selection of poems for this song cycle is inspired. As well as the privilege of working with such evocative text, this commission has also allowed me to revisit the rich combination of soprano and strings first used in my early work *Are You Worried About the Rising Cost of Funerals?* for soprano and string quartet, which Mr McFall's Chamber and Susan Hamilton performed so brilliantly last year in the PRSF New Music Biennale.

The poems in *black apostrophe* are imbued with images of the sea – always a catalyst to my musical conception. Water, the sea, journeying across the sea, are recurring themes in much of my music – whether in such works as my operatic cycle *ANOTHER AMERICA*, *When the Wet Wind Sings* (for forty unaccompanied voices) or in my own popular songs, which I perform myself.

In setting the poems by Walcott, Hamilton Finlay, Scott and Goodison, I have tried to illuminate the distinct atmospheres of each and, through the world of sound and musical thought, to bring out other dimensions and possibilities.

Programme notes often include the texts that have been set to music. It is not always easy to understand the words fully when sung, given melismatic setting, repetitions, altered word stress and music interludes, so the original layout of the text in stanzas (in the case of poems) can be useful for an audience to see. Here are the poems I wrote for the setting of *Are You Worried About the Rising Cost of Funerals?*:

Are You Worried About the Rising Cost of Funerals?

Five Simple Songs

1 Beehive
(Song of the Priest, the Pall-Bearer and the Hanging Man)

Oh, I've seen so much of that
Seen so much of that
That thing, that desperate thing,
Those desperate tears.

The wailing and the gnashing and the beating of breasts,
The fighting and the clawing
But for me –
That bee has no sting.

Take me to that beautiful place,
Drop me in the water,

Curl my eyes into my toes,
Take this lamb to slaughter,
Pray for sinners everywhere,
The hive is high.

They've done so much of that,
Done so much of that,
That sin, that terrible sin,
The sin of them all –

The shirking and the lying and the staying out late,
the fighting and the boozing and the stealing
   and the cheating
and the fornicating
Oh Lord,
That bee's gonna, sure gonna
Sting.

Take me to that beautiful place,
Drop me in the water,
Curl my eyes into my toes,
Take this lamb to slaughter,
Pray for sinners everywhere,
There's nowhere to hide.

Buzz goes the bee.
Buzz goes the bee.
Buzz goes the bee.
But I'm strong enough
And I'm good enough not to be

Stung
By the . . .
Bee.

2 Mary

Without,
Without hope of any kind
She walked.

'Come now,
Take a chance,
Take a ride.'

Mary was such a child
She took him for his word.
Mary was a worry.
She'll fall and hurt her head.
She never ties her laces.

And everywhere that Mary went,
He'd surely go.

'Come now,
Take a chance,
Take a ride.'

3 White Christine

Pristine.
Pristine, so

Clean
In her front room.
Clean, clean,
Clean.

Clean and understated house,
The hearth is filled with white tiles,
White knots, reef knots, granny knots.

Christine.
So still
in her front room.
Her sister wipes away a drop of tea
That fell onto wood.

Christine.
With white knots, reef knots, granny knots.

Around her head.

4 Guru

I have the answer.
The answer's in the bottle,
The bottle's on the mountain
And the mountain's by a river
And the river runs to me.

I have the answer.
And it's what you want to hear
And I'll tell you what to eat

And I'll tell you what to wear.
And the road is not too long
And the way is not too hard.
But I, only I have the answer.

For nobody wants to be alone,
Nobody wants to be a fool
And you want to live forever.

And nobody wants to be alone
Nobody wants to be a fool
And you want to live forever
I'll set you free.

And the answer's in a bottle
And the bottle's on a mountain
And the mountain's by a river
And the river is mine.

Nobody wants to be alone
Nobody wants to be a fool
And you want to live forever –
I'll set you free,
Free from yourself.

I'll set you free,
Free from yourself.
I'll set you free.
Free from your money . . .

5 End of My Days

And so to the end of time
This life is surely come
Now embrace me one more time.

And so to the dark I throng
No tears will fall on me
All is done and all is gone.

Joy, Bliss,
Now.

No doubt to the winds
My tatters fly,
This shambling heart turns to dust
And so shine,
Shine without faith.

Joy, Bliss now,
Now.

Joy, Bliss
Gone desire now,
Gone hope.

And so,
And so shine,
Shine without faith.

And here is my programme note for this work, *Are You Worried About the Rising Cost of Funerals? (Five Simple Songs)* composed in the aftermath of flu-induced delirium:

Songs figure quite largely in my compositional output. I have composed over ninety songs on my own texts, many for myself to perform, as well as settings of poetry and several operas including *Four Figures with Harlequin, ANOTHER AMERICA: Earth, ANOTHER AMERICA: Fire, ANOTHER AMERICA: Air, ANON* and the words for *PRINCIPIA*, and *Spirit in Motion* composed for the opening ceremony of the London 2012 Paralympic Games, and *Diamond Greenwich* for the Queen's Diamond Jubilee. The texts of *Are You Worried About the Rising Cost of Funerals? (Five Simple Songs)* portray a wide range of characters, while the subject matter common to all is death. 'Beehive' is couched in the biblical language of the sinners and the saved and the music draws from the gospel tradition. The narrator gives a witnessing of the temptations and sins of the world, but proclaims his salvation through baptism imagery ('Drop me in the water') and evasion of retribution ('That bee has no sting').

'Mary' is a character of youthful innocence (with a veiled reference to the nursery rhyme 'Mary Had a Little Lamb') succumbing to a calling voice luring her to destruction ('Come now, take a chance, take a ride').

'White Christine' is the most elliptical of all the texts, hinting at a murder mystery and the relationship between two repressed sisters.

In 'Guru' (adapted from my opera *Four Figures with Harlequin*), an imaginary, powerful personality is the narrator, here promising to reveal the secret of life and happiness to all supplicants: 'I have the answer and it's what you want to hear.' Identifying herself with the elemental forces ('on a mountain', and 'the river runs to me'), the guru offers an alluring alternative to the loneliness and banality of ordinary life.

The final song, 'End of My Days', is a farewell to life offered as an exaltation of the soul. Without regret or sadness ('No tears will fall on me, All is done') the narrator reaches for the peak of emotional fulfilment ('joy, bliss now') in leaving life without the reassurance of an afterlife ('Shine, shine without faith'). The music bears the influence of Scotland.

The title of the work, and indeed the work itself, was inspired by a local council leaflet seen in a window in London. The piece was commissioned by the Birmingham Contemporary Music Group and is featured on my CD *The Girl in My Alphabet*.

*

So here I am, on a plane from Belize, crying all the way to Miami. ROMEO TURN.

THE PHOTOCOPIER

I started my composing career in the age of pencil, ink pens, transfer paper and Tippex. I wrote everything by hand. If I were composing a piece for several players or more, a copyist would copy the parts from my score by hand, and if the deadline was looming, there could be several copyists working on the same piece at once; there could be several dead-of-night trips delivering and collecting scores and parts.

The second time my little grey car, my 1955 Austin A30, was stolen (the first time was when it was used as a getaway car in a jewellery robbery*) the boot contained a nearly completed full score, handwritten. There was no copy. I hadn't made it to the photocopier yet.

Everyone lived for the photocopier, which is how I met George and Janette Wilkins. They were from Australia and at the time owned and ran three second-hand bookshops in Greenwich. One of the shops had a photocopier, for which customers were charged a very reasonable rate to make copies. When I was composing my Concerto for Percussion and Orchestra I photocopied it there – going back and forth many times as I completed sections and movements. George was intrigued, eventually revealing his own love for music, telling

* Needless to say, the thieves didn't get very far in a car that huffed and puffed at thirty miles per hour . . .

me that he was a trombonist. We all became fast friends, and George and Janette told me of their passion for Admiral Lord Nelson, eventually commissioning my cantata *Our English Heart*. Their photocopier was responsible for the commission!

By the time I did my MPhil at Cambridge, music notation software was available, and it was the Sibelius program, developed by Ben and Jonathan Finn, that became the publishing industry standard in the UK. I didn't start using the software seriously until around 2001 when the commissioners for whom I was composing a community opera gave me a copy, in lieu of a copyist. It was possibly not ideal to embark on such a steep learning curve while contending with composing an opera – one of the most complicated scores to make with its combination of various types of text as well as musical groupings and layout.

Sibelius has since been bought by Avid and I live in iCloud. Anything I write is now automatically backed up in the ether and even on my phone. As I finish a score, I email it and it reaches the conductor, orchestra, publisher and performers simultaneously without ever needing to go to paper. The conductor will read from a hard copy of the score but many performers don't ever use hard copies as they play directly from iPads, which they can annotate with a special pencil for marking in fingerings, articulation, dynamics, slurs and notes.

The process of creating a score for performance has changed so much since I composed my Concerto for Percussion and Orchestra, but then I might not have met and made such fast friends with George and Janette in their Greenwich bookshop.

DEEP RIVER

Neptune

God placed me here by water
So that I could tell the tale
Of all the comings and goings,
The hellos and goodbyes,
The friendships and enmities
And partings and gossipings,
The nature of waves.

It's dead groovy here
Amongst the mermaids,
Who give me hell
And occasionally let me pat their breasts
In turn – avuncularly.
But wait, I have tenure here, ahem
And much research to do, reports, theses and ahem,
Suchlike.

Besides, I am documenting
The tides, their overtones and tunings
To the satisfaction of the boss
Who is thinking of composing the world
In E flat.

What is it about water that captivates us so? Is it its shifting colours, the nature of its texture, the sound of its weave that moves us to sing and write about it? Crossing water, floating across its breath, moving in its mirrored arms, feeding from its curling whispers, we 'sing, each to each'. The sound of a guitar or harp reminds the listener of water; the sound of a guitar playing the blues *is* water – and blood. In the texts of spirituals, crossing the river means crossing over into camp ground, to deliverance and redemption. I live far from my Abyssinian ancestors but it is the knowledge of water that connects us still. I crossed over to freedom but I need to keep recrossing it to both remind myself that I am free and to forever reclaim my freedom in the ritual that only black people know.

Whenever I return home to London after travelling, I don't feel settled, really home, until I have crossed Waterloo Bridge – the bridge commemorating battle and built largely by women. I love rivers, not least because of their intimation of the sea. Water is the element beyond our control and from which we are made. Many seas have I crossed to be here and I live by the Thames, near another sea-faring girl, the *Cutty Sark*. The river is the first thing I see in the morning and the last thing I hear at night.

Mellis, Suffolk. Walnut Tree Farm. I call it the 'outside in house'. Leaves and animals know to come in. My man, Roger Deakin, has grey curly hair and a Suffolk moat (not to be confused with the kind around castles in fairy stories). He sits at his desk. I sit at my piano. Cosy. I'm composing

Horseplay for Tom Sapsford and the Royal Ballet; Roger is writing his book *Waterlog*. I'm so worried that it will kill him (particularly after the computer crash when he thought he'd lost the entire thing – which wasn't backed up) that I've been more caught up in his anguish than my own pressing deadline. I have left only two weeks for the orchestration of this fifteen-minute work. I have to keep going.

I sit plucking little jangly sounds out of the wooden relic that is the piano Roger bought at a country fair for me and which was delivered to Walnut Tree Farm on a cherry-picker. Roger suddenly says, rather ruefully, that I 'find composing easy'. I haven't thought about this before, but it's true that I happily let notes occur to me and after years of practice in letting the chaos in, I have got used to the process of unknowing – it has become normal to me, if still occasionally painful. Roger is so torn up that his book, his first, should be a bestseller that he seems to be making himself ill. He woke up last night practically crying. When I tried to calm him, he said, 'You don't understand. The nation is waiting for my book!'

Writing for instruments one can't play is, in fact, one of the perks of the job for me, although a continuing mystery for many to understand. I get a real kick out of giving musicians parts that display virtuosity, flair and bravura as well as music that is highly expressive and delicate, even though I can't play their instruments. This is what the craft of composing is – understanding that the performers who convey the message of the music must actually be free to fly but can do so only within certain confines of what their instruments can do. A harp can't whistle. But here's the thing: a great performer transcends their instrument – music becomes music. And a composer must write music that can transcend any imperfections in performance. The performer and the composer need to find where the spirit lies and lock that in. Composers train and study the technicalities and idiosyncrasies of each instrument of the orchestra in order to find out how to get the utmost from their properties and sometimes push the edges. When I first sit down to orchestrate – that is, to write for a crowd – the choices and endless decision-making about which instruments, which hue or timbre to go for always intimidates and unsettles. Even though the framework may be complete and the important musical notes are there in short score, there is still so much to do in the detail of the final full score.

The point of orchestrating is to find the right instrument or combination of instruments not only to evoke the atmosphere but to highlight precisely the line and contour of the music. Instrumentation can reveal the music's form and energy in a way that makes the work clearer and, in this stage of the process, raw invention continues through the adding of instrumental lines as the foreground, middle-ground and background textures are worked out and start to emerge. I feel like a visual artist and it is rather like moving from a maquette to a fully realised sculpture, or from a pencil sketch to a finished painting. I wouldn't consider handing over orchestration to anyone else as I consider the choice of instruments and added movement to be an intrinsic part of the composition process.

It was at Mellis that I first had a powerful dream about a horse, *the* horse. Roger liked it and even suggested exploring the idea of horse as archetype. I proposed the idea to Tom and he loved it. We were off. Tom's canvas was four male dancers – Michael Nunn, Jonathan Howells, Justin Meissner and David Pickering. Tom and I both slaved over the rhythmic possibilities of triplets, leaps, athleticism and lyricism combined, syncopated beats and the occasional sound of jingles, as from the trappings of a horse. It was the search for the perfect jingles for the London performances and for the eventual recording that took me to Empire Drums, a large warehouse beneath the railway arches near Waterloo, a cornucopia of visual and aural delights. Steve and Tony, the proprietors, let me choose from their treasure trove of percussion, regaling me with each instrument's fascinating history.

Horseplay was part of a mixed bill that toured the UK. The opening was at the Lyceum Theatre, Sheffield. At the first performance I barely recognised my music.

Only two rehearsals had been scheduled and this, compounded with a lack of communication with the conductor, meant that there was a rupture in the joyful process that Tom and I had enjoyed with the dancers and the rehearsal pianist where we had all worked out the tempi in every section in great detail and sent the recording and video of the rehearsals to the conductor before the rehearsals with the musicians. The dancers were panicking as the tempi with the full ensemble had changed after weeks of carefully setting and rehearsing all the correct speeds with the rehearsal pianist who marked them into the score. Fixing the correct tempo is crucial for dancers, especially when there are leaps to negotiate. If the speed of the music is too slow, a dancer has no way of building up impetus to get their body off the floor; it's a bit like trying to jump over a vault from standing position.

Working on *Horseplay* was not the first time I had received an object lesson that a stage work, like a racehorse, can fall at the last hurdle (no pun intended). Everyone in the company needs to be facing in the same direction, not least in the transition from rehearsing with a piano to rehearsing with all the instruments. Tom and I had had such a fruitful collaboration in creating the piano score. He was able to ask me for specific things in the music and to be frank about what he needed in the score for his choreography. Every suggestion was based on his deep knowledge of me and my music.

On one occasion when we were rehearsing in a large studio at the Royal Opera House, Anthony Dowell sat in. *The* Anthony Dowell, one of the great *danseurs nobles* of the twentieth century. How I had pored over my ballet books as a child, looking at photographs of him dancing with Antoinette Sibley, Lesley Collier, Margot Fonteyn, Merle Park, Jennifer Penney, Lynn Seymour . . . ! I was so conscious of trying to do everything I could to make the music just right for Tom, I don't think I even stopped to realise that here I was, actually working with the Royal Ballet led by one of the stars in its firmament.

I am not a diva. I am, however, extremely ambitious for the notes and always hope for excellent performances. I feel a responsibility to the music to try to make it the very best it can be, and then I need to find the extra 15 per cent to make it even better. Whatever I compose I hold in mind the standard of my hero, Johann Sebastian Bach. I am part of the tradition of Western classical music. I am part of a centuries-old tradition of putting marks on a page so that a musician or a group of musicians who know the meaning of these marks may release the shaped sounds back into the air. The idea of serving one's art form is the same in the ballet world: the tradition of training for self-discipline and high artistic aims, passed on from one generation to the next, one century to the next.

After the premiere of *Horseplay* I felt I had let Tom down, even though the music received great reviews. I thought that I'd miscalculated terribly in my orchestration of the score, that it was too difficult. When I came to record my first CD release of my classical music for the album *The Girl in My Alphabet* with the Continuum Ensemble, I leaped at the chance to record *Horseplay* and to set down, for good or ill, the music as I had written it. The music is indeed a challenging work with nowhere to hide technically for either conductor or musician. I am grateful to Philip Headlam for bringing it to life on the commercial recording and for allaying my doubts.

Horseplay is a ballet for four male dancers. The composer's idea of the horse as archetype was the impetus of the work.

Each movement has its own colour and word or image associated with horses: the first is 'dark' and brooding, the second is 'swift' and is a winged horse cutting brightly through the sky. The word for the third movement is 'rocking' which sways beautifully but uneasily, and the fourth, 'race', gallops on to the climactic finishing post.

— Tom Sapsford

*

I carry every single work I have composed within me and I continue to think about them long after they have received their first performance. Composing is a learning activity and if I feel I haven't fully cracked a technical or conceptual issue I will go back to these things in another way in another new work.

There were seven years of deep grieving after Rory died. Though the clatter of everyday life continued, the only place I could truly settle was in music. *Horseplay* was composed during this mourning period, yet is a work full of exuberance, light and shade. When Rory was in his last days, lying in a coma, I wasn't allowed to visit him. During those ten days I decided to confine myself to my flat in Greenwich and to concentrate every waking second on thinking only about him. Thinking about all the things he had ever said to me and all the experiences he had ever shared with me. I could be with him in my mind and we could be together there. Words of comfort came from Trish, who said, 'Don't worry

Erlsy, when he dies he will go everywhere.' But when Rory died I kept imploring the darkness, 'Where has he gone?'

One night I had a dream in which I was looking out over a moonlit lake in the very depths of night. Rory was walking, naked, his back towards me, to the other side. At last, solace.

Composers love water for they recognise that, like music, like air, it goes everywhere. Bach's name means, literally, 'little stream'. When I came to compose *Mighty River*, to mark the two hundredth anniversary of the Slave Trade Act, it was to water I turned, water as a metaphor for freedom, used so often in spirituals and gospel music. And when we ponder the elements – fire, water, air, earth – what do we recognise but that they are music's progenitor?

The inspiration of water underlines most of my music and I need to be next to it, part of it, in it. I often think that if I could spend enough time looking out to sea and notate it in all its dancing torment, record its formidable serenity, only then would I have cracked the secrets of music. I think the same thing when I look up at the night sky up here in Scotland too. So much of the universe's water is produced as a byproduct of star formation.

Barcarolle

Still now, the small boats nod to each other
At the shore
And a fox slivers by to maul at scraps
Outside the council flats.

Moon bright,
Stars various and questioning.

'Does the lady know
The sea runs through her veins
Like vitriol?'

And in a moment it will be
Time to unchain the pleading mascot
And hurl another history to the winds.

For what runs black
beneath the pavements
Is the slow, sweet singing of men,
Blood running in their teeth.

The singing for women
Whose own charred songs
Have burst their hearts
In defiance of the new language.

It is eleven years later. Roger has been dead for a while and I've just returned from New York where *Horseplay* was premiered by the New Juilliard Ensemble, conducted by Joel Sachs. I was virtually mobbed after the performance to which I took my little cousin Mimi.

Things come around, depart – then return in the strangest of ways.

All the hellos and goodbyes.

DIDO: PART II

Composing *Dido's Ghost*

What is it about a subject that holds your attention for a lifetime? What are the roots of its fascination? For me and for so many people, the story of Dido and Aeneas has a resonance that has endured way beyond the Latin textbooks in which many of us first encountered it.

At school in East Sussex, I was not to know that the Latin class would also pave a path for my future work. I was placed into Remove (the name of the class between fourth and fifth forms), the girls of which had already been learning Latin for a year. I was given a grammar book with the instruction not only to catch up on a year's tuition by myself but also to join in the taught classes with pupils already in their second year.

Needless to say, I didn't comply with these instructions, which is why, to this day, my Latin grammar is somewhat approximate. In the first classes, we studied Caesar's *Gallic Wars*, from which I learned words and phrases that would have equipped me well for battle: cohorts, hand-to-hand fighting, forced marches – quite possibly useful for a child growing up in Tottenham. These Gallic Wars were a series of military campaigns in which my classmates and I had, as you can imagine, less than a passing interest. They were waged by the Roman proconsul Julius Caesar against numerous Gallic

tribes between 58 and 50 BC and culminated in the decisive
Battle of Alesia in 52 BC, in which the Roman victory resulted
in the expansion of its republic over the whole of Gaul (i.e.
present-day France and Belgium). I still remember all that.

Our genial teacher, the retired headmaster of a boys'
public school, Mr Sadler (nicknamed 'Saddlebags', and
commonly remembered for the Bentley in which he drove
to school), was clearly fascinated by military history in general. He was kind yet entirely without ambition for us. I
still remember his open-mouthed shock at my not knowing
what the opposite to 'front-to-front fighting'* was, when I
replied to his question, '. . . back-to-back?'

After the Gallic Wars were out of the way, we got to the
poetry of Catullus, then Virgil and Ovid. These really moved
me. Rather than the battles, I fell in love with the myths,
with phrases such as 'dearer to me than mine own eyes', with
their deep meditations on being a human being and the complexities of life, even though I did not yet fully know these.
Two of my obsessions date from this time – the story of
Daedalus (from Ovid's *Metamorphoses*) and the story of Dido
and Aeneas (in Virgil's *Aeneid*). I have now set both these
stories to music, even though I had vowed, when I first began
to know about opera, never to set classical mythology, simply
because that's what everyone else seemed to have done.

The first operas, performed in Italy in the seventeenth

---

* To be fair, Saddlebags used the proper term of 'hand-to-hand combat'
first but, in stupefaction at my ignorance was determined to wring the
correct answer from me.

century, were mostly based on classical myths: *Dafne*, *Euridice*, *Orfeo*, *Poppaea*. The first opera I ever saw was Cavalli's *La Calisto*. As I grew up, I realised how many twentieth- and twenty-first-century composers have drawn from Greek myth for their stage works: Stravinsky (*Agon*, *Apollo*), Harrison Birtwistle (*The Minotaur*), Thea Musgrave (*Clytemnestra*), Mark-Anthony Turnage (*Greek*). I decided that in my operas I wanted to tell stories from our own time. Which is what I have done up till now. Yet my twentieth opera, *Dido's Ghost*, returns me to those classics of my childhood, and I now understand why composers have been so attracted to Greek and Roman mythology.

Dido's Ghost combines my love of myth with my love for Henry Purcell and his opera *Dido and Aeneas*. The work I was composing when I glanced at the television by chance and saw Steve MacLean's space shuttle go into orbit was, in fact, for Dunedin Consort – *Comfort Me with Apples*, a setting of The Song of Solomon, which featured Matthew Brook (who sings the part of Aeneas in *Dido's Ghost*). After that premiere it was suggested that I might like to think of a companion piece to *Dido and Aeneas*. I was immediately excited and asked my friend Wesley Stace (novelist, singer-songwriter, polymath) to be the librettist. Eventually we found exactly the right director for such a project: Frederic Wake-Walker.

Over the next ten years, we tried to interest various venues and institutions but it wasn't until December 2019 that Paul Keene, then classical music programmer at the Barbican, hearing about *Dido's Ghost* for the first time, jumped at it. The opera was scheduled to receive its premiere on 6 June 2021, giving us very little time – but, in a sense, we'd had all those intervening years during which ideas had been percolating. Several other co-commissioners – Mahogany Opera, Buxton International Festival, Philharmonic Baroque Orchestra and Chorale (based in San Francisco), and Edinburgh International Festival – then gathered around us.

In the initial discussions, Wesley remarked that he had come across a sequel to the story of Dido, in Ovid's *Fasti*, which begins when Dido's sister washes up on Aeneas's shore after he has landed in Italy. This became the scaffold for our opera. John Butt liked the idea of weaving Purcell's *Dido and Aeneas* into the new opera so that the older opera would work as a masque performed within the new scenario, therefore also operating as an uncanny flashback. As the work developed, the two operas began to flow in and out of each other more seamlessly.

Then the Covid pandemic befell the world.

I was living at my lighthouse in the very north of Scotland with only the sea and my piano for company. Most of *Dido's Ghost* was composed there. Looking out at and listening to the waves every day, I thought about my characters, not to mention the many technicalities I had to deal with.

The sea was therefore my muse for this opera – together with the memory of my first childhood encounter with the story of Dido and Aeneas in Saddlebags's Latin class.

*

As I often complain, I don't much like writing programme notes, particularly when I've just completed a work. I'm exhausted and find it nearly impossible to find the words to describe the journey I have just been on. Words seem so long-winded. A combination of PTSD and amnesia takes hold and I even find it hard to remember the plot, even though I've been immersed for weeks, months and years in it. In a programme note, I initially baulk at the prospect of finding the best way of directing the listener. How does one choose the most pertinent features to prepare the audience for the performance experience? Some programme notes I've read give a detailed map of the work, drawing attention to the structure as well as motifs, harmonies and concept. But programme notes can sometimes take you far away from the crux of the composer's intentions. Then, too, the composer might find it difficult to verbalise those intentions, which is when words can obscure and obfuscate. After composing *Dido's Ghost*, I couldn't put into words what I had done – and, to be honest, I didn't actually want to explain anything at all. The language and reasoning for the work was in the work itself.

In the end I did write a programme note for the Barbican in London, where *Dido's Ghost* premiered and it was during the act of writing it that I realised just how my ideas for the opera had been incubating since childhood.

*

I am back at the lighthouse having travelled up from London the day after the world premiere of *Dido's Ghost*. I write this the day after that. I feel so very strange, as if all the edges of me have melted into a blur. I don't quite know who I am any more. I keep seeing the face of Matthew Brook as Aeneas, bereft, looking up into the air in almost childlike bewilderment as the chorus gently sing Nahum Tate's words to Purcell's music:

> Great minds against themselves conspire
> And shun the cure they most desire.

Dido is now gone forever. There is no more to do than for Aeneas to sing her great Lament and the opera ends with a short coda derived from my earlier duet for Aeneas and the ghost of Dido, blending the music of Purcell and Wallen, the music taken from my song 'Of Crumpling Rocks' composed decades earlier.

I sat next to Frederic Wake-Walker for the premiere on Sunday 6 June 2021 at 8 p.m. I was surprised at how uncomfortable and distracted I felt. It is one thing to compose music when most of your time in the final adrenalin straits is spent on details and the flat-out labour of getting notes onto the page; it is yet quite another to sit through the unveiling of it in real time – the days, weeks, months and years it took to conceive and compose it all rolled into under a couple of hours. As a way of keeping myself rooted and alert in order to critique my efforts (no opera is ever 'finished'), I find it useful to remember the physical situation of composing the work. This situation might seem haphazard to some, but it is also basic and, in every sense, undressed, involving, as it does, whole days spent lounging about the lighthouse in pyjamas and dressing gown. I force myself to remember the feelings of struggle, boredom and restlessness that accompany the experience of thinking deeply about every aspect of making an opera. I remind myself that although I have pushed through the pain barrier and got to the finish line of the first performance, it does not guarantee that the work is any good; the end of that first struggle merely marks the beginning of the next, the journey of *Dido's Ghost* into the world.

At each stage of composing *Dido's Ghost*, I'd posted photos on Twitter of my feet in a variety of socks – socks for the vocal-score stage, new socks for making the full score, orchestrating and proofing stages. Jo Buckley, chief executive of Dunedin Consort, gave me a gift of a pair of Barbican socks before the premiere – socks with the architectural outline of the building.

In a performance I always try to feel the same thing the audience is feeling, and try, somehow, to forget that I am the composer. I watch out for when the audience collectively loses concentration or when there is a 'lag' in the work. What I remember about the premiere of *Dido's Ghost* is just how quiet the audience was; there were so many moments when the auditorium was completely hushed.

My job as a composer when making an opera is to find ways of identifying and isolating specific emotions introduced in the libretto and dispassionately, almost mechanically, set about intensifying them in music. The gut, the chisel and the stopwatch.

An hour before the dress rehearsal on the day before the show, our magnificent electric bass player, Tim Harries, was forced to leave the production. Tim is a lifelong friend and collaborator; the bass part of *Dido's Ghost* was conceived for his playing. Tim is one of the most gifted musicians around, and his knowledge of music – from thrash metal to Webern – is encyclopaedic. He is intuitive, creative and has ears on stalks.

Tim had been contact traced through the Covid app and had to leave the building immediately after he told management. We were both nearly in tears but Jo Buckley had immediately to set about finding a new player for the premiere without them even having a dress rehearsal, and we had to do the dress rehearsal without the bass guitar. Luckily, we found someone to step in – a young man with nerves of steel, Conor Chaplin. He had been playing at Ronnie Scott's until the early hours, so James Gambold (percussionist) and I could go through the part with him only just before the final rehearsal the next morning, the day of the show. John Butt hadn't expected Conor to play the entirety of his part – but Conor did indeed play every note. There is a standout section where Dido's Ghost sings an aria underpinned by an ostinato in the bass guitar that has to remain rock steady and have a focused and groovy sound. Conor nailed it.

This was the first time a classical music audience with

simultaneous live stream had come to the Barbican since the Covid-19 lockdown. Everyone wanted to be there. It was particularly lovely to see David and Simon, friends of Howard Hodgkin (a group of us call ourselves 'The Howardites'), in the front row.

Freddie and I did a brief pre-concert talk and, as we walked on stage, the audience clapped and clapped. Because the talk was also being live-streamed I was able to wave enthusiastically down the camera lens to Wesley, who was watching in Philadelphia and to my bestie in New York, author David Grand, who first introduced me to Wesley.

I had a new mobile phone and realised I didn't know how to turn it off, so made sure it was on silent and hoped for the best that I didn't interrupt my own music.

The whole evening felt a bit like an out-of-body experience. But there was a charged atmosphere emanating from the stage and myriad memorable moments. One such moment was when Dido bids her final farewell and stands high above the stage, about to disappear forever, the hem of her dress fluttering. Magical. I turned to Freddie but he said it wasn't his doing; there was no wind machine.

Perhaps that night we were all, audience and performers alike, hovering on a celestial breeze sent by the gods to bless this commemoration – and to bless our long-awaited return to live theatre.

At the curtain call the audience clapped and clapped and clapped and clapped! Goodness. I wasn't smiling in my usual excited way. Rather, I felt empty; yet deeply relieved that the show had gone on and that Covid-19 or even wrathful Juno (in her own month!) had not brought about its cancellation, though we had come close.

At the dress rehearsal I'd been knocked sideways by the powerful emotions in the opera and was particularly deeply affected by the end section. It made me sad for days afterwards; the story of searing passion, thwarted love, misunderstandings and miscommunication has been experienced by most of us. The work traces the journey of loss and reminds us that it isn't about the past or the future but rather the state of being human. Every joy is but momentary. Decisions made cannot always be undone even though they are revisited. I was reminded that in my twenties I had written somewhere that one of my objectives as a composer was to explore loss. This new work, which had come out of my body, required me to dig deeply emotionally, fulfilling the younger composer's intention. I was wrung out.

We had an intense week of rehearsals up to the premiere. Because of Covid restrictions rehearsals started without the benefit of a sing-through and it was only at the dress rehearsal, the day before the premiere, that we ran the entire opera. I had submitted the first draft of the vocal score in February and after individual Zoom sessions with each of the principal singers I adjusted each part to fit the contours of each singer's voice more closely. Everyone had that score by the end of April. For the second draft I also aimed to make each vocal part more closely delineate the characters.

It is that process, the second, third or fourth pass over

a vocal score, that makes the difference to the full shade, colour and atmosphere a character brings.

I cannot start orchestrating until the vocal parts are absolutely finished and the characterisation is clear. It meant that for *Dido's Ghost* I had only three weeks to orchestrate the full score. I got up at either 5 or 6 a.m. every day and when visitors came to stay at the lighthouse, I just had to leave them to fend for themselves.

Every time I begin the orchestration process, I forget that I do know what I'm doing. I'm not sure why I have this crisis of confidence, other than perhaps it is better not to be smug when creating anything and to begin with a new and open mindset. To Purcell's string orchestra and continuo of harpsichord and theorbo I added electric bass guitar and assorted percussion including two handpans, which I had had specially made in Bristol. Orchestration requires not just imagination but the willingness to put up with slow drudge and indecision – putting notes onto instruments, checking that they are the right notes, then moving them onto other instruments and then changing your mind again and again. I really didn't want this stage to sound like a rush or unfinished in any way, even though I was impossibly pressed for time. The orchestration in an opera is the psychological backdrop to everything and gives vital clues to what is going on dramatically. The orchestra is a multilayered, multi-voiced engine that propels the drama forward.

There was a certain amount of panic from Dunedin even before the submission deadline of the full score. This was the first time they had mounted a contemporary opera and they were worried that my music would be beyond the limits of period instruments. I did my best to keep going – I knew that I had been here before. Pressure is something composers live with on a daily basis but, as author Philip Pullman said, an artist should work as if they have all the time in the world. For the sake of a week or two I didn't want my opera to fall short of what I knew it could be. When orchestrating I feel as if I come face to face with the crux of the composition. It's not just a case of colouring in; I have to bring out important lines, create new strands in melody, harmony and rhythm and add another layer of drama through my instrumentation. There is also the question of the interaction of the instruments with the voices; sometimes vocal lines are doubled or harmonised and I have to think of practicalities, including where vital cues can be given so that the performers can comfortably get the right notes for their entries.

In the history of opera, this final stage is so often squeezed in, and when I look back on my previous nineteen operas, it is the libretto that can, through oversight, have the most time afforded it. The libretto and its dramaturgy are crucial to get right but writing words is inherently a hundred times quicker than producing a score, even with the help of notation software. Moreover, it is the music that adds the final layer of dramaturgy. An opera libretto should not be considered a play – there needs to be space for the music – and there can be a temptation for the writer to imagine the words as being spoken rather than sung. I calculated that, from beginning to end (from the vocal score, revisions and full score), I composed *Dido's Ghost* in less than seven months, but I was grateful that I had been thinking about the musical possibilities for the previous ten years and that Wesley Stace was, despite this being his first libretto, the most perfect collaborator.

Getting up early was relatively easy as the days in north Scotland were getting longer each day – bright mornings and bright evenings. Nevertheless, due to the pressure I was working under, emails went unanswered and admin went virtually out of the window, though I kept up my teaching. After the orchestration was finished, it was on to the proofing and answering questions from the musicians. Olly (Oliver Muxworthy), my trusty copyist, was very fast and I had to make sure I was available to answer his questions. Because my score wove in and out of the Purcell, that score also had to be checked carefully and decisions made as to what we used, thereby conjointly creating a new edition of the Purcell alongside the new opera.

The majority of my music is conceived for big, full-fat sounds with plenty of vibrato in my string writing, so this opera, to be performed on harpsichords, theorbo and a baroque string orchestra playing on gut strings* with hardly any vibrato, gave me a good deal to consider when thinking about the orchestration. However, this wasn't my first time composing for period instruments, and my previous work for Dunedin Consort, *Comfort Me with Apples*, was a commission

---

* Modern string instruments use strings made with steel or synthetic material.

for soprano, baritone and baroque ensemble. Matthew Brook sang the solo baritone part in that work and I was so pleased to be able to return to the sound of his expressive, rich voice as Aeneas in *Dido's Ghost*. It was this search for expressivity that dictated my addition of electric bass guitar and percussion to Purcell's ensemble. The bass guitar, as performed by the inimitable Tim Harries, provides a soundscape – not just rock 'n' roll. It was very important to me to allude to the sound of North Africa, Dido's world, and, at times, to convey a sense of the dreamworld. By using handpans (instruments rarely encountered in classical music) alongside a range of other percussion instruments, I had an intriguing range of textures at my disposal. James was playing twelve percussion instruments: marimba, triangle, shakers, bass drum, tam-tam, two handpans, drum kit, suspended cymbals, crotales, whip and djembe. I was quietly anxious as to whether the handpans (bought by me for £3,000 and made to my own specifications) would be loud enough in the ensemble.

I was mesmerised by the sound of the handpan. It shares some similarities to the sound of the steel drum but is much mellower with a different resonance. I had used it in my duo *Bertha* for violin and handpan and I asked Rosie Bergonzi, who had recorded *Bertha**, to come and play the handpan in the weekend workshop we had in London in October 2020. Pandemic restrictions had slightly eased. The weather was cold and rainy but, to comply with government guidelines,

* With Sara Trickey, violin. Recorded by Gerry O'Riordan at The Sound-house, London

we had to keep the doors and windows of the rehearsal room open. I used the workshop to try out the combination of percussion with Tim on electric bass and voices (three singers trying out snippets of arias and duets for Dido's Ghost, Aeneas and Lavinia). That was the one and only workshop we had for the opera but it confirmed I was on track musically and that the palette of sounds was fitting.

A week before I was due to go to London for the rehearsals I was contacted by the visual artist Sonia Boyce to ask if I would participate in a recording for her show in the British Pavilion for the 59th Venice Biennale. I had admired Sonia's works for years and the timing seemed to work out, just. The recording and filming was due to take place at Abbey Road Studios.

Not having left the lighthouse for five months, I was a bit anxious about entering the maelstrom that is London. The rehearsal week of *Dido's Ghost* was going to be intensely busy and I was also hoping to go to Maida Vale to attend a BBC Singers rehearsal of *PACE* conducted by David Hill. But from day one, *Dido's Ghost* appeared just as I'd imagined it; the performers were extraordinary. John Butt led everyone with enthusiasm, calm and good humour and swept everyone in his wake. We had just one week to get everything together, including costume fittings and interviews. The first rehearsals were with the soloists, then soloists and covers; next the chorus joined. I was pleased to hear the opening of Scene Two where the chorus represents Aeneas and Lavinia's court; I had asked Wesley to give me some Latin and I composed that music while in Glasgow working with Martyn

Brabbins and the BBC Scottish Symphony Orchestra brass section who were recording my arrangement of *PACE*. A new flavour of music came out of me for that Latin chorus. It was challenging, both rhythmically and harmonically, but Dunedin's chorus was resplendent. Everything was sounding better than I had imagined and Freddie and John worked brilliantly together. Paul Keene at the Barbican had asked for a concert version with minimal staging. I was fascinated to see how Freddie drew from the music in his adding of the physical and dramatic layers.

It was only at the dress rehearsal that we all saw and heard the whole work in its entirety (except for the electric bass) and I was taken aback by the shape of the piece and its inexorable journey to Aeneas singing Purcell's famous Lament. When this move was decided, I wasn't entirely sure of how it would transpire and what it would feel like. But, having seen and heard it, I knew there could be no other way. Matthew Brook's devastating performance was also aided by keeping the aria in its original key but sung an octave lower – in performance those falsetto notes on Fs and Gs took us into the ether to which Aeneas is beckoned. For days after, I was sad for Dido, sad for Aeneas. Sad for every heartbreak and loss. Sad for us all. But throughout Wesley and I had had a deep – though not academic – conversation with Nahum Tate and Henry Purcell. We four held hands across the centuries.

At least twenty years previously, before I knew I was going to compose *Dido's Ghost*, but obsessed with Dido nonetheless, I decided to write a poem about Dido. As she faces

death by her own hand she looks forwards and backwards
into the widest universes of time. Her final gaze is on those
who grapple with their own human predicaments, who stare
back from the future in wonder at her, all those who have
remembered her and who will remember her:

Of Crumpling Rocks

Further, further,
Further in I go
Wider, wider –
My arms stretch to tackle the universe,
This universe of crumpling rocks.

And yes,
I am off my face
With the terror of freedom
Yet here I am
And no one knows.
No one knows me –
I am nameless
And nearly nothing

Thin air I am become

My body's commitment fallen
And something still falls
From where my womb was –
Dead cold, dead cold

You and your furious ink,
You in your own committing

You shall in flame,
In flame
And without tears

Remember me

When writing songs for myself to sing I almost always write the words alongside the music. I almost never set my own poetry to music but years after writing 'Of Crumpling Rocks' I decided to turn it into a song, which I included in the song cycle, *The Queen and I*, and recorded on my album *Errollyn*. I had woven the musical language of Purcell with my own and towards the end of this song the melody of Dido's Lament creeps in.

In Act Two of *Dido's Ghost* there is a duet between Dido's ghost and Aeneas. I decided to use the music 'Of Crumpling Rocks' to set to Wesley's libretto:

Aeneas (*Terrified*) DIDO!

Dido is silent.

Are you here for your revenge?

Dido (*Disdainfully*) My revenge?

* Ccommissioned by The Brook Street Band.

Aeneas On me.

Dido I have not come for you at all.

Aeneas But you have haunted me for years.

Dido Not I. Your memory of me.
  Your guilt.

Aeneas Why didn't you speak to me in the underworld?

Dido I had nothing to say.

Aeneas What would you say today?

Dido To you? Nothing.

  I said when I was cold
  That I would join you: here I am
  But I have not come to haunt you
  I do not need to any more
  I do not want you any more
  I was summoned by the moon
  To save my sister

  I said when I was dead
  You couldn't lose me: here I am
  But I have not come to haunt you
  I have not followed you with fire
  Nor come to brand you as a liar
  I won't torment you with desire
  I was summoned by the moon

Summoned by the moon
To save my sister

As I write this, the announcer on BBC Radio 3 says that
my recording of 'Of Crumpling Rocks' will be played on
the radio in just a few minutes' time. Errollyn's Ghost . . .

Why have I been so long obsessed with Dido? I am not
alone in this obsession. Listening to Jeff Buckley and, while
I was working on *Dido's Ghost*, hearing Lisa Fischer sing
the Lament reminded me that Purcell truly brought Dido,
Queen of Carthage, back from the dead and made an aria
for all time and for all people.

As undergraduates we could choose between studying
the nineteenth century or Baroque eras. As a nineteen-year-
old steeped in the avant-garde music of my time, I found
Romantic music often indigestible, so it took but seconds
for me to choose the Baroque era for my special study. For
O levels we had studied Bach's Brandenburg Concerto
No. 5 and the previous summer I'd seen Dance Theatre of
Harlem perform Balanchine's *Concerto Barocco* to the music
of Bach's Concerto for Two Violins. Baroque music is both
deeply expressive and lean. As first-year undergrads, in our
techniques classes, alongside our Palestrina counterpoint, we
also tussled with Corelli trio sonatas and later Bach fugues
before tackling Schumann and Beethoven. We had to
mimic the styles of these composers. It was these techniques
classes that led me on to composing. It was so hugely enjoy-
able trying to put oneself in the mind of another composer

through studying and mimicking their style. I have written several pieces where I meditate on another composer's work (*Concerto Grosso, Spirit Symphony, Louis' Loops, The Girl in My Alphabet, When the Wet Wind Sings*). Working with music of other times opens up the most wonderful compositional conversations and, for me, illuminates the work of the composer like nothing else. I can get especially close to another composer this way.

In music history classes the music of the French Clavecin School intrigued me (I revisited that period in my work for toy piano, *Louis' Loops*) and I shall never forget a lecture by Christopher Wintle when he traced the adventurous journey of a single note in a Bach fugue. I've been captivated by the music of the Baroque for most of my life.

I came across Dido's Lament before ever hearing Purcell's opera in its entirety and I've been haunted by it since I was thirteen years old. When I later wrote my own songs I realised that it is no exaggeration to say that the Lament is one of the most complete, artful and masterful arias ever written, which, with the utmost economy, conveys the deepest emotion. This music had a massive impact on me when I first heard a recording by Janet Baker. Just before settling down to compose *Dido's Ghost*, I met Janet Baker at the Royal Philharmonic Society Awards. I held her hand and thanked her. So many singers, from classical to pop and jazz, have covered that song and it works in any style. When I sing it, I sing it transposed down a fourth to D minor – my preferred key for sombreness.

The original score of Purcell's *Dido and Aeneas* is missing. I understand now why opera scholars will continue talking for hundreds of years about the relationship between the libretto and the score and their differences. No libretto stays in exactly the same shape in which it was originated by the time the composer has set music to it. In my own case, setting a libretto to music means that there are lots of adjustments, repetitions, and many changes, small and large, to the text – because of how words sound when sung and because of practical dramaturgical demands, which become clearest when composing. I like to think that I can look at a libretto and calculate exactly how it will be realised through music, but it is only when actually working on the words together with notes and rhythms that I get a true understanding of how the drama will unfold in time. In each step of the journey of any opera – from concept, to page, to rehearsal, then to the stage – there are adjustments being made all the time, and these continue with each production of the opera in different spaces. Sometimes music is added or taken away for something as practical as a scene change or for getting a performer on or off stage. Those changes don't always make it back to the original libretto, as everyone has moved on and refers to the score, which, after all, has the most complete and recent information. It would be wonderful to have the original score of *Dido and Aeneas* to see first hand what decisions and changes Purcell made in response to Tate's libretto. I am certain he would have made further modifications, however small, for subsequent productions.

Purcell's work is constructed very differently from my opera. His proceeds in formal closed numbers, many of which have repeated sections and through which emerges a unique musical voice, which, centuries later, we are still moved by. My opera has a variety of forms, some of which are inspired by Purcell, some of which are purely my own. I tried to burst through the psychological barrier of my immaculate, computer-engraved, edited and printed score of *Dido and Aeneas* by imagining Purcell the man, sitting down, perhaps unwashed, absorbing and reacting to the words of Nahum Tate, inking out his response and, little by little, bringing the words out of the shadows through the musical notes he gave them. There have been so many enchanting surprises, the greatest surprise being the way the original Purcell tells its own sequel when folded into the Wallen.

While composing this opera has revealed to me how indebted I am to the Baroque (the power of the bass lines, agile rhythms, triads and modes), what I have brought to it is modern dissonance. Several moments pre-echo the Purcell and, at times, as in the duet with the ghost of Dido and Aeneas, I consciously blur and blend both musical languages. At other times, my music is in stark contrast to Purcell's, particularly when I push the wildness of extreme psychological states. Wesley Stace and I have given Aeneas a lot more to sing than he has in the Purcell – our opera provides the opportunity for Aeneas to look back on his past and to confront the consequences of his actions, both as a mortal and as a prisoner of fate. At its heart this new opera, *Dido's Ghost*, through combining the old with the new, speaks to the timeless, universal emotions of monumental love, loss and sorrow.

*

I think I am happiest when I'm trying something new – and making life difficult for myself. I relish composing instrumental music but I do have an innate dramatic instinct and what I love about composing operas is that this collaborative form combines every artistic and technical skill. Composing an opera forces a composer to dig deeply into so many areas of life's experiences outside one's immediate knowledge.

And did it all start with those large square place mats on our dinner table at 74 Seymour Avenue? Each mat had a different scene from *Carmen*. I remember their lurid orange-red hue and the matadors and the dancing women dressed in billowing white blouses and brightly coloured skirts. Opera. I didn't really know what opera was then but as a little girl there were several months when I hurled my warbling self around the house, imagining I was an opera singer. Little did I know that I would compose twenty-two operas . . . and counting.

DECIDING

Right at this very moment I can hear at least three types of hum, the distant splashing of the sea, the flapping of my letterbox and the wax in my ear cracking.

There were so many times when things did not go well. But there was a particularly difficult patch when I was penniless, in debt, and was somewhat rejected – indeed, considered to be at the outer fringes. I was not unhappy, as I am always fizzing with music inside and was steadily composing. But I was certainly on my uppers.

I sat myself down and said, 'E, this is how the rest of your life could remain. Go away and think clearly about your likely future . . . living in poverty and debt, still trying to make it when no one is playing your music. Still sending out scores and recordings with no response, tired, bitter and lonely. Could you still see yourself continuing in these conditions? This could be the very best time to get out and do something else. I want you to think about it for a couple of days then come back with your answer.'

So I went away and thought about it. For a few days. Seriously.

I came back quietly and said to myself: 'Right, E, we're doing this.'

DAEDALUS

Camden Town, in my studio – my 'London palace'.
Daedalus day.

It was merely the inkling of an illusion of an allusion – but
I felt a strong hankering to live in the world of the chords
of Anglican hymns, Tim Harries's liquid, expressive bass
playing and the mythical character of Daedalus, whom I'd
been as long possessed by as I had been by Dido, Queen
of Carthage. It wasn't long until the first chord appeared
beneath my hands and it quickly led to the next chord, and
then the next. The words were kept to a minimum and in
them I hid Daedalus's secret. Listening to the song, you
wouldn't actually know the song was about Daedalus; the
lyrics are a series of questions that anyone could ask themselves: 'Is this the life you would have hoped for? Is this the
life you would have died for?'

When the song was finished, I played it to Tim first
and we first performed it with my band. Tim was playing
his beautiful fretless bass. No one plays like Tim Harries.
'Daedalus' sounds simple but to achieve the fluid joins from
verse to chorus took practice. As I played, I pushed and
pulled the tempo and the band had to learn how to follow.

Songs started to burst out from me again in my twenties.
Unbidden and in a style that blurred all kinds of borders

and boundaries. They were for my pleasure and composed for me to sing and play. Although I had no confidence as a singer and didn't consider myself the pianist I had hoped to become, I had a yearning to sing. At first I couldn't have imagined that it would be possible for me to play some of my more complicated piano parts and sing at the same time but with practice I did; my own particular way of playing becoming an essential part of the musical picture. The piano is my home and I now find it strange singing without the anchor of my hands on the keys.

'Daedalus' is a song I also perform solo and I eventually recorded on my solo album *ERROLLYN*. I recorded it in Chelsea at Snake Ranch Studios with Gerry O'Riordan (Geraldi to me). I *always* want to be working with Geraldi in the studio – we are a great team. The budget to make the album was modest and I decided against specially hiring a Steinway, as the piano at Snake Ranch was pretty good. We had to record everything in about three or four days. On the second day we came to recording the piano part for 'Daedalus' and it was the held chords and single notes that made it clear that I needed to hire in a Steinway, even though it would take me over budget. The song required that the single hushed notes played on the piano would hover in the air like silver shards and that the bass would open up a cavern below without losing any definition in the centre of the sound. The decision to change piano was the correct one and we abandoned recording for the rest of the day.

A Steinway was delivered and installed the following

day. We had a squeaky piano stool, which was mercifully fixed by the congenial Steinway tuner Nigel Polmear, and Gerry and I got on with re-recording the tracks I'd already recorded on the other piano and then came 'Daedalus'. In the version I made for the album, the song lasted eight minutes twenty-seven seconds. The opening introduction, which I improvised, took flight, inspired by the beauty of the piano. I then recorded my vocals on top of the piano part and the song was the first track on the album.

I have always been unfashionably passionate yet I am often described as 'cool' (meaning 'à la mode', I guess) but all I can say is that there is a fire in me, which, living in British society, where it is actually 'cool' to be cool and where deep emotions don't always seem to matter that much, is something I can never quite get my head around. I don't ever want to blunt my responses to events or the world around me, which is why I cannot compose music that is ironic or cynical. However painful, I need to examine feelings, not least to try to imagine someone else's psyche. I see this as my job as an artist and as a human being.

The first song I wrote that was meant for me to play and sing was 'What's up Doc?' Composed at an old baby grand at a boyfriend's flat in Putney, it somehow splurged out in half an hour. I found myself playing a marimba-like riff on the piano that was silly but very jolly – I liked the way the pattern shaped under my fingers and how the words presented themselves, ready formed.

In the beginning, I set out to write songs that avoided the

word 'love' even if the song I was writing was *about* love. This restriction has been fruitful for my lyrics. That is not to say that love is never mentioned but that, certainly in the beginning, I was trying to make my lyrics work harder by refusing to settle for that overused word. I also like working with opposites – 'What's up Doc?' is about depression, but the music is lively; and always a favourite with babies and toddlers to dance to.

When we performed 'Daedalus' in the band version, Tim would improvise an opening riff using harmonics, quietly mysterious with a gentle, rolling rhythm. When I came to notate 'Daedalus' and to play the work solo, I tried to capture the same mystery Tim had conjured. The introduction to this song feels like a different scene to the song and is the place where, when I'm playing it, I see Daedalus sitting at the edge of the sea, his face half shadowed by branches, contemplating the recent loss of his son, Icarus.

I've always marvelled at the playing of jazz pianist Erroll Garner and admired the way his musical introductions often bear no clue as to the melody of the main part of the piece – they are complete pieces in themselves. When I came to arrange 'Daedalus' for the Brodsky Quartet for their album *Moodswings* (released a couple of years after *ERROLLYN*), I was thinking along similar lines and made an introduction that contrasted with the held chords of the verses.

Before the Brodsky arrangement I had included 'Daedalus' in a show I took to the Edinburgh Festival Fringe. It was in essence a song cycle with film by the honey brothers (Mark

and Daniel Goddard) that ran the length of the performance, which included dance solos by Tom Sapsford, who
was a member of the Royal Ballet at that time, and music
performed by a string quartet. Paul Bull was our indefatigable
and devoted sound engineer, production manager and roadie.

The film section for 'Daedalus', which Mark and Dan had
shot in a swimming pool, showed Tom swimming dancelike under water. He could have been flying. The first night
of our two-week run there were four people in the audience
and I knew three of them. A woman in the audience, whose
flat I was renting for the duration of our time at the festival,
came up to me at the end and said that she felt fated to hear
that song; it was meant for *her*. Every word in it spoke to her
own recent tragedy – the drowning in a swimming pool of
her four-year-old son just a few months before.

Through the years since her son's death, she has kept in
touch with me and her therapist even advised her that I
should perform the song for her on what would have been
his eighteenth birthday. 'Daedalus' has remained her talis-
man through these years of loss.

When I came to record the string quartet version of
'Daedalus' for the Brodsky Quartet, it was one of the last
recordings made at Snake Ranch Studios, the studio where
Gerry and I had recorded my labour-of-love first album,
Meet Me at Harold Moores. Emotional.

During the day, Elvis Costello and Ron Sexsmith recorded
their songs for *Moodswings* and I sat in on their sessions. After
they had gone, we put the quartet part down and, when the

quartet left, I went into the vocal booth and sang into the vintage Neumann valve M49 microphone (which Gerry had borrowed from Keith Grant) for the last time in that much-loved studio, which closed a week later.

What is it about playing and singing simultaneously that brings about such a sense of belonging, of being exactly in the right place? Also on the Brodsky's album was 'Real Emotional Girl' by Randy Newman, which Elvis Costello sang. When I went to see Randy Newman perform a solo show at the Royal Festival Hall, I thrilled at how his songs, sung and played by him, songs that have been covered by countless superb artists, sounded brand new in his rugged, unfettered voice.

When I started to teach composition I thought it was very important that in the first lessons I had with my students, they should have the experience of composing a song, complete with their own words, for themselves to sing. One year I invited my students round to my flat and in impromptu fashion they performed their songs to each other. That proved to be the first Errollyn Wallen Song Club. Subsequently, for about a year, I held one every month at The Green Carnation in Soho and at Netil House, Hackney. During the pandemic I hosted my Song Club online with Katie Melua as part of Spitalfields Festival.

When, in 2011, I was approached by producer Ewan Marshall to compose the music for the four-part TV drama series, *One Night*, I had to audition along with other composers. We were all asked to compose a theme tune that would encapsulate aspects of the four main characters, determined by our understanding of the script. I wanted that job *so* badly – it was a superlative script by Paul Smith. I also had a large credit-card debt. Never before have I wanted a job so badly that it physically hurt; and the sheer nervous anxiety of waiting to hear whether I'd got the job or not caused me to eat five Mars bars in a row. I came up with not one but two theme tunes and recorded them at Will Mount's studio – I had met Will through the Errollyn Wallen Song Club. Reader, I got the job (!) and proceeded to work on the incidental music, starting on it while I was performing at Tanglewood Music Festival in the Berkshire Hills of western Massachusetts. The director, David Evans, would send me clips from the day's filming so I could start to get a feel for the main characters. Then David came across a recording of 'Daedalus' on my website. That was it – he had to have both versions of the song for the opening and closing titles. The BBC executives wanted a popular hit song, but David stuck his neck out for me, insisting that the song was perfect – not only for its mood but in the way the lyrics reflected each main character. When the show was broadcast, 'Daedalus' went to the top of Apple Charts for one day. My score went on to win the FIPA d'Or for Best Music for a Television Series.

One summer's day I was invited by a friend, last minute, to go with her that evening to a Bobby Womack concert at the Royal Albert Hall. My friend Juliet Jackman brought two other friends, a couple, with her. It was a great band and a fantastic concert. During the gig I noticed that at several points a man dressed like a butler would go on stage and take drinks on a tray to Bobby. Towards the end of the gig, one of the couple turned to me and said, 'Let's go and see Bobby back-stage and see if I can give him one of your business cards.' We got to the stage door in time to see the same 'butler' carry-ing out a tray of sandwiches, drinks and snacks, which would have been the dressing room rider. As Bobby got into the lim-ousine, my friend's friend gave him my card . . .

Two days later I receive a call. From the 'butler'. 'Hello, this is Arthur. I look after Bobby Womack. He would like to work with you.' Blow me down.

I speak with Regina Womack, Bobby's wife, and tell her about the idea for an album I have called *Myth*, for which I collaborate with various artists to present songs related to the Greek myths. I tell her about 'Daedalus' and Bobby is keen to sing it. Regina tells me that Bobby thinks of himself as a classical composer.

I receive another call from Arthur some days later as I am driving to Walthamstow to visit friends April and Ewan for dinner. 'Bobby is playing with Ronnie Wood at the Royal Albert Hall tonight and asks if you'd like to come down and hang out backstage?'

I was so excited to work with Bobby Womack and it proved to be the one true moment of credibility I had with my two sisters. After my mother's funeral, when everyone had left (apart from cousin Harrison) Karen and Judith played every one of Bobby's recordings and danced all night singing along to the words. Thank you, Bobby, for aiding family entente.

I saw Regina several times in New York and at a party held for the launch of my album *PHOTOGRAPHY*. We became good friends.

Then Bobby suddenly died. His life-wizened, scorched voice will now never sing 'Daedalus'. But I do know that there will be a musical tribute from me to him one day soon.

I love imagining how other singers will connect to my words and music and when 'Daedalus' was programmed by tenor Nicholas Phan for his Collaborative Arts Institute of Chicago (CAIC), not only did it lead to many other singers singing it but I was able to share performance notes with the singers and ask what images *they* saw in their mind when singing that opening verse. Did they also picture Daedalus standing by a tree at the edge of the water, after his son Icarus has fallen into the sea? Grief-stricken yet haunted by his old secret: 'Is this the life you would have wished for? Is this the life you would have killed for?'

Not only can a song cross 110th Street; a song can travel across a thousand lives, through a thousand voices, through a thousand selves. I think of my song's journey to outer space on the STS-115 space shuttle with Steve MacLean. I dream at night of its plangent resonance forever whirring into infinity.

BOWING CLOTHES

Bowing – as in acknowledging the live audience's applause after a work has been performed.

I genuinely like disappearing and being 'backstage', which is where a composer truly belongs. Unless we are performing our own music, our essential selves are brought forward by other people, the performers. Sitting in a concert hall or theatre, being exposed after a new creation has just beamed into the world, causes conflicting emotions as I walk up onto the stage to take my bow. I am shy/happy-relieved/awkward. But before all of that, what to wear?

As a child brought up by a chiropodist, I could only look with envy at other little girls wearing pointy black patent leather shoes. I had to wear Tuf shoes, those leather, round-toed, sensible shoes – my Uncle Arthur's doing. No child of his was going to be running around in synthetic footwear that pinched and mis-shaped their feet, causing years of agony in later life.

I compensated for Uncle Arthur's then under-appreciated prudence when, having 'discovered' clothes only in my twenties, I went on to covet designer attire in my thirties, merrily squashing my toes and heels into stilettos, wedges and too-tight thigh-high boots. I have finally made peace with patent leather – and with Uncle Arthur – with several pairs of round-toed patent leather flat Doc Martens . . . and I've just come across a complicated thigh-high pair to add to my collection.

Living in uniform night and day at Holly Park was no bad thing for teenage girls. There was no comparing how expensive or designer-labelled your clothes were but, rather, how you customised your uniform could say a lot about your personality. Artfully frayed jacket sleeve cuffs, knee-length socks only a quarter pulled up, hands stuffed into the inner lining of your blazer, your Aertex sports shirt ripped at each side, culottes worn as short as possible. These were the hallmarks of a girl of discernment – a girl you could have a crush on.

As a teenager out of school uniform I dressed like the frumpy nerd I was, with occasional forays into suede hot pants and flared nylon trousers. Though in the miserable years of my late teens, when I was at home instead of being at school, my spirits withered away in beige corduroy and knobbly cardigans. At Goldsmiths, a high point was achieved with Laura Ashley dresses and short, sleek hair. But there were a lot of sensible brown shoes and in between (or because of) the eating disorders, tight, bright red jeans and woollen tank tops. The earliest photograph I have of me taking a composer bow is at Goldsmiths, after the world premiere of *Deaths and Entrances* – my setting of Dylan Thomas's poetry. I accompanied my friend, baritone Stephen Roe, and am wearing a colourful waistcoat over a black polo-neck jumper and long skirt. I look conventional, geeky and prim with my librarian glasses. I was obsessed with classical music rather than the creation of my image or persona, and I didn't want to draw attention to myself.

Things might have been different if I had been obsessed with pop music, I suppose. I was an introvert, while also being gregarious and loving of laughter. After my transformation in my mid-twenties, Kene would lift an eyebrow when I bought myself clothes: 'Got yourself new clothes, Linny?' – as if this act was selfish and extravagant. As a young woman, from a poor working-class family, she nevertheless had worn very fine clothes as a young woman and would go without and save a month's wages to pay for a new dress, skirt or shoes. Kene had dainty feet but suffered in high heels. I think she often missed her young courting days when she looked like a movie star.

Until I was nineteen, I had little control over the clothes I wore as I didn't have my own money, and there wasn't the variety of inexpensive fashionable clothes and designer copies that are available now. As children we would pore over the mail-order catalogue – staring and pointing at the models, all of them white, in various states of dress and undress. We were often dressed identically and on occasions when we could wear different clothes from each other, I was encouraged, as the eldest, to only wear 'sensible' colours – navy blue or brown. Kene sometimes made our summer dresses from patterns and would sit at her Singer sewing machine. It must have been quite a struggle to keep up with three fast-growing girls.

My mother would often wear corsets and more than once, as a very young child, I would be bustled into a public lavatory while she peeled the thing off. My mother was very happy in her body with its marshmallow-soft folds of fat, and changed into comfortable loose clothes as soon as she got home. Barbara had wardrobes and drawers of lovely clothes and jewellery but in the last twenty years of her life she hardly went out unless she was being driven. She really didn't dress up at all. The smartest she looked was in her coffin, her striking white hair and white gloves folded onto a beautiful dress I'd never ever seen her wear.

In my twenties I played loads of gigs and dressed very loudly: PVC dresses, leather miniskirts, dangly diamanté earrings, heavy necklaces, skyscraper shoes, neon lipsticks and a very short, gamine haircut. A friend from Holly Park was often chiding me for not dressing like a 'proper' feminist but, after years of impersonating a Miss Marple librarian, I wholeheartedly embraced dressing for the stage, even when at home alone or out shopping. I always looked stage-ready.

I asked Jenny Packham, a young up-and-coming designer I'd met on a shoot for a newspaper article on young up-and-coming creative women, to make me a black and white halterneck tutu of silk and tulle for a performance with my band at Hackney Empire – the first time I was singing out front and not from behind a keyboard. I should have asked Jenny to put a label in it for posterity's sake (she went on to design a number of dresses for Kate Middleton). I loved giving parties at my London flat and wore the Jenny Packham frou-frou 'Cruella de Vil' creation, though the volume of the tutu skirt meant that guests could get nowhere near me. I was like a teenager let loose with this sudden passion for clothes and the many types of fabric from which they are made. The passion continues.

Clothes are a way of being modest, keeping warm and for expressing predilection and colour and shape preferences. A composer lives in the world in three different ways when it comes to what to wear, depending on where they are in the process of creation. My first stage, when starting to compose a piece of music, involves remaining in nightwear. It's better to get to work immediately after breakfast. If I wait until I get dressed, I will get sidetracked by bath bubbles and emails. The second stage is when I am attending rehearsals. I dress in a relaxed but purposeful way – jeans, shirts, lipstick and smiles. Then come the bowing clothes. What the hell to wear? I sometimes enjoy the distraction of this consideration, usually occurring at the final stage of composing, and it can spur me on to finish a work to think of what I will put on my body and feet.

Sometimes I can be just plain vain. For the premiere of *Carbon 12* at the Millennium Centre in Cardiff I was determined to wear my new, towering Terry de Havilland leather and metal wedges though they were way too precarious to walk in all night. Therefore, when it came to bowing time, I walked in sensible shoes to the side of the stage with John Binias, my librettist, and hastily pulled out the wedges from the plastic bag clutched in my hand, just so I could stagger on stage in footwear no one in the audience could probably even see.

But what *do* you wear when you take a bow for a symphonic work in a concert hall or an opera premiere in a gilded theatre, for a brand-new work or a work that has been performed many times before? One of my first premieres was televised (my Concerto for Percussion and Orchestra in BBC's *Young Musician of the Year* competition) and my friend James Bailey brought me a long gold-sequinned dress. It was, frankly, over the top, as I wasn't one of the young finalists, but James said that the glamour made up for the stress I had endured during the process of composing the work. A fairly early work was *Spirit Symphony – Speed-Dating for Two Orchestras*, a companion piece to Handel's *Music for the Royal Fireworks*, broadcast live on BBC Radio 3. Petroc Trelawny was the presenter. My friend Anda Winters had given me a beautiful striped Betty Jackson black and white knee-length jacket in which I bounded down the steps of the Royal Festival Hall. Petroc described this coat and my general attire in lengthy detail. I have adored him ever since.

Many composers will admit to feeling very uncomfortable in the audience for a world premiere. Part of that is the nervousness of having to go up on stage after you have exposed your soul, although I realise that an audience loves to see the creator of the work. But however much clapping and cheering there is, it's as if I can't hear anything – my ears, which have been so alert to the quietest nuance, seem to close up. Memorable bows include the one after the premiere of *This Frame Is Part of the Painting* at the Proms. I wore an unusual jumpsuit by a favourite designer, Junya

Watanabe. Because it was more than slightly tight, I had asked Gail, the excellent dressmaker and seamstress in Thurso (above Betty's the haberdasher's) to help. She suggested buying 1½-inch-wide ribbon that could be inserted into the outside seams of the trouser legs. The only ribbon of adequate length was a vivid green – actually perfect for celebrating Howard Hodgkin. The outfit was in keeping with invention and the painter's unique sense of pattern and shape. I had to stand up carefully to avoid a split before taking my bow. Memories suddenly flashed back of when I was playing with PULSE at Henley Festival. I wore a skirt so tight and so short there was absolutely no space for underwear. When my skirt ripped mid-performance I couldn't come out and take a bow and was thankful for having a keyboard to hide behind.

When my Concerto for Percussion and Orchestra was performed in Mexico in the Cervantino Festival, I arrived in Mexico City late afternoon before the long drive to Guanajuato where my music was being performed the next day. My luggage had been lost in transit from Italy. In Guanajuato I stocked up on clothes I wouldn't normally ever wear but I managed to find sequinned flip-flops in gold and silver and rather ill-fitting dresses and skirts. Someone lent me their shawl and I took my bow after the performance. The stage was very high and there were no stairs up to it, so I reached up to shake the hand of the conductor. Later, at the reception, a woman, not realising I was the composer, commented on how remarkable it was that I was so overcome that I felt impelled to run up to the stage, like a superfan. Perhaps my clothes did not suggest 'composer bowing' or was it simply the colour of my skin?

I bought a silk quasi-tartan Vivienne Westwood dress for the premiere of my opera *YES*. The seating, with set design by the director John Lloyd Davies, was in the round. A friend later told me that my dress was quite short at the back, which meant that the audience at some point would have had full sight of my underwear, if not my bum.

Am I vain? *Moi?* No. I just love colour, texture, shape and the cut of designers such as Vivienne Westwood, Junya Watanabe, Issey Miyake, Alexander McQueen, Dries Van Noten, to name but a few. Dressing up is an antidote to my composing attire, which, these days, is a tired-looking, fluffy pink onesie with pom-poms, one of which has got accidentally yanked off. I smile when I think of my nerdy younger self. That creature was such a puritan snob (probably as an overhang of my nun-aspiring days) who truly believed that excessive attention to adornment was vulgar, indulgent and a waste of time.

I hadn't yet read that the wearing of copious amounts of silk for both composing and bowing did Liszt and Wagner absolutely no harm.

CHRISTMAS 2021...AND AFTER

Another Christmas has come round again. I am driving to my home at the lighthouse on 22 December. I catch the very end of a concert of contemporary carols broadcast live from Temple Church, London, by the BBC Singers. I hear them sing my 'Peace on Earth' and think I can hear the voice of Jess Gillingwater singing in the choir. Jess sang at the first workshops for *Dido's Ghost* and was one of the Witches. She also sang Lavinia in the Buxton performances. I check later and it was indeed her voice I heard. This Christmas I won't be alone and I'm glad of that. Friendship and the feeling of togetherness with other human beings have become priceless. A variant of the virus is raging across Europe and is worse in London.

My mother's birthday is tomorrow. Years before they died, Dad would joke how he would dig a big hole and he and Mum would wheel around and around it together in their wheelchairs until they fell in. I still hear their laughter in my ears and see them jumping up and dancing to music whenever they heard something they liked. I also remember, as an adult, jumping up to lie between them in their huge bed in Brooklyn, the television blaring. It was as if we three instinctively remembered our physical configuration as a new family when I, their first-born, nestled between them in our first months together in Belize.

This beautiful spot in the most northerly part of the Highlands where I live and work, with its supreme quiet and sombre peace, connects me to my past, to my earliest childhood, and to centuries past and to come.

By March 2022, I am shattered. I realise I have completed three operas in a year: *Dido's Ghost*, *The Paradis Files* (for Graeae Theatre Company) and *Quamino's Map* (for Chicago Opera Theater). The last two premiere within ten days of each other. But, really, I'm shattered because, finally, Covid got me (most likely on the second visit of my Wort residency in Cambridge) and I am waiting to see if I will be fit to fly to Chicago in a few days' time. I haven't had a cold or cough for at least three years but the worst symptom is the fatigue. It is a much milder variant than what was around a few months back, but I am laid low. I've been pushing and pushing to try to meet all these deadlines. *Quamino's Map* was the biggest squeeze – having to orchestrate a ninety-minute opera in six weeks called on all my focus and reserves. I bought myself *two* pink fluffy onesies (one for the wash while wearing the other one) complete with white fluffy pom-poms; that is still my preferred composing uniform.

I have had to cancel my trip to Chicago for the first weeks of rehearsals because of Covid-19. *Quamino's Map* was commissioned with only a little more than a year to the first performance and none of the creative team had worked together before. It is crucial for me to be there, to meet everyone, to be with everyone – and to hear my music properly at last.

But instead there followed weeks of evening Zoom rehearsals from a computer screen at Strathy Point to an echoey rehearsal room in Chicago, and Zoom rehearsals from my computer screen to Graeae's rehearsal studio in London.

The premiere of *The Paradis Files** at the Southbank turned out to be a bright spark in the year. An opera that celebrated all physical abilities, both on stage and in the audience. Telling the story of blind pianist and composer Theresia von Paradis (1759–1824) seemed a daunting task at first; I was nervous that we might merely produce a docudrama. But by putting three women at the heart of the action (Theresia, her mother, her maid) we were able to explore the characters and situations more and give full flight to our fancy. Hilde has been a resentful and ambivalent mother. Theresia finds that hard to forgive. It is Gerda who sees Hilde as the vulnerable woman she is, seeking the love and forgiveness of her daughter. The Baron, Theresia's father, is an authoritarian father, typical of the time, who is yet deeply moved by love for his gifted daughter. I drew on my own story of a talented child misunderstood by her family and also highlighted both private/family and public attitudes to people with disabilities.

But before I went to Cambridge for my Wort residency I had made myself finish the orchestration of *Quamino's Map*. I'm so glad I did, as it would be much harder to do now in this enfeebled state. And a wonderful thing happened

---

* Libretto by Nicola Werenowska and Selina Mills; music director, Andrea Brown; stage director, Jenny Sealey.

within an hour of completing it. It was a late Sunday night. I was packing for leaving early and was getting my steps in (I try to do seven thousand a day) while brushing my teeth, when there was a banging on my window and my neighbour beckoned me to come outside. A few nights earlier my friend Les Armishaw had told me that the Aurora Borealis – the Northern Lights – were about. I just needed to look out the window of my lighthouse. Sure enough, I looked and did see white moving shapes, not super distinct, but when I took a photograph I could see the faint colours. The human eye primarily views the Northern Lights in faint colours and shades of grey and white but my smartphone didn't have that limitation. Now this time I went outside wearing only my onesie, the night being calm and very mild, and there was no need to take a photo to check if what I was seeing was the 'Mirrie Dansers', for there I saw them, no mistaking – the Northern Lights in their full iridescent glory.

It was as if the sky was thinking, thinking and dancing – and beckoning in wisps and gusts. Right across the sky, even though the moon was very bright, a show for all to see was put on for our sole entertainment, or so it seemed. A couple of ships were in the distance. I understood how anyone could think there might be a god. God of the sky, thought, music, dance and all of time. Curtains in the sky seemed to part and wreaths of air unfurl. Depths and layers shifting and communicating. If the Russian bombs raining down on Ukraine that night could have stopped and if we could have all gathered to look up at the sky, we might have known that nothing destroyed or nothing created is greater than what is already there in the majesty of our earth. One day I shall attempt to convey in music the wonder I just beheld. Impossible but a small step towards peace.

These days, I require my brain to function at its sharpest so I am finally succumbing to paying closer attention to my health and getting enough sleep. After a childhood where I was often made to feel inadequate, I finally accept that music pours out of me and that performers and audience take pleasure in it. I also realise that my brain and my ears are my biggest assets and I need to avoid any unnecessary disturbance in order to enable their optimum functioning. It has taken me my whole life to be able to do that. As a child, I tiptoed through the quagmire of other people's emotional problems and though I miss my four parents, who are all gone, the world is a lot quieter! There is greater calm and equilibrium; I can hear myself. After a lifetime of familial uncertainty, being pulled between several loyalties, living in limbo, being judged and made to feel a freak, I am finally enjoying what it is to be me and not just a projection of others' perception of me, notwithstanding that mocking inner voice which will always live with me, whispering, 'You're not all that much.'

As a small child I relished time alone and my time is now my own. The lighthouse has opened a new door to composing productivity and personal happiness, calm and purpose. I have complete solitude and quiet when required and treasured company when I want it. I am so very lucky.

I wasn't prepared for the vehement resistance of many people who thought I was mad, irresponsible even, to be moving to a remote lighthouse in the far north of Scotland. It opened my eyes to realise how little is understood about what composers need and how the people around you can feel threatened when you step outside their picture of you – when you change. It was in the first weeks of my year in Cambridge, while doing my MPhil, that I received one of the best pieces of advice for living – from John Butt, who told me, 'Don't even try to fit in.'

After borders reopened, it wasn't easy to leave my Scottish sanctuary but being back in the United States after so long was heartwarming and invigorating. I was able to see my family and friends. Music was live again after all those Zoom rehearsals and online performances. After the three operas composed back to back, I still had a heavy workload and needed to continue working as well as attending Chicago Opera Theater rehearsals, which were often from morning until ten at night. After so long immersed in trying to meet the pressing opera commissions, I was now very behind with my administrative tasks and other commissions. Still suffering from the after-effects of Covid, I nevertheless had to continue pushing myself. But as I looked out from my desk window, there was Muddy Waters playing his guitar, all nine storeys of him – a 130-foot-high mural of a musician in his prime, in his music.

It was while I was in Chicago that I managed to spend

some time with the newly transcribed score of *The World's Weather*, composed in 2000 while in Cambridge.

A few months previously, conductor Martyn Brabbins had asked for a work to open the concert on 11 June 2022 at City Halls, Glasgow, with BBC Scottish Symphony Orchestra featuring James MacMillan's *Veni, Veni Emmanuel* (Evelyn Glennie, soloist) and Elgar's First Symphony. I suggested a couple of works which weren't quite suitable. Then, on a trip to London, I practically stumbled over a score that had been typeset by a fellow MPhil student, Martin Iddon (it had been proofed by Ben Harris who also greatly encouraged me while I was composing it) but I didn't have the original file. So I employed my ex-student John Sturt to transcribe the music digitally onto the Sibelius composing software program and another ex-student and my stalwart copyist, Oliver Muxworthy, to edit it and make the orchestral parts. While in Chicago I listened to the digital playback and was surprised by many of its features, which were unlike anything I am currently composing. Because *The World's Weather* was an old work, I had subconsciously written it off as being inferior to recent works, when, in fact, I had opened a window to another side of my musical personality. I had no recollection as to the nitty-gritty details of how I composed the work but it was a forgotten aspect of my aesthetic and one I'd like to return to in future works. Thank you, Martyn and BBC Scottish Symphony Orchestra, for the opportunity and for what was a brilliant premiere.

ADVENT 2022

The World's Weather wasn't the only circle I closed.

The piano concerto commissioned by Julian Lloyd Webber for Rebeca Omordia was another casualty of the pandemic, so I put the orchestration to one side before having to suddenly take it up again as a new performance date was set. It received its world premiere at Royal Birmingham Conservatoire in autumn 2022 and was also recorded by Resonus Classics with Rebeca and the BBC Concert Orchestra.

And I couldn't let this year's Venice Biennale close without travelling to see Sonia Boyce's show, *Feeling Her Way*, in the British Pavilion, the space it was created for. I went with my friend Sarah Alexander and we had two exhilarating days in one of my favourite cities on earth. Sonia's show was mesmerising and full of layers of history, sound and motion, the whole space devoted to the celebration of women and the power of the voice. It was strange seeing myself on screen and seeing the image of my daisy-appliquéd Doc Martens venerated as part of the handmade wallpaper, but I was overjoyed to have contributed to this landmark work of art for which Sonia Boyce won the Golden Lion.

I have just come to the completion of a run of choral works: 'Road to Refuge', a carol for the latest series of *Carols for Choirs* (Oxford University Press), a new anthem, *Timbrel*, for the Choir and Mixed Voices of King's College, Cambridge, a Magnificat and Nunc dimittis for Westminster Abbey, carols for Salisbury Cathedral ('Salisbury Carol') and Harrow School ('A Spotless Rose') and an anthem, *I Heard a Voice*, for Knox Presbyterian Church in Cincinnati. For Salisbury Cathedral Choir I dedicated my carol to the Queen, who died in September 2022, and my text describes how at the end of the year we all remember those who we have lost. Tears were in my eyes as I composed it. I loved our Queen. Last weekend I attended evensong at King's, Cambridge, and heard the premiere of *Timbrel*, sung as the introit, by King's Choir and King's Mixed Voices.

This year there is a proliferation of recordings and performances of my carol 'Peace on Earth', including a fine recording followed by a performance at Wigmore Hall by Ruby Hughes and Huw Watkins. It was while I was at King's for the performance of *Timbrel* that Daniel Hyde, the director of music, told me that this Christmas Eve 'Peace on Earth' was to be sung in A Festival of Nine Lessons and Carols at King's College, Cambridge, broadcast live on BBC Radio 4 around the world and also televised on BBC Two's *Carols from King's*. I wish my mother and father could have heard and seen it. That little song I wrote, almost on the spot, has been performed throughout the world and was even translated into Catalan last year. This year I will listen with my Butt family to 'Peace on Earth' as it goes out live on radio then later watch it in its television version.

Nine Lessons and Carols with a glass of sherry – a family tradition marking the beginning of Christmas.

Before leaving the Butts I shall send off my last completed work of the year, my new brass quintet, *ONYX*, which I am dedicating to Mike Hodges, the filmmaker, who with his wife Carol have been such dear, kind friends. Mike died very recently. I hope he would appreciate the astringent, upfront character of this work, which saves the tender moments for the very end.

Then it's back to the lighthouse. Back to Strathy Point and to all the new works I have to compose. They have been waiting patiently for me.

I am never bored here. Who could be? The quality of light that greets you every day; the panoramic views of the Atlantic; the sprawling skies that throw all weathers at us.

Yes. All weathers do sail and sing on this unending horizon.

ACKNOWLEDGEMENTS

I am truly grateful to Belinda Matthews who asked me to write this book. Her kindness, patience and encouragement have kept me going. My editors, Emmie Francis, Jill Burrows, and project editor Joanna Harwood have been magnificent – I have learned so much from them. Thank you to Trish Mersh, my childhood friend, for reading the first draft, to John Butt for his perspicacity and to friends Shannon Latoyah Simon, Jamie Edwards and Morgan Burroughs who suffered me reading bits out to them over the phone from the lighthouse.

I am most favoured to have had the expertise and jolly lunches with Peter Button and Stephen Pidcock from Clintons bestowed upon me.

The daily chivvies from Sally Butt and my agent, John Owen, sustained and cheered me even more than cake.

This book is for all the people who have opened doors for me – I am forever grateful – and for all who have enjoyed my music.

COPYRIGHT ACKNOWLEDGEMENTS

'Composing *Dido's Ghost*: An In-Depth Exploration',
Gramophone, 17 August 2021.
'Of Crumpling Rocks' (pp. 273–4)

Image credits

Page One

Henry Wallen seeing his daughter Errollyn off to
  Hollington Park School for Girls. Courtesy of the author.
Barbara Wallen taking leave of her daughters, Karen,
  Judith and Errollyn at Heathrow Airport. Courtesy of
  the author.
Arthur Horatio Douglas Wallen in Paris. Courtesy of the
  author.
The wedding of Renee (Kene) Richardson and Arthur
  Wallen in London. Courtesy of the author.

Page Two

Karen, Errollyn and Judith Wallen outside 74 Seymour
  Avenue. Courtesy of the author.
Edwin Ewart Lincoln Wallen, Winnipeg, 1943. Courtesy
  of the author.
Barbara Wallen with baby Byron and Errollyn, Judith and
  Karen in costume. Courtesy of the author.
Errollyn, Arthur, Judith, Karen, Kene and cousin
  Stephanie. Courtesy of the author.

COPYRIGHT ACKNOWLEDGEMENTS

Page Three

Family with cousins Michael and Lincoln, sons of Molly
(*pictured*) and Edwin Wallen (*taking the photograph*)
and family friend, Kaye McCoy. Lancing, West Sussex.
Courtesy of the author.

Rory Allam on tour with the Royal Shakespeare Company.
Courtesy of the author.

Errollyn and Trish in Italy. Courtesy of the author.

Hollington Park School Choir performing at White Rock
Pavilion, Hastings. Errollyn at the piano, Miss Pearse
conducting. Courtesy of the author.

Page Four

Ernesto and Kishana's wedding in Belize. Courtesy of the
author.

Recording *Meet Me at Harold Moores*, pictured with Nell
Catchpole and Matthew Sharp. Courtesy of the author.

Tim Harries at Edinburgh Festival in rehearsals for
Scottish premiere of *Dido's Ghost*, August 2021.
Courtesy of the author.

With Anthony Parnther, Tai Murray, Isata Kanneh-Mason
and Chi-chi Nwanoku after recording *Concerto Grosso*.
Courtesy of the author.

Page Five

Mrs H's 103rd birthday party, London. Courtesy of the
author.

Grace notes: Portrait of Errollyn Wallen, composer. Oil

painting by Gill Robinson. Copyright © Gill Robinson
Errollyn in dress rehearsal for *Jordan Town*, Royal Opera
  House. Photo credit Cathy Masser
Family Proms, Royal Albert Hall. Photo credit Chris
  Christodoulou

Page Six
Errollyn Wallen at The Ivor Novello Awards at Grosvenor
  House, London, 2013. Errollyn was the first woman to
  receive the award for Classical Music. Photo credit PA
  Images / Alamy Stock Photo, photographer Ian West
Investiture at Buckingham Palace. Photo credit PA Images
  / Alamy Stock Photo

Page Seven
Rehearsing for premiere of Magnificat and Nunc dimit-
  tis at Evensong, Westminster Abbey, November 2022.
  Choir of Westminster Abbey, James O'Donnell, conduc-
  tor, Peter Holder, organist. Courtesy of the author.
Errollyn on Kilimanjaro with a roll-up piano. Courtesy of
  the author.
Backstage at Symphony Space, New York. Courtesy of the
  author.
ERROLLYN floating near the pilot's seat on the shuttle
  STS-115. The CD travelled 7.84 million kilometres
  in space and completed 186 orbits around the Earth.
  Photo credit Steve MacLean

INDEX

317

INDEX

INDEX

Maureen Lyons School of Dancing, 102, 190

Maycock, Robert, 201

McFall, Robert, 236

Meissner, Justin, 251

Melua, Katie, 287

Mendelssohn, Michèle, ix, 152–3

Menuhin, Yehudi, 104

Merwin, W. S., 'Runes for a Round Table', 128

Miller, Graeme, 6

Mills, Serena, 301n

Modibbo, Aishatu ('Tish'), 191, 192, 193, 195

Moir, Jim (aka Vic Reeves), 163

Morison, Catriona, 205, 222

Mortimer, Bob, 163

Mount, Will, 288

Mozart, Wolfgang Amadeus, 33

Musgrave, Thea, 259

Muxworthy, Oliver, 269, 305

National Youth Brass Band of Great Britain, 218

Navigating the Unknown (book), 230

Nelson, Admiral Lord (Horatio), 23, 25, 27–8, 31, 32, 35, 197, 246

Neruda, Pablo, 47

New Cross station, 96, 106

New Juilliard Ensemble, 256

Newman, Jim, 212

Newman, Randy, 287

Newman University, Birmingham, 92

New Notes (magazine), 111, 202

New York, 57–61, 64, 65, 90, 102, 152, 199

New York City Opera, 170

NightWalking conference, 6

Nitro, 'A Nitro at the Opera', 66, 77–8

Nordberg, Jonas, 234

Norris, David Owen, 122

Northern Ballet, *Great Expectations*, 117

Northern Lights, 302

Nottingham Now festival, 41n

Nunn, Michael, 251

Nureyev, Rudolf, 216

Nyman, Michael, 211

Omordia, Rebeca, 306

One Night (TV drama), 94, 287–8

O'Riordan, Gerry (Geraldi), 39, 270n, 283, 284, 286, 287

Osmond, Donny, 40

Other Minds Festival, 110–11, 111n, 212

Ovid, 42, 43, 44, 49, *Fasti*, 260, *Metamorphoses*, 258

Packham, Jenny, 294

Paradis, Theresia von, 301

Paralympic Games (London 2012), 79–80, 82, 169, 243

Parkhurst Infant School, 177

Parry, Hubert, 214, 215, 217

Petrucciani, Michel, 227

Peyton Jones, Jeremy, 207

Phan, Nicholas, 290

Philadelphia Chamber Society, 231

Philharmonic Baroque Orchestra and Chorale (San Francisco), 260

Pickering, David, 251

Pine, Courtney, 160–1

Polmear, Nigel, 284

Pook, Jocelyn, 201

Pook, Laurene, 107

Pope, Laurette, 122

Poppy, Andrew, 171, 207

Porfiris, Rita, 12, 91

Portsmouth Cathedral, 23

Pountney, David, 84

Power, Stephanie, 201

Prévost, Abbé, *Manon Lescaut*, 92, 93

Price, Florence, 210

Proms, 17, 196, 196n, 205, 209, 211, 214, 224n, 296–7

Puccini, Giacomo, *Tosca*, 85

Pullman, Philip, 22, 268

PULSE, 38, 163, 167, 207–8, 297

Purcell, Henry: *Dido and Aeneas*, 140–1, 226, 259, 260, 262, 267, 269, 270, 272, 274, 276, 277–9, influence, 217

Purcell Room, Southbank Centre, 10, 201, 202, 204

PUSH, 83, 83n

321

Raag Ramkali, 223
Radio 3, 102, 110, 219
Rajam, Steven, 219
Reich, Steve, 199, 211
ResCen, 6
Reshetilov, Ivan, 171, 172
Rhaburn, Gerald 'Lord', 107
Richards, Clive, 27
Richardson, Renee. *See* Wallen, Kene
Riley, Terry, *In C*, 207
Risca Male Voice Choir, 86
Roberts, Juliet, 160, 161
Robertson, Martin, 201
Robinson, Jeff, 91
Roe, Stephen, 201, 292
Rospigliosi, Veronica, 127, 128
Royal Academy of Music, 149
Royal Albert Hall, 17, 196, 288, 289
Royal Ballet, 216, 249, 252, 286
Royal College of Music, 39
Royal Festival Hall, 287, 296
Royal Northern Sinfonia, 37
Royal Opera House (ROH), 75, 85, 216, 252
'A Nitro at the Opera', 66, 77–8
RO2, 89
RSA Academy, Tipton, 92
Russell, Mark, 110
Rutter, John, 218

Sachs, Joel, 256
Sadler's Wells, 83
Salisbury Cathedral Choir, 307
Sammie and Rosie Get Laid (film), 162
Sandall, Robert, 110
Sapsford, Tom, 88, 249, 251–4, 286
Savidge, Peter, 122
Scarlatti, Domenico, 161
Schoenberg, Arnold, 60, 206
Scotland, 149–51, 244, 255, 260, 269, 304
Scott, Dennis, 236
Scott, Gina, 108
Sealey, Jenny, 301n
Second Viennese School, 60, 207
The Secret Policeman's Ball, 160
Self, Will, 9
Sexsmith, Ron, 286
Shakespeare, William, 42, 47, 50
Sharp, Matthew, 6–11, 13, 94
Sibelius program, 246, 305
Sidebottom, Frank, 164, 165, 208
The Singing Ringing Tree (play), 163
Slany, Sonia, 201
Slough, 168
Smith, Lucinda (Lucy), 172, 173, 193, 195, 196
Smith, Paul, 288
Snake Ranch Studios, 283, 286
Society for the Promotion of New Music (SPNM), 111, 202
Southbank Centre, 6, 10, 104, 170, 301
Sowande, Fela, 210
Spitalfields Festival, 287
Srivastava, Atima, 66
Stace, Wesley, 226, 259, 260, 265, 269, 271, 272, 279
Steel, George, 170
Still, William Grant, 209
Stockhausen, Karlheinz, 206, *Mikrophonie II*, 209
Stoodley, Amanda, 93
Stott, Kathryn, 11
Stravinsky, Igor: *Agon*, 259, *Apollo*, 259, *Ave Maria*, 120, *Dumbarton Oaks*, 125, *Three Japanese Lyrics*, 116
Sturt, John, 305

Takács Quartet, 170
Tanglewood, 200, 288
Tan, Margaret Leng, 110, 123, 127
Tate, Nahum, 262, 272, 278, 279
Tête à Tête Opera, 79
Thomas, Dylan, 292
Tilbury, John, 201
Tilbury Docks, 66–7
Tilson Thomas, Michael, 12
Tippett, Michael, 217, *A Child of Our Time*, 120–1, 217
Top of the Pops (TV show), 157–8, 167
Tottenham, 59, 89, 99
Trafalgar, Battle of, 23, 27, 31
Trelawny, Petroc, 296
Trickey, Sara, 270n
Trinity College of Music, 103

INDEX